AF304854

Jihadism in Europe

JIHADISM IN EUROPE

From the 1990s to the Present Day

Hugo Micheron

Translated by Cory Stockwell

polity

Originally published in French as *La colère et l'oubli: Les démocraties face au jihadisme européen*
© Éditions Gallimard, Paris, 2023

This English translation © Polity Press, 2026

This book is supported by the Institut français (Royaume-Uni) as part of the Burgess programme.

Map produced by Edicarto.

Polity Press
65 Bridge Street
Cambridge CB2 1UR, UK

Polity Press
111 River Street
Hoboken, NJ 07030, USA

ISBN-13: 978-1-5095-6611-2 – hardback

A catalogue record for this book is available from the British Library.

Library of Congress Control Number: 2025949893

Typeset in 11.5 on 14 Adobe Garamond Pro
by Fakenham Prepress Solutions, Fakenham, Norfolk NR21 8NL
Printed and bound in UK by CPI Group (UK) Ltd, Croydon

The publisher has used its best endeavors to ensure that the URLs for external websites referred to in this book are correct and active at the time of going to press. However, the publisher has no responsibility for the websites and can make no guarantee that a site will remain live or that the content is or will remain appropriate.

Every effort has been made to trace all copyright holders, but if any have been overlooked the publisher will be pleased to include any necessary credits in any subsequent reprint or edition.

For further information on Polity, visit our website:
politybooks.com

Contents

III The Natives – The 2010s

Detailed Contents

Preface

The debate around definitions of Islamism is an old one. The term is used to designate movements that share a conscious refusal to divide religion between faith, culture, ideology, and political system. These movements have the common goal of subjecting social space to a specific regime of religious rules. I will introduce three of its currents here.[1]

The Muslim Brotherhood

Born in Egypt in 1928, this organization, founded by the teacher Hassan al-Banna, initially sought to re-Islamize Egyptian society, fight British occupation, and combat the Zionist movement in Palestine. Its stated objective is to gain power in order to impose the statutes of religious law (Sharia). This model was duplicated across all Arab countries. In Europe, associations aligning themselves with this movement appeared during the 1980s, to deal with the implications of being Muslim in non-Muslim countries. They act in several groupings to obtain an institutional recognition that allows them to negotiate, in a logic of community-based lobbying, their control over the population of Muslim ancestry in the eyes of public authorities. These militants seek to combat and discredit the advent of a theological and liberal Islam, identified with a belief freely lived by each person. To do this, they pursue a strategy of community-based affirmation, which exploits all the resources of democracy (judicial procedures, associations, etc.).

The Tabligh

Contrary to the Muslim Brotherhood, who focus on political action, the Tabligh ("propagation of faith") is a preaching movement that is strictly focused on religious piety. The organization was created in 1927 in the British Raj, near Delhi. Its members insist on the importance of making their behavior conform in a literal way to the model of the Prophet. Among their particularities is the organizing of proselytizing tours that aim to convince the Muslims they meet to follow their model and join their group. The Tabligh expanded rapidly in underprivileged neighborhoods in the 1990s, but has faced competition from Salafism since the 2000s.

Salafism

The Salafist doctrine is very broad, and we will return to several of its aspects. It is rooted in the most literalist school of Islam (Hanbalism) and is partially merged with Wahhabism, the state religious doctrine of Saudi Arabia. Its etymology refers to "pious ancestors" (*al-salaf al-salih*). They are linked to the utopian community of the first believers, who experienced the golden age of the beginnings of Islam, the political model of reference that they wish to restore. Islam, in its pure Salafist version, does not encourage violence, out of respect for the duty to obey the "holder of authority" (*wali al-amr*), which differentiates them from jihadists.

Introduction

Since September 11, 2001, almost 150 Islamist attacks have been committed in Europe, killing 800 people and wounding almost 5,000.[1] To this should be added the hundreds of thwarted attacks from Brest to Vienna, from Glasgow to Milan, and from Barcelona to Oslo.

But jihadism *can't be reduced* to attacks. It is not simply a macabre accounting, even if it is often limited to this. It produces lasting political effects that profoundly and negatively affect the cohesion of European democracies, starting with the political polarization that results from a degraded public debate that confuses immigration, the place of Islam, and terrorist violence.[2] Attacks are a belated symptom of the presence of individuals who adhere to this ideology and its murderous methods. They are not an end, but one means among many employed by sympathizers to intimidate those whom they designate as their enemies. Attacks take place at the end of a process, as the final manifestation of the existence of jihadism at the heart of European societies. Limiting our interest to them alone, and turning them into mere gauges of alert levels, is like judging the quality of a film by watching only the last few minutes. Beyond the issue of security, indeed well upstream from it, there exists the jihadism that lies *between attacks*, which must be analyzed as such.

To gain access to the entirety of the film, along with its subtitles, it may be useful to take the objective numerical data that we have at our disposal as a starting point. To be more precise, one reliable indicator is the number of people who joined a jihadist group during the war in Syria in the 2010s.

For the European Union, including the United Kingdom, the number is 6,000. From this we can draw the immediate conclusion that there is a concentration of the jihadist phenomenon in Western Europe. Almost ninety percent of these individuals come from eight countries: France (1,910, 32% of the total), Germany (950, 16%), United Kingdom (850, 14.5%), Belgium (498, 8.5%), Sweden (310, 5%), Holland (300, 5%), Spain (230, 4%), and Denmark (145, 2.5%).[3]

If we relate these numbers to overall population, Belgium, Sweden, and Denmark jump to the top of the list. As such, and counterintuitively, there was a disproportionate number of departures for Syria from the Scandinavian countries, which have no colonial past and are among the most egalitarian societies in the world. This contradicts a common presupposition, one formulated, for instance, by the American diplomat and former special envoy to Syria, James E. Jeffrey, according to which "Denmark does not produce terrorists."[4] If there is an exception in this general overview, it is Italy. Only 129 residents of this country made their way to the Levant, two and a half times fewer than Sweden, whose population is six times smaller. This number falls to eleven if we include only those born in Italy and holding Italian citizenship. Contrary to its neighbors, Italy did not experience the rise of an endogenous jihadism.

In a previous work, we showed that, in the case of France, jihadism mostly takes shape in specific neighborhoods, and not necessarily the most marginalized ones. Within them, departures for Syria arose within restricted circles — "clusters," families, groups of friends — that had sometimes been involved in the movement for several years.

Three years later, it appears that this observation in fact holds for all the countries mentioned so far. There are about twenty such zones in France and Germany, about fifteen in Great Britain, a half dozen in the Netherlands, and four each for Denmark, Belgium, Sweden, and Spain.

In Germany, the first jihadist network took shape in Ulm and its environs, a peaceful, well-off area with a high student population. Only three percent of documented jihadists are from the former East Germany (and East Berlin), with its weak economy, but thirty percent originate from the *Land* of North Rhine-Westphalia,[5] the most dynamic region of the entire European Union, with a GDP higher than that of Switzerland. In Belgium, only a few departures came from the de-industrialized regions of Wallonia, hit by unemployment and ills of all sorts — the opposite of Antwerp, capital of Flanders and the richest city in the country. The research of Magnus Ranstorp or Henriette Esholdt makes identical observations about the Scandinavian countries,[6] as does that of Robert Leiken or Arturo Varvelli for the United Kingdom.[7] Naturally, certain of the cities in question are confronting serious difficulties, like sensitive areas in English cities (Birmingham, Leicester, Luton, etc.), disadvantaged quarters of Brussels (Melenbeek, Laeken, Schaarbeek, etc.), or underprivileged neighborhoods in France (in Trappes, Roubaix, Strasbourg, etc.). But the same findings are true here as well: within each of these municipalities, departures take place in certain areas, and not in others that are in every way comparable to them. Once again, specific human environments are key. This does not mean that jihadist dynamics are restricted to these zones, or that these are completely "lost" territories, subject to an unbridled and irreversible jihadization. But they are concentrations of a dynamic that must be elucidated.

Johannes Saal's impressive quantitative work on the German-speaking zones of Europe provides us with further information. It appears that the most decisive factors in explaining the number of departures for Syria from any given city is not the level of poverty or the size of the local Muslim population, but the proportion of Salafists within it. Saal notes that, for each of the nineteen German cities in question, the number of departures for Syria is always equivalent to eight percent of local Salafists. In other words: "Jihadism appears as a niche within the Salafi spectrum."[8] The triple finding of a cluster effect, a lack of correlation with the level of poverty, and the importance of the Salafist factor is even more marked for Austria and German-speaking Switzerland, where the raw numbers are smaller. Finally, Saal specifies that individuals from different municipalities are often in contact with one another, which implies that the dynamics of these different spaces are linked.

We're not suggesting that socioeconomic variables play no part in our approach to European jihadism – this would be false. But turning these variables into the main explanatory factor is a shortcut that is as seductive as it is erroneous. At best, they explain only part of the phenomenon, and they tell us nothing about *who* is likely to depart in any given locale; taking into account ideological, genealogical, and historical factors, on the other hand, allows us to determine this in large part. Our analysis must therefore rest at the intersection of these different approaches, and be contextualized in the territories in question.

All of this is congruent with another element relating to departures for Syria. The zones in question are spaces in which veterans of jihad in the 1990s, or their European successors in the 2000s, settled down. Put simply, one finds, behind the geography of European jihadism, the emergence of personal histories made up of men and women. Jihadism didn't fall from the sky or arise out of the earth: it was transplanted by militants.[9] These preliminary observations, which hold for the west of the EU, echo the similar findings of Adrian Shtuni for the Balkans, Nate Rosenblatt in his dissertation on the situation in North Africa and the Middle East, and Shahul Hasbullah for Kattankudy, in Sri Lanka.[10] Taken together, they may sketch out a pattern of the diffusion of jihadism that holds for all territories, beyond the specificities of those on which they focused.

But, even if we don't go quite that far, it does appear that the local development of jihadism exhibits, at a minimum, several common features. The tendency of public debates in Western Europe, however, has often been to try to explain the phenomenon of departures for Syria through the poor functioning of the social contracts of the countries in question, without paying any attention to all the other factors. In France, a debate between the academics Gilles Kepel and Olivier Roy led people to question the role of religious elements in radicalization,[11] but its effects in the political realm have been limited to issues relative to secularism. The latter is suspected, by some, to be too exclusive, generating the resentment and feelings of rejection that fuels jihadism, while for others, it represents a rampart that should be reinforced, and whose continual dilution weakens the republican fabric.[12] Comparable discussions, all more or less lively, have also troubled our neighbors, dividing public opinion on the issue of "communalism" in Great Britain, cultural "differentialism" in Germany,[13] social "egalitarianism" in Scandinavia, and "multiculturalism" in the Netherlands. Every society tends to explain jihadism in the light of its own model, without realizing that the phenomenon is very similar in societies whose political and institutional systems, and relationships with religion, are very different.

Like a drunk person who desperately seeks his keys beneath the streetlight because that's where the light is, this strictly national focus has prevented people from exploring the rest of Europe. But the findings I've mentioned invite us to enact a decentering of the French debate, and not to reduce the explanation for jihadism to the ills of France alone. This means setting forth a scale that is more appropriate for making sense of the general dynamic of all the countries I've mentioned in the north and west of the EU. Despite the diversity of models, these countries share a common political history, and a basis of fundamental values constructed around respect for the rule of law, the guaranteeing of fundamental individual freedoms, and a more or less strong detachment of religion from the public sphere. These societies share similarities where security considerations, and the dynamics of departures for Syria, are concerned, and they have also been the site of similar debates, debates that share many of the same terms. This is true of the spread of Salafism, and also of polemics around the "right to blaspheme" that come up from time to time, in response to events ranging from the death sentence proclaimed against the British writer Salman Rushdie by the Ayatollah Khomeini in 1989, to the assassination of the history and geography teacher Samuel Paty in Conflans-Sainte-Honorine in 2020.

Jihad comes from within – from the mutations of European societies, and from their own history, which includes the settlement of Muslim immigrants, the economic suffering of certain neighborhoods, and unresolved effects of colonialism. But it also comes from the outside, and was in part "reimported" onto European soil by militants from the Muslim world, who, though involved in conflicts that seem remote, are nonetheless interested in putting down roots and acclimatizing themselves to the local political, social, and religious environment. The recontextualization of the jihadist phenomenon in these territories requires us to take local histories into account. The ingredients differ from one culture to another – northern or southern Europe, rural or urban areas, suburbs or city centers, and the varying backgrounds of Muslim populations (the Indian subcontinent for England, North Africa for France, Belgium, and Holland, Turkey for Germany, and the Horn of Africa, the Middle East, and Indonesia for Scandinavia and Holland). But jihadism also arose from transformations undergone by all of these countries over the past 30 years, the most obvious of which are globalization (with its resulting de-industrialization), the digital revolution, and increasing diversity as a result of new population influxes.

In Western Europe during this period, jihadists have tended to group themselves less nationally than linguistically. Over the past thirty years, the French dynamic is often very close to those observed in the French-speaking parts of Switzerland and Belgium, while the Flemish networks overlap with those of Holland. The activists of German-speaking areas, in Germany, Austria, and Switzerland, work in concert, just like those in Scandinavia. The British, custodians of the twenty-first century's lingua franca, play the role of emulators and coordinators of the various regions. This is all reminiscent of the Swiss *Röstigraben*, whereby each canton has its own recipe for potato pancakes, which is the common national dish and the reference point of Helvetic identity beyond cultural differences. The predominance of language in the organization of jihadists in Europe can be explained by the fact that it is the very instrument of political and religious teaching, and is the most important of all the aspects that fuel the spread of this ideology, as we will see.

Those observing this broad panorama often make the mistake of viewing jihadism solely through the lens of Western categories. But even though it has become a European phenomenon through and through, this movement first took shape thousands of miles from the French suburbs, the British and Belgian inner cities, or the plateaus of Sauerland in Germany. It emerged during the extremely violent conflict that tore Afghanistan apart between 1979 and 1989, following the Soviet invasion, and this partially determined its development. This conflict, which from the Western point of view is seen as the death of the USSR and the final episode of the Cold War, and which some qualify, following Francis Fukuyama, as the "end of history,"[14] is in fact the beginning of what the jihadists consider their history. This initial misunderstanding would continue, leading observers to underestimate the breadth of the dynamic that it unleashed. In January 1998, for example, the architect of the American strategy in Afghanistan, the former national security counsellor Zbigniew Brzezinski, told the *Nouvel Observateur*: "What is more important from the standpoint of world history? The Taliban, or the fall of the Soviet Empire? A few agitated Muslims or the liberation of Central Europe and the end of the cold war?"[15] Shortly thereafter, in the morning of September 11, 2001, Al-Qaeda, sheltered in Afghanistan by the Taliban, were able to commit the first wide-scale terrorist attacks by a foreign organization on American territory. Two decades later, jihadism would be debated, during the French presidential campaign, as a domestic political concern. In hindsight, the ideology of "a few agitated Muslims" turned out to be powerful enough to spread, in the space of a generation, from the Hindu Kush to Arab and European cities, to the point of becoming a source of meaning for a sector of young people, and an object of public concern.

High Tide and Low Tide: The Two Phases of Jihadist Activism

Throughout the world, over the past thirty years, the development of jihadism, far from being linear, has followed a sinusoidal path, marked by peaks and then sequences of decline. Militants have tended to act based on how they view the balance of strength with regard to their enemies, and the opportunities offered to them. They have alternated between two distinct periods of activism: phases of action and expansion, when they feel they are in a favorable position, and phases of retreat and reconfiguration, when they see themselves in a position of weakness. These ebbs and flows are reminiscent of the tidal cycle.

At high tide, in phases of ferment, the movement is visible. Sympathizers give priority to armed jihad and actual fighting. The organizations that seek to embody this, such as Al-Qaeda or, more recently, ISIS, plan attacks against chosen targets – Muslim regimes viewed as "apostate," and "infidel" Western powers. They make vehement declarations through spokespeople who are drawn to them, and deploy their propaganda in every possible medium. Their members gather in foreign theaters of operation that become the epicenter of their activism, such as the tribal zones of Afghanistan and Pakistan (in the 1990s), Iraq (in the 2000s), or Syria (in the 2010s). They try to conquer these territories so as to apply the strictest interpretation of sharia law, which they present as a body of perfect laws, a political model infused with the divine, and the only possible expression of Islam. They seek to mediatize their operations to galvanize sympathizers, seduce new recruits, and intimidate adversaries. These periods of affirmation are the periods in which they most often employ terrorism.

At low tide, jihadism seems to have been defeated, and enters into a state of retreat. The very groups that envisioned victory a few months earlier are beset by turmoil. Organizations are dismantled in takeovers that they cause or allow to coalesce, or they tear each other to shreds in fratricidal combats. They no longer have the operational capacity to conduct large-scale attacks.

At this point, their spokespeople advocate clandestine resistance, as when Abu Mohamed al-Adnani called for sympathizers of the Islamic State (IS) to return to the shadows in summer 2016, anticipating inevitable military defeat in Syria.[16] Their emirs, when they are not flushed out and killed in raids, like the Al-Qaeda leaders Osama bin Laden on May 2, 2011 and Ayman al-Zawahiri on August 2, 2022, go to ground or are arrested. Thus, for the external observer, armed jihad seems for all intents and purposes to have disappeared, and its threat correspondingly weakens. Its emblematic figure becomes that of the prisoner with an emaciated face, like the partisans of the IS incarcerated in the north of Syria. For activists, this phase of ebbing is not governed by military logic. The most urgent matter is no longer the direct destabilization of enemy societies, but ideological and intellectual reconfiguration, and quick adaptation in the face of the new judicial or security situation. It's true that there can be attacks during this time, but the threat is greatly reduced. Armed struggle is replaced by ideological subversion from inside or outside of the countries in question. The sympathizers mostly strive to remain under the radar, to convince judicial authorities to reduce their sentences (even at the cost of officially distancing themselves from their former terrorist affiliations), or to downplay the scope of their involvement. Those who admit to being "soldiers of the Islamic State," like Salah Abdeslam, the sole survivor of the commando unit that carried out the Paris terrorist attacks of November 13, 2015, are a minority.

Armed struggle and ideological struggle, visibility and discretion, urgency and patience, attacks and indoctrination: jihadism is an adaptable militant phenomenon that fluctuates according to the context. But it no more ceases to exist in its intermediate periods than the ocean evaporates between its high and low phases.

This wave-like movement remains a poorly understood aspect of jihadist dynamics in the West. The usual approach tends to ignore this pendulum and measure it in static ways, solely from the standpoint of the threat of terrorism, in other words through a lens in which only the phase of strength is visible. Few are interested in the mutations that occur during phases of weakness, which determine the form jihadism will take during the next inversion. European societies, for lack of taking into account the double dimension – political and religious – that is proper to this ideology and the conditions of its propagation, consign themselves to enduring the rhythm imposed by the jihadists, rather than anticipating reorganizations that take place.

The back-and-forth movement between these phases was conceived of by several ideologues, including one of the original sources of inspiration for the Salafi-jihadist movement, the Egyptian Muslim Brotherhood member Sayyid Qutb, who was radicalized in Nasser's prisons and hung by the regime in 1966.[17] These ideologues present activism as a succession of periods of strength (*marhalat al-tamakkoun*),[18] in which open combat is recommended, and weakness (*marhalat al-istidaf*), in which preaching, political struggle, and religious teaching must be privileged.[19]

According to these interpretations, militants must put their faith in the apostolate of Mohammed. The prophet was able to avoid open confrontation when he began to preach, when the first Muslims were exposed to hostility from the pagan tribes of Mecca. After the flight to Medina (the Hijrah of 622, the event that marks the year 0 of the Islamic calendar), they were able to change their strategy, eventually gathering support, leading a campaign against the Meccans, and taking the city, which was the prelude to a long period of the expansion of Islam by way of conquests (*foutouhat*). Almost all militant jihadists know these Koranic episodes, even if they don't make daily references to them to justify their actions. The ideologues among them, who provide intellectual structure for the movement, make free use of them, and adapt them to specific contexts. In this way, such ideologues form a distinctive category, one that conforms to the observations of Louis Wirth, who writes: "In every society, there are individuals whose special function is to accumulate, preserve, rework, and spread the intellectual legacy of the group."[20]

This book deals with the way jihadism, as an ideology, has contributed to the production of a new definition of Islamic identity, and asks how this identity, once transposed into European Islam, has transformed from top to bottom the relationship certain Muslims have with their life in Europe, their country, and their European identity, to the point that they now view themselves as having absolutely and violently broken with the constitutive values of these societies. It aims to put forth elements that allow for an explanation of the expansion of jihadism outside the Middle East, and the political tensions that stem from it in Europe.

Many books have dealt with the evolution of Islamist terrorism in Europe,[21] and countless works have looked at how radical currents took shape there. But regrettably, despite its constant political importance, no *history of European jihadism* has been written. Nor has the importance of this movement outside periods in which attacks occur been the object of any in-depth treatment. In the following pages, I seek to join the different wagons of the history of this phenomenon, by straddling several geographic regions in the Middle East and the Euro-Mediterranean zone. I will attempt to connect local dynamics with the global transformations that converge in the departure of 6,000 Europeans toward the Syria of the IS, and in hitherto unseen reconfigurations since the fall of this organization.

While our account will follow a historical sequence, and focus in particular on the workings of the movement in periods of "low tide," it is not the fruit of the work of a historian, but of a researcher in political science. It is based on the gathering and use of primary and secondary sources, as well as archival material in three languages (French, English, and Arabic) from the vast collection of the libraries of Princeton University, where I taught for two years (2020–2022). This material enriched the abundant work I'd done in France and Belgium, which I began ten years ago, and work I did in prisons with several dozen French jihadists who were active in the war in the Levant before and during the fall of IS. This was complemented by seventy new interviews conducted between 2020 and 2022 in the United States and eight European countries. The book gathers the varied observations of important actors over the course of almost three decades, by Western jihadists, government and security officials, social workers, politicians, imams, former militants and newcomers, and ordinary witnesses of trivial events whose repercussions unleashed global polemics.

Over the past thirty years, jihadism has ebbed and flowed in Europe with astonishing regularity, at a rate of one complete cycle per decade, and this book dedicates a part to each one: 1989–2001, 2001–2010, 2010–2023. Changes from one period to the next take place when historic events occur, major disruptions that bring with them a radical change in perceptions, and shifts in the balance of power, in the places in question.

The phenomenon originated in the war in Afghanistan in the 1980s, put down roots in Europe in the 1990s, spread throughout this continent after September 11, 2001, and expanded to new horizons with the emergence of jihad in Iraq and then Syria, where it changed scale. In the post-IS period, it underwent new phases of mutation, in prisons and within European societies, which makes understanding this broad movement all the more urgent.

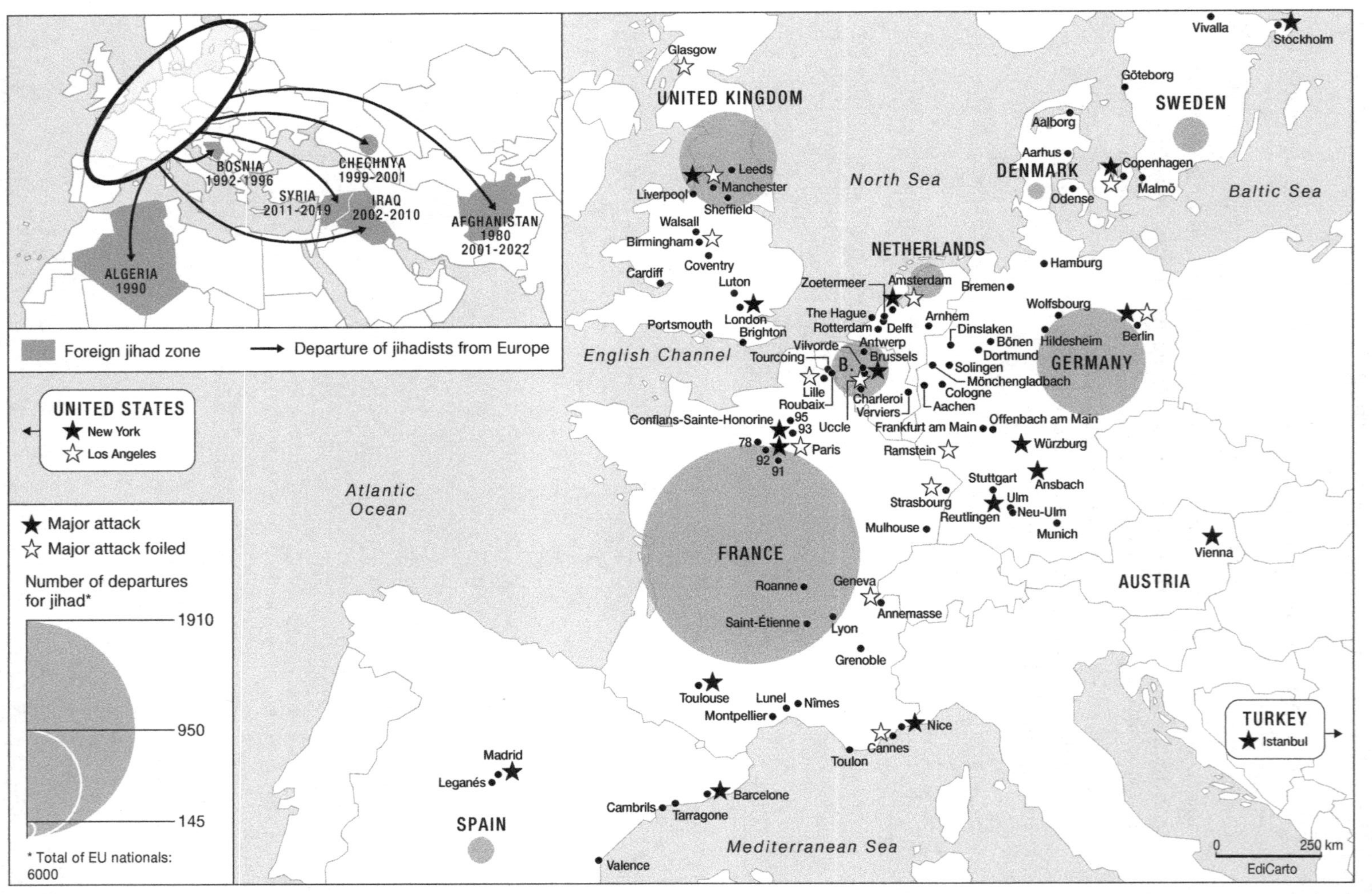

BOSNIA
1992-1996
CHECHNYA
1999-2001
SYRIA
2011-2019
IRAQ
2002-2010
AFGHANISTAN
1980
2001-2022
ALGERIA
1990
Foreign jihad zone
Departure of jihadists from Europe
UNITED STATES
New York
Los Angeles
Major attack
Major attack foiled
Number of departures
for jihad*
1910
950
145
* Total of EU nationals:
6000
Glasgow
UNITED KINGDOM
Leeds
Liverpool
Manchester
Sheffield
Walsall
Birmingham
Coventry
Cardiff
Luton
Portsmouth
London
Brighton
English Channel
North Sea
Vivalla
Stockholm
Göteborg
SWEDEN
Aalborg
Aarhus
DENMARK
Copenhagen
Odense
Malmö
Baltic Sea
Hamburg
NETHERLANDS
Zoetermeer
Amsterdam
Bremen
Wolfsbourg
The Hague
Rotterdam
Delft
Arnhem
Dinslaken
Bönen
Hildesheim
Berlin
Vilvorde
Antwerp
Brussels
GERMANY
Tourcoing
B.
Solingen
Mönchengladbach
Dortmund
Lille
Charleroi
Verviers
Cologne
Aachen
Roubaix
Conflans-Sainte-Honorine
95
93
Uccle
Frankfurt am Main
Offenbach am Main
78
92
91
Paris
Ramstein
Würzburg
Strasbourg
Stuttgart
Ansbach
Ulm
Reutlingen
Neu-Ulm
Mulhouse
Munich
Vienna
Atlantic
Ocean
FRANCE
AUSTRIA
Roanne
Geneva
Saint-Étienne
Annemasse
Lyon
Grenoble
Toulouse
Lunel
Nîmes
Montpellier
Nice
Cannes
Toulon
TURKEY
Istanbul
Madrid
Leganés
Cambrils
Barcelone
Tarragone
SPAIN
Mediterranean Sea
Valence
0   250 km
EdiCarto

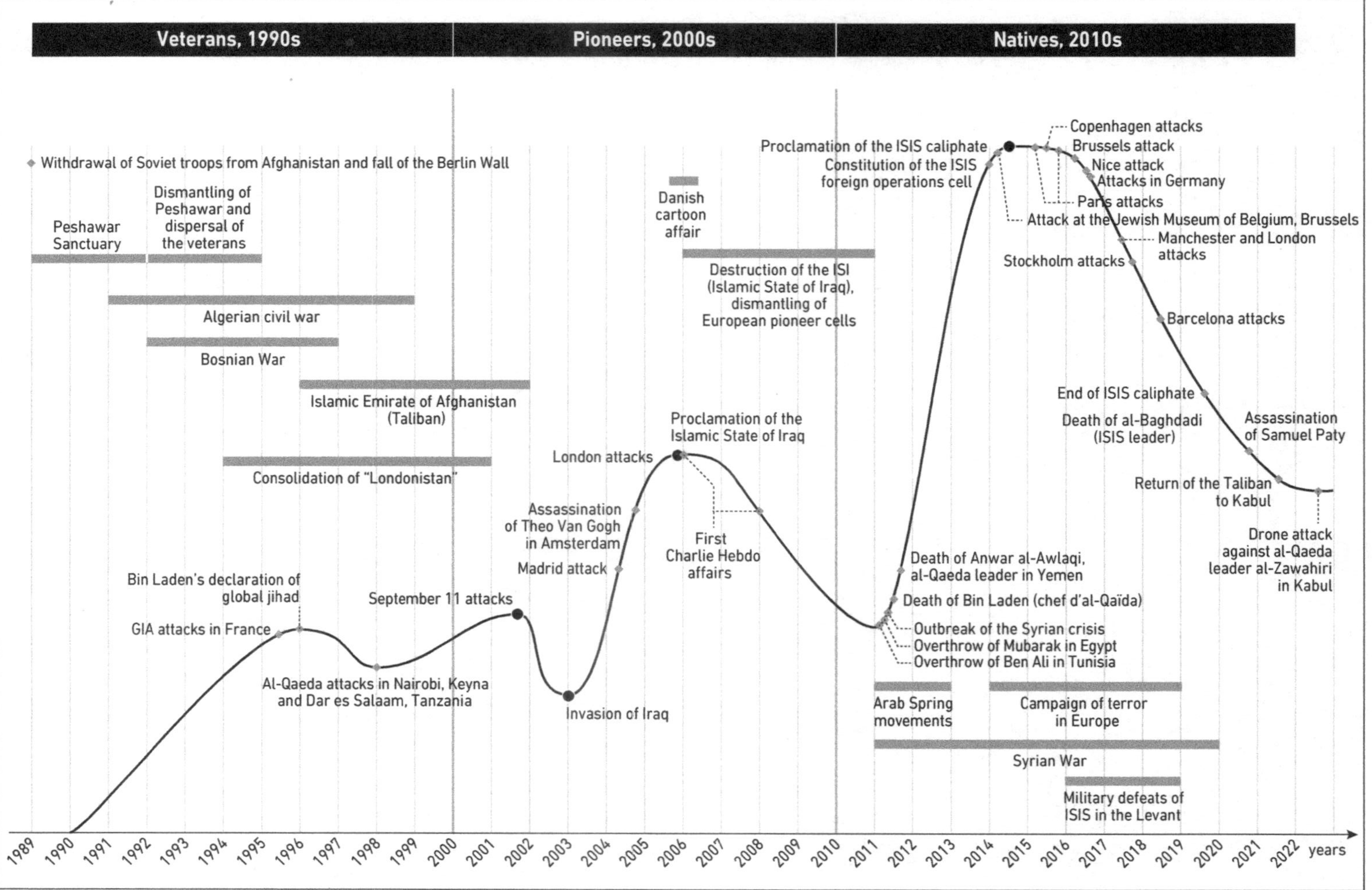

Veterans, 1990s
Pioneers, 2000s
Natives, 2010s
Withdrawal of Soviet troops from Afghanistan and fall of the Berlin Wall
Peshawar Sanctuary
Dismantling of Peshawar and dispersal of the veterans
Algerian civil war
Bosnian War
Islamic Emirate of Afghanistan (Taliban)
Consolidation of "Londonistan"
Bin Laden's declaration of global jihad
GIA attacks in France
September 11 attacks
Al-Qaeda attacks in Nairobi, Keyna and Dar es Salaam, Tanzania
Danish cartoon affair
Destruction of the ISI (Islamic State of Iraq), dismantling of European pioneer cells
Proclamation of the Islamic State of Iraq
London attacks
Assassination of Theo Van Gogh in Amsterdam
Madrid attack
First Charlie Hebdo affairs
Invasion of Iraq
Proclamation of the ISIS caliphate
Constitution of the ISIS foreign operations cell
Copenhagen attacks
Brussels attack
Nice attack
Attacks in Germany
Paris attacks
Attack at the Jewish Museum of Belgium, Brussels
Manchester and London attacks
Stockholm attacks
Barcelona attacks
End of ISIS caliphate
Death of al-Baghdadi (ISIS leader)
Assassination of Samuel Paty
Return of the Taliban to Kabul
Drone attack against al-Qaeda leader al-Zawahiri in Kabul
Death of Anwar al-Awlaqi, al-Qaeda leader in Yemen
Death of Bin Laden (chef d'al-Qaïda)
Outbreak of the Syrian crisis
Overthrow of Mubarak in Egypt
Overthrow of Ben Ali in Tunisia
Arab Spring movements
Campaign of terror in Europe
Syrian War
Military defeats of ISIS in the Levant
1989 1990 1991 1992 1993 1994 1995 1996 1997 1998 1999 2000 2001 2002 2003 2004 2005 2006 2007 2008 2009 2010 2011 2012 2013 2014 2015 2016 2017 2018 2019 2020 2021 2022 years

THE VETERANS –
THE 1990s

1

Afghanistan: Return to the Source

All the people are dying they're willing to give
Every drop of their blood for this freedom to live
All the people are dying to get back their land
And the home of their fathers who died for Islam

Chorus

Afghanistan the land of Islam [repeat]
Afghanistan the land of Islam
Afghanistan, la illa illallah [there is no God but Allah]
Muhammad rasulullah [Muhammad is the messenger of Allah][1]
Alaihi salamullah [the peace of Allah be upon him]

There's five million homeless over one million dead
How can the world go to sleep with injustice up there
All the orphans are crying it's loud and it's clear
For the ones who have heart for ones who can hear [repeat]

Chorus

Ya muslimoun, Ya muslimoun [repeat] [O Muslims, O Muslims]

Oh victory is coming and history will tell
'Cause the disbelieving army is heading for hell

And paradise belongs to the pious and firm
To God we belong and to Him we return [repeat][2]

Chorus

Ya muslimoun, Ya muslimoun [repeat] [O Muslims, O Muslims]
Yusuf Islam (formerly Cat Stevens), "Afghanistan," mid-1980s

Fifty Shades of Red: The USSR and the Afghan Quagmire

Let me give you an idea of how important Afghanistan is. You've probably heard of the pop star Cat Stevens, who converted to Islam in the 1970s and changed his name to Yusuf Islam? For a community that was exposed to so much racism at the time, imagine what it was like to have a star convert to Islam and give up music . . . He composed Islamic songs [*anashid*] for several years, and one of them was about Afghanistan . . . It went like this [he sings the chorus and the first verse]. It was a popular song in the British Muslim community in the 1980s. And so you can see, it had an effect on us: that war was a holy war; it was our duty.[3]

These remarks, made in London in winter 2022 by Usama Hasan, one of the rare Europeans to have gone to the front line in Afghanistan before the fall of the USSR, highlights the singular importance of the conflict in the collective imagination of its time. This Briton of Pakistani and Indian origin, who holds a degree in physics from the University of Cambridge, was a prominent imam in the UK's Salafist community. He continues:

At the time, the Muslim community in England was between 500,000 and a million. Everyone in our circles was talking about Afghanistan. It was huge because fighters from all over the world were going there to support jihad. The idea of holy war was really important. Afghanistan, Palestine, the Middle East, and later Bosnia – we felt we had a duty to act with respect to these causes that we were following in the newspapers, in the brochures of Islamist organizations, in newsletters, on TV, on the BBC. It was close to my heart.

As is clear from these words, the echo of the war in Afghanistan resounded in important ways in certain European homes. In 1979, the invasion of

Afghanistan by the USSR came about in the tumultuous geopolitical context engendered by the Iranian Revolution. The overthrow of the Shah, an ally of the United States, and the establishment of a (Shiite) Islamic Republic led to a change in the balance of power in the region whose effects continue to this day. The Soviet leaders feared that the revolutionary spirit would spread into neighboring Afghanistan and the Muslim-majority Soviet republics of Central Asia. On Christmas Eve of 1979, the Red Army began a military intervention in the country. The plan was to replace the communist regime in power, which developed in a context of chronic instability and outside of the Soviet Union's sphere of influence, with a new government aligned with Moscow. Channels of communication were interrupted and the main cities were occupied, while a straw man was installed as the country's leader. The objective seemed to have been accomplished. But the country's rough and hilly terrain and harsh climate limited the maneuvers that could be undertaken on its territory, which was never conquered or unified in a lasting way. The generals underestimated the effectiveness of local resistance and the ability of the United States to exploit what was the first incursion into Muslim lands by the USSR since the Second World War. Bruce Riedel, at that time in charge of the Afghanistan dossier at the CIA, speaks of how the American administration viewed the Kremlin's recklessness:

> The Carter administration saw an opportunity. Here was the USSR trying to stifle an insurrection in a huge country with an extremely devout Muslim population. In many ways, it was the perfect place to inflict on the USSR what the Carter administration and other Americans believed they had done to us in Vietnam. The idea was to drag the Soviets into a quagmire that would cost them a fortune, both financially and in terms of wounded and killed soldiers, with very little prospect of victory. The added advantage was that, just as the Viet Cong had a sanctuary in North Vietnam, we had a sanctuary for the mujahideen in Pakistan. The Pakistanis were willing to . . . well, no, they were eager to support the mujahideen. So we had someone to do the dirty work while we sat back and watched the Soviets get wiped out in an endless conflict they couldn't win.[4]

Four years after the humiliating evacuation of Saigon, and a few weeks after American diplomatic personnel were taken hostage in Iran, support for the Afghan resistance became the lynchpin of the fight against the USSR. During the 1980s, the United States employed a method they'd used since the beginning of the Cold War, to contain the advance of communism in Muslim-majority countries: namely, supporting, in the name of the defense of Islam, proxies who feared, and were galvanized by, the atheist tenets, anticlericalism, and emancipatory promises of Marxism and Leninism.[5] This maintained American investment beneath the threshold of open conflict, thus preventing a nuclear escalation between the two superpowers. The result went beyond the expectations of Washington strategist. Bruce Riedel continues:

> At the beginning of the war, the general feeling within the CIA and the government was that the Russians would bloody their noses, not that the Afghans would defeat the Soviet army. We are talking about the same Red Army that was victorious in World War II, that sustained twenty million casualties against the Nazis; they would surely find a way out. But starting with the second Reagan administration [1984–1988], it became increasingly clear that the Russians knew they were losing. At first, we wanted to make things difficult for them, but in the end it became the decisive battle that would lead to the end of the Cold War.[6]

The consequences of the invasion of Afghanistan are now well known. On the Afghan side, the price of a decade of confrontation turned out to be astronomical: more than a million dead, and far more who were severely injured and displaced. On the Soviet side, what was expected to be a short-term operation became the one to which every superlative applies: it was the longest, costliest, and deadliest conflict in the history of the USSR.[7] The miscalculation was fatal. The Berlin Wall collapsed on November 9, 1989, a few months after the military withdrawal, and the Soviet Union disappeared two years later, on December 5, 1991. On the American side, the Afghan war was the most important operation in the history of the CIA, and one in which a very low investment resulted in huge dividends.[8] The fate of the Cold War, was not settled by a nuclear apocalypse, but in the slurry of the Hindu Kush. The iron curtain fell and the liberation of Central and Eastern Europe was achieved without any American losses. Nonetheless, the hidden costs of this victory turned out to be colossal: nothing less than the birth of the matrix of contemporary jihadism.

The Arrears of Afghan Jihad

The importance of the war in Afghanistan for the rise of contemporary jihadism has been abundantly documented in academic literature, notably since September 11, 2001.[9] If we want to understand the uniqueness of this phenomenon, three of its aspects merit further attention. First, the acts of volunteers in Afghanistan was guided by international considerations that from the start largely went beyond the framework of Central Asia. Second, jihadism did not appear within the Afghan conflict but at its peripheries. Third, jihadism flourished there at least as much as an intellectual matrix as on the front lines.

During the whole of the 1980s, the Afghan cause was promoted in important ways in Muslim-majority countries. The Pakistani and Saudi security services and religious networks played the initial roles, with the benediction of the United States. They put in place a vast program of financial, military, humanitarian, and logistic support for the various factions of the Afghan resistance, which led most of the combats.

What is usually referred to as jihad in Afghanistan took shape in the middle of the 1980s, both through the channeling of aid and the arrival of thousands of volunteers from the Muslim world, referred to in the international press as "Afghan Arabs." Their recruitment was facilitated by a circuit of Islamic NGOs, many of which were located in Gulf states, and their satellites in the various capitals of the Arab world.[10]

At the end of the 1980s, several regimes in North Africa and the Middle East sustained broad protests, due to an economic downturn, political paralysis, and a delay in demographic transition. The reinforcement of authoritarianism and the destruction of opposition movements allowed Islamic movements to become the sole bearers of political alternatives, whose most extremist elements began dreaming of revolution. Several regimes – including Algeria, Egypt, Syria, Jordan, and Saudi Arabia – saw the promotion of jihad against the Soviet Union as an outlet for appeasing these tensions. The departure of Islamist groups for the faraway peaks of the Himalayan foothills offered a precious distraction for domestic repression, a low-cost way of redirecting the energy of dissenters toward a common foreign enemy. For radical activists who were persecuted in their countries, meanwhile, the Afghan war offered a form of exile and the hope of constructing a sanctuary that could become a base of operations.

Beyond the attraction of fighting against the Soviet Union, the Afghan region became an unexpected meeting ground for dissidents from across the Muslim world, who hadn't necessarily given up on the aim of overthrowing the systems in their home countries. These mixtures gave rise to new forms of synergy, of which today's jihadism is the outcome.

Fifty Shades of Green: The Intellectual Matrix of Jihadism

Jihadism was structured behind the Afghan front lines. The Pakistani city of Peshawar is the place in which volunteers converged and new ideas were born.[11]

Situated in the northwest of Pakistan, in a majority Pashtun region, Peshawar was the main gateway toward wartime Afghanistan, through which both military convoys and international aid passed. The seven parties of Afghan resistance set up their headquarters there, and held authority over the camps that housed hundreds of thousands of refugees. Innumerable NGOs installed their local offices there. Both information services and private donors were active. The Afghan Arabs landed there by the thousands, but blended into the scenery of this operational hub, which was indispensable for everyone active in the war. One such Afghan Arab, during a meeting in London in February 2022, gave the following overview of the situation:

> There were many NGOs, often Westerners who were working with refugees [. . .]. Arab volunteers were in the minority; they weren't at the center of the action in Peshawar, there were only a few thousand of them, including drivers, teachers, those who had settled in with their wives, and those who lived in guest houses.[12]

In 1984, the Afghan Services Bureau (*maktab al-khidamat*), the initial welcoming point for the Afghan Arabs, opened in Peshawar. This unassuming building, which resembled a business incubator, served as an office, mosque, gathering place, and accommodation facility for foreigners who sought to offer their services to the Afghan cause. Its founder, Abdullah Azzam, would become one of the most renowned figures of global jihadism. At that point, he was a well-known professor of Islamic theology, a member of the Jordanian Muslim Brotherhood, and enjoyed privileged access to the Saudi religious establishment, whose ulamas[13] are major promoters of Salafism, and sponsors of the Afghan jihad. This support allowed him to take on high-profile responsibilities in the transport of foreign aid from the Gulf countries, and in the coordination of Afghan Arabs. According to the Norwegian scholar of Islam Thomas Hegghammer, who wrote a long and rich biography of him, Azzam established himself, by turns, as a preacher, a recruiter, a combatant, a militant theorist, and an ambassador of jihad in Afghanistan.[14] His son-in-law, an Algerian who was one of the first to arrive in Afghanistan, and who assisted him in the creation of the Services Bureau, explained the aim of the Bureau in an interview conducted in 2022:

> Among the Arabs, some were from the Muslim Brotherhood, others were Salafists [. . .]. Abdullah Azzam wanted to find a way to bring some unity to it all and find a role for everyone who came to help, whether you were a doctor, teacher, driver, religious scholar, or former soldier.[15]

Azzam established around thirty branch offices of the Services Bureau across the world, the aim of which was to raise funds, broadcast propaganda, and recruit new candidates for jihad. Their workings benefited from the generosity of one of its first disciples, the son of a Saudi construction magnate, a billionaire named Osama bin Laden, who in 1986 established his own camp in Afghanistan, which focused on the training of an elite fighting force that would become the main global jihadist organization: Al Qaeda. Azzam was the first to understand the unprecedented enthusiasm for Afghanistan on the part of Islamists from across the world, and he tried to shape the movement in its initial stages. For this reason, he is to this day the object of emphatic respect from almost every major player in the Jihadist movement. Osama bin Laden, for example, said the following in an interview with Al Jazeera in 1999, ten years after Azzam's death: "May God have mercy on him. He was a man worth an entire nation. Since his assassination, Muslim women haven't been able to give birth to a man of his caliber. The people of jihad who lived through that era know that no one did as much for jihad in Afghanistan as Sheikh Abdullah Azzam."[16]

On the intellectual front, Abdullah Azzam brought together disparate elements from various Islamist currents who were present in situ, and in so doing confirmed himself as the original ideologue of what has since been named "Salafi-jihadism."[17] His main contribution lies in the way he revisited principles of jihad that had been debated for centuries in the Islamic tradition so as to make jihad the focus of this religion and insert it into a modern worldview, adapting it to the context of the war against the USSR. He drew from the famed theses of Sayyid Qutb, the ideologue of the revolutionary fringe of the Egyptian Muslim Brotherhood, and adapted them to Salafist doctrine. His writing inscribes action against the Soviets within the time frame outlined by the Koran, and is based on this text's conceptual categories. Jihad in Afghanistan becomes the motor for the renewal of a Muslim history abandoned since the fall of the Abbasid Caliphate, in the thirteenth century, and marked by continuous decline.[18] He takes stock of the disastrous state (in his view) of the Muslim world in the 1980s in the light of the divine promise formulated in the Koran more than thirteen centuries earlier: the conquest and Islamicization of the entire world. According to him, the resumption of Koranic history, which will end with the accomplishment of this promise, requires a return to original dogma (which is nothing other than Salafism), and the circulation of this dogma by way of jihad. The forces that oppose this movement, and which must be annihilated, have taken the form of Soviet invaders in the case of Afghanistan, but take on different forms in other places. The Israelis and their American benefactors, in Palestine, the Spaniards who have "occupied" Muslim Andalusia since the *Reconquista*, or those regimes in the Arab world that oppress "true" Muslims like him, are so many avatars of this.

According to Azzam, the international mobilization to repel the Red Army is an example of healthy reaction that must be imitated elsewhere. It is the task of this "avant garde," composed of determined militants (the Salafi-jihadists), to enlighten other Muslims, who may then intervene wherever conditions are ripe for doing so.[19] In his writing, the war in Afghanistan is thus merely one landmark on the road of jihad, which leads toward a return of "true" Islam, and is a decisive step for the accomplishment of the Koranic promise: the advent of the caliphate and the worldwide spread of Islam, the universal truth breathed by God.[20]

It should therefore not be surprising that in the writings of Azzam, and those of many of his followers, participation in holy war has become an essential component of Muslim identity, a sort of sixth pillar of the religion. According to him, jihad to "liberate" Muslim territories is a religious obligation incumbent upon all believers (*fard ayn*), wherever they may be in the world. In order to concretize this narrative, he introduces elements that create a cult of the contemporary martyr-combatant, presented as the best way to assure entry into paradise and atonement for sins committed on earth, and hence the symbolic fuel for the rise of militancy. The intellectual matrix set forth by Azzam thereby moves well beyond the framework of Afghanistan so as to nourish the reflections of Islamist movements throughout the world.

No sooner were they published in Peshawar than his writing spread abroad via the journal *Al-Jihad*, which he founded in 1986, or by way of his magnum opus *Ilhaq bil-kafila* ("Join the Caravan"), a compilation of his articles that appeared in 1987. Copies reached the shelves of certain Islamic bookstores in London, Brussels, and Paris. An antiterrorism police officer in Brussels, who at the time was the only member of his unit who had learned Arabic and was interested in militant literature, recalls:

> At that time, in certain mosques that were just beginning to become politicized, pamphlets such as *Al-Jihad* [Abdullah Azzam's journal] could be found. Using their phone number, we learned that these people had an official office in Belgium, and that fundraising was done for them.[21]

Azzam himself traveled abroad to bring awareness to the cause. His presence in the west bothered no one, as Bruce Riedel, head of the CIA's Afghanistan dossier, observes:

> Azzam traveled extensively to raise funds, including to the United States. It's hard to imagine in 2022, but in the 1980s, Muslims coming to the United States to raise funds wasn't something the FBI monitored. Especially since he was raising funds for a war that we were also financing . . . So if someone else wanted to foot the bill, that was even better, it saved American taxpayers money![22]

At the end of the 1980s, the entire spectrum of Islamism was present in Peshawar. Aside from the followers of Azzam, who remained the most important figure, several more or less rival poles coexisted. Members of the Egyptian group responsible for the assassination of President Sadat (the Gamaa Islamiyya) established their own guesthouses and their own journal. Some of them later sought refuge in Denmark and played a key role in local jihadist structures, as we will see. Like the Egyptians, the Algerians had their own brigades. In 1987, the Afghan Abdulrab Rasul Sayyaf, who was close to the Saudi networks, founded a "University of Jihad and Preaching."[23] Several of today's most renowned jihadist ideologues had classes in Peshawar at that time, such as the Jordanian Abu Qatada and his compatriot Abu Muhammad al-Maqdisi, who would be the mentor of the founder of the Islamic State in Iraq. The entire milieu turned into a site of so much intellectual fermentation that Peshawar, as time went on, became the final destination of many volunteers. The indoctrination in Peshawar's institutes by way of eminent figures who rushed to the city and vied to be the most radical of all became more attractive than crossing the Afghan border and exposing oneself to the ruthlessness of the front lines. Bruce Riedel, the CIA agent in charge of the Afghanistan dossier, said the following about the situation:

At the beginning of the war, there was only a small number of Arab fighters, mainly Saudis, such as Bin Laden. Most of the others arrived much later, in the late 1980s. Around 15,000 Saudis traveled to Pakistan, but 95 percent of them never crossed the border into Afghanistan. They were there for a "photo op," dressing up in combat gear and taking pictures. They would return home and say "I took part in the great battle." Very few were actually killed in action. Bin Laden is a special case because of the combat experience he gained.

There were others like him, but the vast majority of what are known as Afghan Arabs ended up working in hospitals and shelters for the millions of Afghan refugees who had fled to Pakistan. The reality of what they did on the ground is far less glamorous than the mythology they later developed, which consists in saying that they defeated the Soviet Union, and that the Afghan Arabs were instrumental in the victory . . . None of that has any connection with reality. It's a very effective myth, and for reasons of their own, the Saudis wanted to propagate this image. It made them key players in defeating the atheist Marxists.[24]

In the cauldron of Peshawar, the neighborhoods in which militants gathered turned into a new kind of laboratory, giving rise to the birth of the first jihadist ecosystem. The original diversity of the movement was a key element of its internal dynamism, but also the marker of its structural instability, which would haunt its development for the next three decades. In the manner of a true symbol, Abdullah Azzam was assassinated in Peshawar in 1989, in a car bombing for which no one has ever been charged.[25] The dynamics he initiated in Peshawar survived him and would be exported, especially to Europe.

Peshawar, 1992: Ground Zero

Contemporary jihadism emerged as a movement not at high tide, at the peak of the war in Afghanistan, but at low tide, after the Soviet occupation of the country, when its initial raison d'être had disappeared.

The number of Arab volunteers in Peshawar continued to grow after the withdrawal of the Red Army in 1989.[26] Most justified their presence by the need to overthrow the communist president Mohammad Najibullah, who remained in power in Kabul until 1992. But many of them returned to what had been their initial objective: the fight against the regimes in place in their own countries. Peshawar thus became the staging ground not for the fight against the Soviets, as it had been, but for international jihadism, as it had been conceived by Azzam and his auxiliaries. The Egyptians in particular stand out. Between 1989 and 1993, they instigated three assassination attempts against the Ministers of the Interior and the head of government. An attack on President Hosni Mubarak, while he was visiting Ethiopia, failed two years later, while the Embassy of Pakistan was struck by an explosion, which led to the closure of the Services Bureau by the authorities. In the meantime, the neighborhoods inhabited by the Afghan Arabs and their families in Peshawar came to be highly sought after, places where these people could live amongst themselves in isolation and follow a routine of daily life regulated by the strictest religious laws.[27] Certain veterans of the jihad lived there because they couldn't imagine returning to their own countries without facing torture. These included Azzam's son-in-law Abdullah Anas, who explained:

> When I decided to go to Afghanistan in 1984, I was alone. In 1992, I was married and had two children. She [his wife, the daughter of Abdullah Azzam] is Palestinian with Jordanian nationality. I am Algerian and I cannot return to Algeria at this time because of the repression.[28]

At the same time, Peshawar was still the gateway to the jihadist training camps in Afghanistan and the tribal areas, including those established by Al-Qaeda. The city attracted militants from across the world seeking to take on a sheen of legitimacy within international Islamist circles. Abdullah Anas, who took up arms against the Soviets, deplores these "posers" who were enthroned as mujahedeen for the simple fact of studying in local madrasas:

> From the moment you said "jihad in Afghanistan" or "Abdullah Azzam," people [in Islamist circles] automatically came to listen to you because of the aura it gave you . . . I was very surprised to see certain people, certain "big names," who had never been to Afghanistan [only Peshawar] and who boasted of being jihadists.[29]

In this way, the movement had a concrete existence in physical spaces from the very beginning. The centrality of Peshawar in the cosmogony of jihadism demonstrates that the latter cannot be reduced to fighting or dying as a martyr, and even less to terrorist attacks. As the place where everything began, Peshawar inaugurates a paradigm of the gathering and functioning of activists in actual territories.[30] It allows us to understand that Salafist Jihadism can take shape in "background" sanctuaries even more than on front lines, and that the gathering of activists who are driven by the same utopian images gives rise to attempts to organize movements and also the territories onto which these movements project themselves. Abdullah Azzam and the Afghan Services Bureau were the first incarnations, but the myriad of religious schools and ideologues that came about in his wake shows that the model is easily emulated and duplicated.

Starting in 1992, the fall of the communist government in Kabul gave rise to a violent civil war between the different victorious Afghan factions.[31] In Peshawar, the situation underwent a serious deterioration. Economic difficulties were felt immediately, and poverty became the norm as the creditors of the Gulf States paused their massive funding. Added to that were internal struggles, themselves the product of ideological, ethnic, and cultural rivalries, and the ravages of the war against the Soviet Union, which left Pakistan with the burden of hundreds of thousands of refugees. Between 1992 and 1994, most of the veterans fled the city. They benefited from the tacit support of local authorities, who were subjected to the pressure of foreign governments (in particular those of Saudi Arabia and Egypt) who were worried about their citizens settling in what appeared to be the base of operations for an increasingly globalized terrorism. The last burning embers of the Cold War would soon be rekindled in a new locale, Europe, though this would not be understood until after September 11, 2001.

2

The Preaching Machines, from Peshawar to London

During the 1990s, thousands of "Afghan Arabs" and veterans scattered toward new horizons. It was thus that jihadism spread to the Euro-Mediterranean zone, first in Bosnia (1992–1996) following the implosion of Yugoslavia, then in Algeria during the "Black Decade" that devastated the country (1991–1999). Other militants, hunted in their own countries, settled in Europe, creating clusters similar to those that had been glimpsed in Peshawar.

Preaching Machines in Europe

The situation in the Pakistani city at the beginning of the 1990s at first seems to have little in common with those of London, Brussels, or Copenhagen (which are already very different from one another) in the same period. By the same logic, these cities have little to do with those of southern Tunisia or northern Syria twenty years later. And yet very similar mechanisms took shape in these different spaces, following more or less the same blueprint.

The starting point for these situations is (1) a group of Salafi-jihadist militants, who (2) gather in certain neighborhoods that they identify in advance, and (3) where they establish training structures, collectively organize preaching, and build support networks. All of which results (4) in the creation of a new Islamic frame of reference for the locality, one that is impregnated with Salafi-jihadism, which these militants can then disseminate beyond the bounds of the neighborhood.

30

As we will see over the course of the following pages, the actors in question seem to identify the territories they seek to "shape" on the basis of whether Islamist movements are already present, which was the point of departure for the entire dynamic of Peshawar. In the 1990s in Europe, most of the groups in question developed within the galaxy of the Muslim Brotherhood or the Tablighi Jamaat. In the 2000s, it was most often the Salafists, and in the 2010s, of environments that were a mix of these different influences. Salafi-jihadists tended to adapt their modus operandi to the religious, political, social, and economic situation of the places where they settled. There is thus a connection between the nature of the environment (whether the zone in question is socially, ethnically, or religiously marginalized, blighted by drugs, home to other Islamic movements, etc.) and the shape their activism ends up taking.

Once they have settled into a particular neighborhood, these activists establish "preaching machines," which reflect the methods and techniques, but also the religious and community structures, that they employ to propagate their unique conception of Islam in a given environment. Whether in the public sphere or the virtual sphere, their activities include "ordinary" forms of activism and proselytism: going door to door, or organizing sociocultural, sporting, educational, or spiritual activities. They enriched their offerings with new initiatives as the breadth of their financial and human networks grew: they opened independent schools, held seminars and colloquia, invited radical preachers to speak, etc.

Over time, preaching machines often bring about an Islamist ecosystem that is more or less radical and more or less anchored in its territory, which can produce effects in surrounding areas, especially those focused on by activists. We will observe this in particular in the case of "centers" of militant geography that are created by Salafi-jihadist activists in Europe, such as Londonistan or certain districts of Brussels.

In all the places we consider, and regardless of the size of the preaching machine, the activists in question strive to transform the political and social aspects of the human environment. Where religion is concerned, they seek to gain a foothold at the heart of the Muslim community, and create within it a faction that will fight the influence of all other forms of Islam. In so doing, they aim, whether by persuasion or intimidation (depending on the balance of power in the given community), to have the injunctions of the doctrines of Salifi-jihadism applied to all of the faithful. One sees the results of this in dress and in the extolling of the signs of belonging that are valued by the canons of conservative Islam (niqab, qamis, etc.), but not only there. One also observes it in the way people focus on an "ideological" adhesion to the project. We will see several examples of this, particularly in London, where the first Salafi-jihadists insisted on this as soon as they arrived.

Where politics is concerned, the activists advocate a break with the society designated as that of the "unbelievers." The militants' efforts aim at neutralizing the dynamic of integration in European societies, and showing that young people of immigrant background are not part of the social contract of these countries. They denigrate acts that show adherence to citizenship (for example, voting), to the State (for example, holding a job in public service), and to commonly recognized values and principles, such as the equality of the sexes and freedom of choice and expression. This explains why they often seek out face-to-face confrontations with xenophobic groups in the places where they settle, for this allows them to designate these groups as the true "faces" of European democracies. They espouse identity-based dynamics that the Islamic groups who preceded them also followed.

Starting in the 1990s, the first militants defined the new Muslim identity as morally superior to Western culture, but also as unjustly belittled. They were assisted in this by a general feeling of exclusion, whether real or perceived. As we will see, one of their most frequently used instruments was the denunciation of Western political interventions in the Middle East: "iniquitous" support for Israel, participation in wars in Iraq, Afghanistan, and Mali, and lack of concern about the persecutions of the Palestinians, Rohingyas, and Uyghurs. Their claims aimed to insert legitimate political preoccupations within an all-encompassing narrative according to which European democracies were waging an unspoken but active and indeed "institutionalized" war against Muslims, both at home and abroad. In this scenario, Western leaders demonstrated hypocrisy in their political priorities (defense of human rights but not of the Palestinians, etc.), and their true aim was to destroy Islam. Incarnations of this included the separation of the spiritual and temporal realms, something the constitutions of European countries have in common, and the affirmation of the superiority of the state of law over religious rules and guidelines.

For the jihadists, the political and religious realms, while distinct, nonetheless complement one another – neither can work without the other. As the work of Abdullah Azzam shows, the jihadists' aim to change the world takes as its starting point an interpretation of said world that rests on Salafist ideology.

Ismaël, a 28-year-old jihadist from Grenoble with whom I met when he was in prison in 2016, defines the nature of his engagement thus:

> Jihadism is political activism through and through. It is indissociable from the religious sphere: the more involved you get in religion, the more you become politically active, the more you become an activist – they go hand in hand.

Activism, when given free rein, tends to have important radicalizing effects on those exposed to it, leading to a rejection, simultaneously, of society and its founding democratic principles, of other forms of Islam, and more broadly of anything that differs from itself.

In France, where the principle of secularism is famously problematic for the Salafists, preaching focuses on political elements, notably the way these elements neutralize religion. Conversely, in England, where Muslim environments are far more structured and developed, Salafi-jihadists have long attacked the dominant currents of British Islam and of rival Islamist movements – all of this takes place on a far more religious level than in France. All hostility demonstrated by jihadists toward the English model must be understood within this framework. Identity- or community-based organization ("communalism," in the English context) grants English jihadists more freedom to act than in France, where the withdrawal into such forms of organization stands out more, is perceived negatively on an ontological level, and thus more fiercely denounced. Salafist activism in France is thus more overtly political and hostile. Such activism is not weaker in Great Britain, but is expressed more in the religious sphere, often in ways that are much deeper. The situations of the other European countries, which we will look at below, can be situated between these two poles.

London, the European Peshawar

Wembley Stadium, London, August 7, 1994

Omar Bakri, a man in his early thirties with a thick brown beard, is sitting behind a podium. The atmosphere is electric. He steals a glance at his audience from behind his thick glasses, straightens his shoulders (which are wrapped in an immaculate tunic), and addresses the crowd of almost seven thousand participants who have come to listen to him:[1]

OMAR BAKRI: What do we want?

AUDIENCE: Jihad!

OMAR BAKRI [*in a louder voice*]: What do we want?

AUDIENCE [*in a louder voice*]: Jihad!

A MAN IN THE CROWD: Fi sabil illah [*in the way of Allah*]!

OMAR BAKRI [*cheerfully*]: We want jihad in the way of Allah for Bosnia, Palestine, Kashmir, nobody disagrees with that! What do we want every time someone attacks Muslim territory?

AUDIENCE: *Ji-had!!!*

What has just taken place at Wembley Stadium, under the low sky of London on a cool and cloudy summer Sunday, hardly registers in the minds of Britons. Three months earlier, Manchester United's players raised the FA Cup in this very enclosure, the consecration of a successful season for the Scottish manager Alex Ferguson and his whirling French forward "King Eric" Cantona. Like this team, which was on the verge of reconquering European football, England was at the dawn of a cultural, political, and economic rebound. It was no longer the time of the punks, who shouted their slogan "No future!" during the preceding decade as unions were losing their final battles against the intransigent prime minister of the time, Margaret Thatcher. It was the time of neoliberalism, the financialization of the economy, the rise of the City. The musical scene was dominated by the lingering tunes of Oasis and Blur, and the press would soon be stirred by the international phenomenon of the Spice Girls. Public discourse enjoyed an unhindered freedom of expression, and British society took pride in having become, over the course of this final decade of the twentieth century, "Cool Brittania."

It was slowly turning the page on thirty years of conflict in Northern Ireland, and had placed its hope in a new political order with Tony Blair's New Labour. Its leaders extolled a gentle, multicultural, and decentered model, more open to the world than ever before, modernizing (and revealing the outdatedness of) the Victorian slogan "Rule, Brittania" from the imperialist era of the preceding century.

At the time, it was unimaginable that the decomposition of the Afghan front, thousands of kilometers away, could have any importance for the future prospects of living in harmony in the British Isles. But just like Omar Bakri, who won renown for himself at Wembley in August 1994 (and to whom we shall return), numerous ideologues who had passed through Peshawar, or who were in direct contact with the local jihadist ecosystem, brought about the rise of a new form of activism in Great Britain.

In the 1990s, London was a center that was open to all possible influences, shaped by the solidity of its legal framework and a long tradition of hospitality. For these reasons, it became a unique kind of world city. It succeeded Cairo and Beirut as the seat of the most important Arabic-language newspapers.[2] The City, all the while that it assesses the price of crude oil, also gathers within itself the banking and financial networks of the Gulf, and the largest number of Islamic charities, ensuring a wide circulation of capital between these various poles. It is also the center of opposition from the countries of North Africa and the Middle East, from the most uncompromising Islamists to the most viscerally atheistic Marxists. The representatives in exile of Al-Nahda, the party of the Tunisian Muslim Brotherhood, Egyptian defenders of human rights, political refugees of every stripe are active in London. Usama Hasan, who at the time was a Salafist militant, explains this density:

> I remember meeting representatives of the [Afghan] mujahideen who had their office here. [. . .] The Muslim Brotherhood [from various countries] had lots of offices in London. There were also Libyan opponents of Gaddafi, Pakistani Islamists, Egyptians fighting against Sadat and Mubarak – people from all over had branches here.[3]

The repression of Afghan Arabs in the Arab world meant that many of them preferred the sanctuary of London. Osama bin Laden went there several times in 1993 and 1994, and financed a local branch, given the task of transmitting his viewpoints while claiming to be a Saudi dissident group. Dozens of veterans and other ideologues who had passed through Peshawar found asylum in England, bringing with them, along with their suitcases, their conceptions of Islam, their worldviews, and their ways of operating.

The Emirs of Londonistan

Many books have examined the presence of propagandists for the jihadist cause in London in the 1990s. Most researchers have noted the clear connections between networks already in place and those woven on the Afghan front.[4] But the tendency has been to see Londonistan as its own unique situation, an "anomaly" in Europe. Above all, most authors have focused on the paths taken by veterans, while spending much less time on the homegrown dimension of preaching. But the sustainability of the militant universe is of fundamental importance for the understanding of the meteoric rise of jihadism in Europe, which in the 1990s had seemed inconceivable. With thirty years of hindsight, we can undertake the autopsy of Londonistan with the help of new tools: by focusing less on the pedigree of the jihadists themselves, and more on the blueprint of their actions and the way they made their ideas viable through mechanisms that were proven in Peshawar and then duplicated elsewhere in Europe.

The activities of three "Londonistan emirs" have been abundantly documented (with good reason). We need to introduce these men here.

The first of them, known as Abu Qatada, was born in Palestine in 1959. He holds a doctorate in Islamic Studies, and gained respectability in the radical circles of the University of Peshawar in the late 1980s. He became a professor, was thereby exposed to the entire range of perspectives expressed in this setting, and played a key role among Afghan Arabs. He spent time in the company of several of Azzam's disciples, including Bin Laden, and did not acknowledge his affiliation with Al-Qaeda until the 2000s. In 1992, the deportation to Jordan of a compatriot, Abu Mohamed al-Maqdissi, also an influential ideologue, sent a clear signal to the movement in Peshawar. The following year, Abu Qatada was granted asylum in England, where he and his family were granted refugee status for four years. He remained there until 2013.

The second individual, who goes by the demonym Abu Hamza,[5] is an Egyptian who went into exile in the UK in the 1980s, gained citizenship by way of marriage, and bloomed in a setting opposite from that of Abu Qatada: he was joint manager of a strip club, where he also appears to have worked as a bouncer and a pimp.[6] As he personally evolved, he gradually drew closer to Salafism, and met Abdullah Azzam during a pilgrimage to Mecca in 1987. He claims the encounter "changed the course of his life," and described the father of contemporary jihad as "a great man" who, in his eyes, embodied "the future of Islam."[7] In 1989, Abu Hamza moved with his family to Peshawar, where he lived for almost four years, until it ceased to be a place of refuge. Little inclined to erudition, he sought to shine through his operational skills. While preparing an attack on the Pakistani border, an error in handling an explosive device led to its detonation, which deprived him of his left eye and both hands. He overcame this injury by having two metal claws implanted in the place of his hands. This earned him a nickname on the front page of the British tabloids: Captain Hook. One member of a London Islamist movement described him as a caricature of an extremist, one that might be found in the pages of *Charlie Hebdo*.

He returned to England in 1994, then went to the front lines of jihadism in Bosnia, before becoming, as we shall observe, the face of radical Islamism in London. His gained exceptional exposure from his dual status as a "returnee" from Afghanistan and Bosnia, and his standing as a disfigured war veteran lends him credibility.

The third individual is a Syrian named Omar Bakri Mohamed. Born in 1958 into the Sunni bourgeoisie of Damascus, he sympathized with Islamist circles at university. The growing repression of the Muslim Brotherhood, perceived as revolutionary by the regime of Hafez al-Assad (Bashar's father), prompted him to flee Syria and settle in Lebanon, where he is said to have taken part in the civil war against the Christian phalangists. He then went to Saudi Arabia, where he completed a doctorate on the concept of the caliphate in Islam. In 1983, he moved to Pakistan, where he lived for a time in Peshawar. In 1986, he was granted asylum in England for himself and his family after being expelled from Saudi Arabia, which pleased him greatly. In London, he became head of European operations for Hizb at-Tahrir, an Islamist organization to which we will return later, implementing the ideological consciousness-raising program that has earned him *persona non grata* status in Saudi Arabia, a country that follows the most conservative current in world Islam, Wahhabism. He gained widespread notoriety in London when he publicly called for the death of the then British Prime Minister, John Major, after the outbreak of the Gulf War. An application to deport him was rejected in compliance with the right to asylum. This led him to understand the importance, in his own words, of "the London media."[8]

From that point on, he never ceased to exploit the negative attention he generated, using it as a weapon to spread his ideas across the Channel. Bakri, who likes to describe himself immodestly as "the catalyst of political Islam in Europe," is one of the figures who has most consistently and profoundly impacted the environment of European jihadism, and his work merits reconsideration.

The trajectory of the three "Londonistan emirs" has much in common with those of other extremists of the same ilk who make up their entourage, and who will appear from time to time in the pages that follow. They have all been marked by their personal or intellectual encounters with Azzam. They are all his heirs (each in his own way), and openly align themselves with Salafi-jihadism. All three passed through the cauldron of Peshawar: the importance of this stage in their journey is clear, and it demonstrates the diversity of this milieu. All three believe that Britain can be a land of preaching. Their temperaments, however, differ greatly. Abu Qatada is discreet, even though he is the ideological reference point for the international jihadist movement. Abu Hamza is an inflammatory agitator and a rugged leader of men. Omar Bakri is a polemicist, a specialist in grotesque and provocative antics that conceal a cunning individual who constantly skirts the borders of illegality. All three have played a key role in the construction of European jihadism. They competed for control of sympathizer networks in London, but complemented each other in style, and presented a united front against the British authorities.

The Paradoxes of the Establishment of Jihadism in the West

One of the most misunderstood paradoxes of the way jihadism took hold in the West is that the very propagators who chose Europe for the exceptional guarantees and protection they enjoy under the rule of law at the same time denounced these foundational democratic principles as outrages from which Muslims must be fully protected.

Until September 11, 2001, the British authorities believed that the fringe elements linked to the Afghan conflict, themselves just a small number of the oppositional voices from the Arab and Muslim world, were not a direct threat. The terrorist risk in Great Britain was embodied by the Irish independence movement (IRA), the surveillance of which used up more than half the resources of MI5, the internal security service, until the end of the decade. Peter Clarke, former head of Scotland Yard, sums up the prevailing perception of Londonistan's emirs:

> They were mainly perceived as polemicists, activists. But did they pose a threat to the United Kingdom? An ideological problem, perhaps, but ideology as such, especially at that time, was not perceived as a direct threat. [. . .] It was known that several countries were concerned about what was happening in London, and the term "Londonistan" was beginning to be used.[9]

The belief, at that time, in the omnipotence of the Western democracy, which had triumphed over communism and whose model would define a new global norm, was widespread. British leaders had little reason to doubt the prevailing social contract, *communalism*, which at the time facilitated, if somewhat inconsistently, the integration of the most diverse minorities into a multicultural society. Throughout the 1990s, they constantly reminded their European partners, who were concerned about the establishment of extremist groups across the Channel, of England's long history of political and religious tolerance. The asylum offered to radical preachers was part of a long chain of decisions that, while controversial, were part of a tradition of which Great Britain is rightly proud. As such, Omar Bakri and his accomplices followed in the footsteps of Victor Hugo, who spent twenty years in Jersey and Guernsey (1851–1870), and, before him, Karl Marx, who lived with his family in exile in Soho. British politicians justified their refusal to extradite certain terrorists by arguing that the same principles had enabled General de Gaulle, then considered an enemy of France by the Vichy regime, to organize the French Resistance. In addition to underestimating the security threat, the British authorities failed to see how politically subversive these individuals were. Their attitude was dictated by the feeling that the Londonistan emirs were "under control." Usama Hasan, then active in Salafist circles after having himself been to Afghanistan, agrees:

> I think most of the British authorities believed that they [the emirs of Londonistan and their followers] would not lash out at Britain, which had offered them political asylum. [. . .] I believe the British sincerely thought that London would never be targeted.[10]

The same sentiment prevailed among journalists, who tended to perceive Abu Hamza as a clown, a character of no importance. And indeed, the "Londonistan emirs" provided many guarantees to the police, starting with that of not inciting attacks on British soil.[11] But at the same time, they set up a preaching machine and gradually created a jihadist ecosystem in the capital, the diversity of which has never been matched in Europe. It relies on the daily activism of hundreds of militants who are slowly but surely brought together by veterans in demonstrations and various places of worship. London's appeal to preachers seems to have been little anticipated: it was a gateway to the European Islam that was in the process of asserting itself.

Omar Bakri's Project: Transforming European Islam

The work of Omar Bakri bears witness to an unceasing ambition to revolutionize Muslim identity and transform the field of religion in Europe.

In the early 1990s, he oversaw the activities of Hizb al-Tahrir in Great Britain. This Islamist movement was founded forty years earlier by a Palestinian, Taqi el-Din el-Nahbani, who had broken with the Muslim Brotherhood. The organization advocates the return of the Caliphate to the land of Islam as an absolute goal, and promotes non-violent methods to achieve it. Its hierarchical structure is based on the indoctrination of followers. Its militants are young, often middle-class and foreign-born, and undergo intensive intellectual and ideological training. They are typically recruited from schools, having been identified for their high potential. Under the leadership of Omar Bakri, Hizb at-Tahrir gradually won almost all student union elections on London campuses, and already had four hundred members by 1990.[12]

Rashad Ali was exposed to the ideas of Hizb at-Tahrir in his early teens by a teacher at his college in Sheffield, northern England. After becoming a member of the group, which he later left and denounced, he explained how indoctrination leads people to redefine their relationship with the surrounding society:

> It is a totalitarian ideology; it covers everything. When you adopt it, it changes your whole way of thinking. [. . .] They have a very specific morality that they teach you [. . .]. Socialists have their truth, capitalists have their truth, etc. If you are Muslim, from their point of view, there is only one truth, which is their way of thinking, derived from their Islamist ideology. And they have principles that apply to everything. In the end, not only do you think in only one way, but you reject everything else. Everything is black or white; it is a very specific moral, political, and ideological system.[13]

This is a clear indication that Omar Bakri's approach is more than just speeches and fiery preaching. The members of the group disseminate a worldview and the intellectual tools to enable followers to reason and to independently shape themselves within a conflictual ideology. Ultimately, it leads them to distance themselves from the rest of British society, and from Muslim communities that do not fall into line with these precepts. In 1993, a student of Bakri's translated, for the first time into English, a dissertation, defended at a Saudi university, on the principle of "loyalty and disavowal" (*al-wala wal-bara*) in Islam. The concept is nothing less than the intellectual pillar of the development of jihadism in Europe. Usama Hasan, a leading Salafist at the time, looked back at this turning point:

> I remember the English translation of Mohamed Sayed Qahtani's book on loyalty and disavowal;[14] he even came to give lectures in London at the time. The concept means that a Muslim should only ally himself with other Muslims and trust only Islam. He must disavow, that is, hate and detach himself from any form of loyalty to non-Muslims and anything that has nothing to do with Islam. This is a fundamental principle for the people of Al-Qaeda and ISIS. They take it very seriously. If you look at their rhetoric and propaganda today,

they constantly come back to it: the idea of "them against us," that love for one's own goes hand in hand with hatred for the other, and that all of this is a divine commandment. It's a very powerful idea. The book was published in London by someone who published a lot of jihadist books in the 1990s and was a fan of Abu Qatada, Abu Hamza, and all those people.[15]

Originally theorized by Mohammed Ibn Abd al-Wahhab's grandson to dissuade the Saud family from forging an alliance with the Ottomans in the nineteenth century, the principle of "loyalty and disavowal" is now well known in all Salafist and jihadist circles.

Reinterpreted in late twentieth-century England, it posits that the worship of Allah has as its inseparable corollary the detestation of all those who do not follow suit.[16] This binary opposition extends to all the relationships that make up everyday life in a society: the faithful must constantly choose "their camp" between two systems that are presented as antithetical and in conflict with each other. A perfect "Islamic" register is opposed by a corrupt "democratic" register, divine justice (sharia) is opposed by the injustice of human laws, and loyalty to Muslims is opposed by enmity toward infidels. There can be no bridge between good and evil.

Young Britons exposed to this logic are faced with a Shakespearean choice of identity: to be or not to be a Muslim, to be or not to be a British citizen, that is the question. The answer is eminently political. For the internalization of this principle, which gradually incorporates all aspects of life, leads to the affirmation of a new Islamic identity, and hence a completely different outlook: instead of imagining himself as a British citizen of the Muslim faith, the individual imagines himself as a faithful member of a Muslim nation (ummah) that is itself orphaned from its political system (the caliphate) and exposed to human injustice so long as sharia law does not reign on earth.

Other Muslims, who are responsible for the situation because they have fallen asleep, must be "awoken" by the vanguard, through preaching. According to this vision, not only is the very idea of "integration" for English Muslims absurd, it is above all a religious failing, since Islam cannot comply with anything that does not originate within itself. On the basis of this understanding, Omar Bakri began to systematically denigrate British Muslim communities. He invited his followers to renounce their nationality, to refuse to recognize the legitimacy of English law, and to abstain from voting. Even as he negotiated with the authorities, he admonished anyone "prepared to sacrifice the *shahada* [the Muslim profession of faith] in exchange for an English passport."[17] Conversely, any policy seeking to coordinate Muslim worship, or to facilitate the integration of Muslims who have recently arrived in the UK, is stamped with the seal of illegitimacy. Bakri variously accused Muslims of being too confined within their ethnic groups (of being too "Pakistani," too "Indian," too "Bengali"), or of integrating into the life of society and becoming too "British." Drawing on the identity-based tension felt by many second-generation European Muslims, Bakri argued that soon they wouldn't even be able to call themselves "Muslims" – which would leave them as eternal second-class citizens in a diabolical system designed to crush Islam. At no point is Bakri interested in dispelling anxiety; on the contrary, he employs it to persuade his interlocutors to join him in the ideological war within Islam and against society.

For the culprits behind this state of affairs are also malevolent powers, of which England is a prime representative. The term with which Omar Bakri branded the country in the 1990s was *Rās al-Kāfirīn*, literally "the head of the infidels." Over the past twenty years, the term has been used by various Salafi-jihadist organizations to refer successively to the United States, Denmark (during the controversy surrounding the Muhammad cartoons in 2005) and France (since the late 2010s). This shows that the logic of opposition and conflict inherent in the concept of loyalty and disavowal is constructed in the same terms, independently of national contexts, social contracts, and the political circumstances of a given moment. Ismaël, a young Frenchman imprisoned for his association with various terrorist activities in 2012, sums up in his own way the application of the concept to the whole of Europe:

> There's a religious basis, if you get what I'm saying, there's a foundation, it's *al-wala wal-bara* [loyalty and disavowal]. Knowing your religion is the most important thing, it's the foundation. Once that's clear, Germany, Belgium, France, for us it's all the same thing, the same shit. Once you've reached that point, you say to yourself: "I'm surrounded by my enemies," so I'm planning my death [*a terrorist act*]. It's obvious.[18]

As we see in these remarks, and as we also saw in Usama Hasan's testimony, the concept of loyalty and disavowal has become more and more popular since it first entered circulation in Londonistan's Islamist circles in the 1990s, to the point that it is now the cornerstone of contemporary jihadist arguments.

Omar Bakri was one of the first preachers in the West to so ardently and publicly draw a symbolic boundary between British and Muslim identity. This division is now found throughout the areas that interest us, and it did considerable damage within European Islam in the 2000s and 2010s.

3

Bosnia and Scandinavia: The Periphery of European Jihadism?

In the early 1990s, Yugoslavia imploded. In 1993, the Serbian army launched a territorial annexation campaign based on methodical ethnic cleansing, particularly of Bosnian Muslims. The international community botched their intervention, and the horror of the massacres reached millions of homes in Europe, thanks to abundant media coverage.

Slags from the Bosnian Hearth

The Afghan jihad officially ended in 1992, just as the conflict in Bosnia began. Hundreds of veterans thus took part in the war. They set up their own brigades alongside local troops overwhelmed by Serbian firepower. In the eyes of the militants, the configuration of the conflict was a mirror image of the situation in Central Asia, with the Bosnians taking the place of the Afghans who had to be rescued, and the Serbs in the role of the Soviet aggressors. The Balkans became the site of the first contemporary European jihad. For months, sympathetic networks in London and elsewhere moved in support of the cause. A British Salafist recalls the departures from within his entourage:

> One of the members of our [Salafist] movement, an Afro-Caribbean convert from Reading [in southern England], gave his life in Bosnia fighting Serbian forces. His name was David. He took part in a legitimate jihad, and we see him as a martyr.[1]

Omar Bakri's networks organized conferences and fund-raisers, and distributed videotapes of unbearable acts of violence during Friday sermons.[2] The Western powers, who hesitated to intervene in the early months, bore the brunt of much of the blame, and were portrayed as complicit in Serbian atrocities, hypocritical, even partially responsible for the Bosnian tragedy, which was viewed in the same terms as the crises in Palestine and Kashmir.

Similar dynamics were at work in other localities, involving ever-increasing numbers of comparable figures. In Germany, Dr. Youssouf, who would come to play an important role, was one of them. At the time, he was a well-known doctor based in Freiburg, and enjoyed a stellar reputation. What people didn't realize was that before seeking refuge in Germany, he had belonged to the radicalized branch of the Egyptian Muslim Brotherhood, and had been imprisoned following the assassination of President Anwar Sadat. With a view to contributing to the Bosnian war effort, he founded a humanitarian association called People for the People, which helped finance brigades. Among the young people he sponsored at the time was another German of Egyptian origin, Reda Seyam, who died in Mosul in 2018, having risen to the position of ISIS's "minister" of education. In the 1990s, Seyam was still a Salafist who felt it was his duty to support his brothers in the Balkans. Upon his arrival, he at first took part in the fighting, but soon decided to settle with his wife in the Guča Gora camp, a kind of phalanstery dominated by puritanical religious codes and closed to the outside world. He lived there for four years, until well after the end of the war.[3] Several similar communities sprang up, including in the village of Gornja Maoča. As in Afghanistan, the foreigners in these places were just as interested in applying the most conservative religious precepts to the Islamic lands they had come to "liberate" as they were in the armed struggle. They disseminated a vision of Muslim dogma strongly influenced by Salafi-jihadism, which was in stark contrast to Bosnian Islam.[4]

At the time, these dynamics, transposed from Afghanistan to the heart of the Balkans, still seemed far off and difficult to grasp. The Islamist brigades, the story went, had attained visibility, but were hardly likely to have meaningful effects on sections of European youth. The number of Westerners involved in the conflict remained very low, around a few dozen, a far cry from the thousands who made their way to Syria twenty years later.

The Blind Sheikh and the Danish Refuge: The First World Trade Center Attacks

The Scandinavian countries form a coherent whole in their approach to European jihadism. Located at the heart of the North Sea's political and commercial system, they share a modest size and social models considered among the most egalitarian in the world. They're at the top of the standings in terms of human development indices, social redistribution, quality of education, and healthcare, and have some of the lowest unemployment rates in Europe (around 4–6%). These countries have little colonial past and, unlike their neighbors, did not follow a program of importing workers from poorer regions, in particular the Arab and Muslim world, during the prosperous postwar years. Their populations have long been characterized by strong social and cultural homogeneity, and a preference for consensus, compromise, and institutional stability.[5] Non-European immigration essentially began in the 1990s, when the region welcomed populations exposed to systemic violence of all kinds. It took shape with the arrival of Palestinians under the Oslo Accords, victims of civil war in Lebanon, those suffering political repression in Egypt, and populations fleeing crises in the Horn of Africa (Somalia, Eritrea, Ethiopia) or Central Asia (Pakistan and Afghanistan). Today, these countries are relatively cosmopolitan (twelve to sixteen percent of the population is of immigrant origin), and their diplomacy has established the region as a humanitarian "superpower."

The distinctive nature of the Scandinavian model would not protect these countries, however, against the very early development of jihadism in forms similar to those described above. Jakob Scharf, Director General of the Danish Security and Intelligence Services from 2007 to 2013, shared the following observations:

In the 1990s, there were already clear links between extremists based in Denmark and Sweden, those based in other European countries, and those outside Europe. They had largely forged links in Pakistan, among veterans of Afghanistan, but also within terrorist groups such as Gama'a Islamiyya [Egyptian jihadists].[6]

In the early 1990s, the Gamaa Islamiyya was a group known worldwide for its brutality and radicalism. Their spokesman, Abu Talal,[7] one of the movement's most important representatives in Europe, turned up on the streets of Copenhagen. He came from the university benches of a working-class city in Upper Egypt, where he was active in the Muslim Brotherhood, before joining the radical fringe of the Gamaa, which advocates the overthrow of the regime and the establishment of an Islamic state. He was convicted of involvement in the plot to assassinate President Anwar al-Sadat, who was assassinated in spectacular fashion in 1981 during a military parade.[8] In 1989, Abu Talal managed to escape during a prison transfer, and made his way to Peshawar, where the Gamaa had its own guesthouses. There, he joined his group's command in exile, which included Ayman al-Zawahiri, future right-hand man of Osama bin Laden. He took on important responsibilities, such as overseeing the publication of the propaganda newspaper *Al-Morabitoun*, and partici-pated in the fighting in Afghanistan. He and his colleagues constituted the hardest line of the nascent jihad movement. They rejected as "too moderate" the ideas of certain leading lights of the cause such as Azzam, whose assassination they were suspected of having plotted in 1989. After his time in Peshawar, Abu Talal, who was sentenced to death in absentia in his own country and took on an assumed name, was granted asylum in Denmark.[9]

Like other veterans in London, Brussels, and Madrid, Abu Talal focused, from the moment he arrived, on spreading his highly singular conception of Islam. His status as a well-known opposition figure, the aura granted to him by his time in the mountains of Afghanistan and Pakistan, and his intense character led him to be treated as a guest of honor in the small Islamist circles of the Danish capital. Abu Laban, a member of the Muslim Brotherhood of the Levant, and whose role in the 2005 Mohammed cartoons affair we will examine later, welcomed Abu Talal into the Vesterbrogade mosque, not far from the city center, and then the Dortheavej mosque, in the northeast of the city. Abu Talal moved to this district, and regularly gave the Friday sermon in the mosque, educating the faithful about jihad in Afghanistan and Bosnia, and the legitimacy of fighting against "apostate" regimes in the Arab world. He was also offered the position of imam on a weekly TV show broadcast on a community channel. Despite his extremism, he managed to emerge as a prominent preacher. In a Danish context in which Islam was not particularly well organized, he was able to spread his jihadi sympathies. One Lebanese teenager, who took refuge with his parents in Denmark and who also played a key role in the cartoon affair, shared his memories of meeting Abu Talal in Aalborg, in the north of the country:

> As a young man, I used to attend a small mosque in Aalborg, and I quickly realized that the religious sphere was divided between different groups and factions, some leaning toward Sufism, others the Muslim Brotherhood, others the Tabligh and still others who were very focused on jihad, the idea that Islam calls for armed struggle and demands victims. And one of the people who was there in the late 1990s – I was still a novice, I didn't know much – was an Egyptian, Abu Talal. He had been imprisoned in Egypt for involvement in the assassination of Sadat, and after escaping [. . .] he ended up in Denmark. He was ill and diminished, but he preached, and in many places he won the sympathy of young people, won them over to his cause and his mission.[10]

Abu Talal was close to a prominent speaker from Copenhagen, Saïd Mansour. There is a very important factor at work here, one that lies at the heart of most successful attempts to implant jihadist ideas in a given territory: the access and support that seasoned militants enjoy from radical entrepreneurs. The latter are sympathetic to the cause, but are mindful of their public image and the need to remain within the law, and thus present themselves to the outside world as "intellectuals" with conservative ideas.

Indeed, Saïd Mansour was already a point of contact for extremist networks that had moved to Europe. He arrived from Morocco in 1983, and three years later founded the Al-Nour bookshop in Copenhagen, the first of its kind to publish important booklets on Salafism and international jihadism.[11] He claimed to know personally (without being close to them) some of the most renowned ideologues of this movement, such as the Jordanian Abu Mohamed al-Maqdissi, mentor of the man who founded the Islamic State of Iraq (the prototype of ISIS) in the mid-2000s. Mansour was involved in organizing socio-cultural activities for newly emigrated communities. He presented himself as a "mediator" between these communities and the public authorities, and organized study and exchange groups for young believers.

Abu Talal and Saïd Mansour thus held complementary positions in local preaching. The former was driven underground after being hunted down for decades by the Egyptian secret service. Although he knew how to maintain his public image and was in no way one-dimensional (as shown by his television work), he did most of his work in the trenches. Saïd Mansour, by contrast, was not battle-hardened. His role as preacher, entrepreneur and propagandist made him visible, but kept him away from weapons and high-profile responsibilities. He facilitated the work of the most virulent actors, but did not participate in their activities, allowing them to surface and return underground. For instance, he gave Abu Talal and a few of his followers access to the Toveshøj mosque in Aarhus, the country's second-largest city. Founded a few months earlier by Palestinian and Tunisian Salafists, this place of worship was to become their base of operations in western Denmark, and the most important site for radicalization in Denmark in 2015.[12]

Having once advocated the fight to the death against the Egyptian regime, and taken up arms in Afghanistan ten years later, Abu Talal turned his attention to Bosnia. From Denmark, he made increasing contact with former companions in Milan, and participated in setting up a pipeline of fighters to the Balkans. He even went there himself, as did Saïd Mansour, who wanted to meet the mujahedeen and document their actions.

In 1993, just as Londonistan was taking shape, a van filled with explosives was left in the basement parking lot of the World Trade Center in New York. The detonation killed six people and injured 1,000, but proved too weak to cause the Twin Towers to collapse. Eight years before 9/11, terrorists linked to al-Qaeda's operations bureau were already targeting the symbol of American financial power. The FBI's investigation quickly traced the attack to a cell that met in a room on Atlantic Avenue, in Brooklyn, under the leadership of the man who called himself the "blind sheikh" (his real name was Omar Abdel Rahman). Spiritual leader of the Gamaa Islamiyya, the blind sheikh was not just any militant, but one of the most renowned figures of the cause. His journey alone sums up the extent of the network built in the West since the war in Afghanistan. He went to Peshawar in the mid-1980s to join his former professor at Cairo University, Abdullah Azzam. After the Soviet withdrawal, he settled temporarily in London before moving to the east coast of the United States.

It is quite possible that Abu Talal was aware of the preparations for what is in fact the first act of jihad on American soil. Indeed, Abu Talal was a disciple of the blind sheikh, and Mansour hosted him in Denmark during a memorable tour a few years earlier. Matias Seidelin, a journalist and the author of the only biography of Abu Talal, notes that the blind sheikh was like a rock star in these circles, with people coming from all over the country to meet him.

Following the blind sheikh's arrest in the United States, Abu Talal and Saïd Mansour appeared side by side in Aarhus in a show of public support for him. Shortly afterwards, the FBI's investigations unexpectedly turned towards Denmark. A regional police investigation into what appeared to be an honor killing by three Egyptian residents of Aarhus led to the discovery of bomb-making equipment, jihadist propaganda, and a map of the area surrounding the Israeli embassy in Copenhagen. A diary containing the addresses and telephone numbers of guest houses (including that of the Services Bureau) that had hosted Egyptian fighters in Peshawar, where two of these individuals had briefly stayed, was also uncovered. The fingerprints turned up by this investigation matched those found on some of the explosive components used in the USA, as well as on forged passports used by the blind sheikh's cell. Finally, videos of Abu Talal preaching with the blind sheikh were found in the apartments of the conspirators. Investigators on both sides of the Atlantic gradually became convinced that the cases were linked. The evidence proved insufficient, however, and the three Egyptians were convicted in Denmark on ordinary criminal charges. As soon as the trial began, one of the three defendants expressed his hostility to the court: he refused to identify himself and threatened his two accomplices before being expelled from the hearing. The next day, he expressed his "repudiation" of the Danish judicial system, suggesting that mere human justice was unimportant for him. The imperfect translation of his remarks at the time captures only part of their meaning: "He's proud to be a Muslim. All the others in the courtroom are infidels, and he cannot accept being judged by the godless."[13] Although he was born in Egypt and given a religious upbringing, he sought to present himself as an unbeliever who has "returned" to Islam, which, in his telling, occurred when he joined the Gamaa jihadist group. He characterized the Egyptian population as a whole as having "left Islam"; for him the only way to belong to the religion was through adherence to the purest principles of Salafist doctrine. These remarks, which take on their full meaning only in the ideological register in question, were considered by his lawyer and then by the court to necessitate psychiatric care. The individual was sent to a hospital in Aarhus to be examined, and joined al-Qaeda in Pakistan upon his release.

These jihadist hubs in Denmark in the early 1990s are examples of how individuals who first joined the movement a few years earlier in Afghanistan came to use their position in Europe as a place of refuge from which to operate. They disseminated their ideas in a few places of worship in Copenhagen and Aarhus, and linked up with new areas of jihad, in this case in the Balkans. Some in their circles were already involved in planning attacks abroad, and their choice of targets shifted from leaders in their former homeland – Egypt – to civilians in New York.

In 1995, while Abu Talal was in Zagreb (he was on his way to Bosnia), he disappeared. According to several versions of the story, including that of his family, Croatian police arrested him in his apartment and then handed him over to the Egyptian authorities. An Egyptian representative declared at the time: "His arrest proves what has always been said, namely that these terrorist groups operate on an international scale, using places like Afghanistan and Bosnia to train fighters who then return to the Middle East. European countries like Denmark, Sweden, Switzerland, England, and others that offer refuge to these terrorists should now realize that this will come back to haunt them at home."[14]

As for Saïd Mansour, he was not troubled by any of this. He continued to play a key role in the regional structure of Salafi-jihadism until his first conviction in a terrorist case in 2007. More on this later.

4

Algeria and Belgium at a Crossroads

The first city to be affected by departures to Syria, Brussels is also the place where the members of the commando group behind the November 13, 2015 attacks prepared, before falling back into the shadows. Since the 1990s, jihad "veterans" have used Europe's capital as an unobtrusive nodal point. The particularity of the Belgian case lies in the fact that it is a condensed version of many dynamics observed elsewhere. While the jihadist circles in Brussels were more modest than those of Great Britain at the same time, their influence was more lasting, and attracted little political or media attention until the rise of ISIS.

Brussels, Molenbeek, and the Canal Municipalities

The municipalities of the Charleroi canal were the first to be affected. The best known of these is Molenbeek, which, along with Anderlecht, Saint-Gilles, Saint-Josse-ten-Noode and Schaerbeek, form a crescent-shaped swathe of poverty in Brussels. Geographically, they are a continuation of sorts of the city center, and form a compact and coherent whole. One moves easily from one to the other, and since none of them is more than a ten-minute walk from the Gare du Midi, they are certainly not far-flung suburbs. Molenbeek is home to a high proportion of foreigners and the vast majority of the capital's residents of Moroccan origin, and thus takes on the appearance of a small enclave. The city's inhabitants of Turkish nationality or descent live mainly in the neighboring municipality of Schaerbeek. Social and residential mobility in these neighborhoods is lower than elsewhere, and most residents have lived there for a long time. Forms of social solidarity and networks of affinity are interwoven. The majority of those living in these communities have a strong sense of belonging to them, a sense enhanced by the fact that these immigrant populations often include entire extended families. Whether because of the schools, the foot traffic, or the small shops, or the fact that neighbors know and recognize each other, these municipalities have a village feel to them.

The history of the canal municipalities is closely linked to the industrial revolution. Until the end of the eighteenth century, Molenbeek, whose Flemish name means "Mill Creek," was a site of pilgrimage for 2,000 souls, famous for its annual St. John's Day processions. On June 24, those afflicted by mental illnesses would gather here, dancing and singing in the manner of Salome, who, according to the Gospels, was responsible for the martyrdom of John the Baptist. Crossing the "brook" bridge was synonymous with purification and temporary healing. The processions of mad *Molenbeekois* entered into European cultural heritage through the paintings of the Dutch Renaissance master Pieter Bruegel the Elder in 1592, and certain engravings by Hendricus Hondius in 1642, whch are now in the British Museum. The rapid industrialization of Brussels, driven by Walloons and French-speaking Flemings, led to the emergence of the historic canal districts in the early nineteenth century. The square and seaport of Molenbeek came to be known as "Little Manchester."[1] They housed the headquarters of the companies that controlled the bulk of the Belgian economy, and were the site where major strikes and workers' uprisings began. The Brussels metro, first built by Dutch-speaking Flemings (who had arrived in Brussels as a result of the rural exodus), then by Italian, Spanish, and finally Moroccan immigrants, passes through the historic heart of Molenbeek, of which it is a symbol.

Densely populated, the urban space is shaped by workers' houses and modest stone buildings, sometimes stylish, often dilapidated, which stand alongside narrower, more recent constructions. Once known for the hundreds of small cafés where laborers gathered after work, these neighborhoods reverberate with the echoes of folk tales and songs that have entered the pantheon of Brussels culture.[2] From the 1970s onwards, Moroccan migration became more feminine thanks to family reunification policies, at a time when the industrial crisis was taking its toll. This period of economic uncertainty was accompanied by a change in perspective, as for recent immigrants, the prospect of returning to their countries of origin, also in the throes of change, became more remote. New arrivals abandoned the dream of "returning to the *bled* [village]" and settled down; this took place in the context of mass unemployment, but one marked by the absence of trauma linked to the colonial past. The question of how to practice Islam and transmit it to younger generations, which was of secondary importance so long as people considered their presence in Belgium to be temporary, now came to the fore.

The Structure of Belgian Islam: Salafists, Brothers, and the Question of Grooming

The Belgian State turned to the Gulf in order to bring structure to Muslim worship in the country. In 1974, against a backdrop of soaring oil prices, Saudi Arabia was entrusted with the organization of Islam in Belgium, in exchange for a preferential agreement on the supply of fossil fuels. This pact, the only one of its kind in Europe and the subject of intense controversy, had the immediate effect of setting in motion a top-down Salafization of Belgian Islam. It also guaranteed a strong Saudi presence in the heart of Europe, as Belgium gave the Kingdom a location to host the European headquarters of the Muslim World League, which is tasked with the responsibility for spreading Wahhabism throughout the world. Alain Grignard, a member of the Belgian police's anti-terrorist unit, is one of the first people in his position with a strong knowledge of Arab culture. He has observed the changes in Belgian radical movements over the past forty years, and offers his insights into this period:

Belgium is not a secular state like France. Religions are recognized by the state and subsidized. Prior to 1974, these religions included Judaism and Christianity (not only Catholics, but also Protestants and Orthodox), but not Islam. So, in 1974, the Muslim religion was recognized. [. . .] The Saudis came to us and said: "Don't worry, we'll take care of everything." The politicians thought it made sense. [. . .] But a lot of problems arose. In particular, the influence of the commando groups of preachers they sent us, who didn't even speak French.[3]

At the same time, other Islamist organizations were taking shape, such as the Tablighis. As was the case elsewhere in Western Europe, they pursued a "re-Islamization" of consciousness from below. Alain Grignard continues:

> The first Tabligh mosque was the An-Nour mosque in Schaerbeek in 1974. By the 1980s, there were sixty Tabligh mosques in Brussels and three hundred in Belgium, most of them founded by the Tablighs. And on this basis of re-Islamization, other more political movements began to emerge. I'm speaking, of course, of the Muslim Brotherhood.

The first Muslim Brotherhood groups, which were small, appeared in Belgium in 1964 within university associations.[4] From the 1980s onwards, their presence was reinforced by the arrival of student networks, mainly of Syrian and Tunisian origin. In Brussels, they moved into traditional Muslim communities, particularly the conservative Moroccan setting of Molenbeek. In 1985, the Syrian branch was behind the founding of the municipality's largest place of worship, the Al-Khalil mosque. A few years later, a series of controversies erupted locally. The first so-called headscarf affair, which certain Brotherhood members used to their advantage, took place not in France but in two public schools in Schaerbeek and Saint-Gilles in 1987.[5] Two years later, at the height of the French controversy following the expulsion of three veiled pupils from the Gabriel-Havez school in Creil, a similar incident occurred in a school in Molenbeek. After that, demonstrations against the publication of Salman Rushdie's *Satanic Verses* broke out in the center of the municipality. A portrait of Ayatollah Khomeini was raised, and the municipal authorities came to be concerned about the presence of "fundamentalists."

In the early 1990s, Islam was on the point of becoming the majority religion in some areas of the canal municipalities, including in the center of Molenbeek. Religious practice there was quite conservative and traditional, in line with that of the countries of origin, meaning the social and commercial environment was not saturated by Islamic norms. But the influence of Salafist preaching, and that of movements close to the Muslim Brotherhood, was beginning to have an effect. Although these groups were rivals, their local representatives were converging. Their positions in Brussels appear to be complementary.

Representatives of the Saudi current were able to count on the influence of the Brotherhood with the public authorities to compensate for any loss of momentum and to avoid being labeled as responsible for "fundamentalism." In return, the Brothers were guaranteed full Islamic legitimacy by the Salafists, who began gaining influence among young people. The situation has produced a Salafi-Brotherhood hybrid that is unique in Europe, which starting in the mid-2000s began to spread to the rest of Brussels, and then to Switzerland, France, and elsewhere in Europe. In Molenbeek, members of both groups launched associations, established schools, and optimized the territorial network of Brussels's poorer municipalities.[6]

The changes taking place in local Islam were very poorly understood by the authorities, who became both hostages and accomplices of these changes.[7] The arrival of a new municipal mayor, Philippe Moureaux, changed the situation. He launched a policy seeking the institutional-ization of Islam, in coordination with the most visible local leaders. This turned the representatives of the aforementioned Salafi-jihadist circles into official interlocutors, conferring upon them the staus of *de facto* leaders of the local Muslim community. Under Moureaux's leadership – he remained in power from 1992 until 2012 – Molenbeek underwent spectacular transformations. The population of the center doubled and the socio-religious environment came to be completely based in religious and ethnic identity. The long-standing director of the Al-Khalil mosque explained in a 2016 interview that the "Islamic veil" case was a turning point in this respect. The court dealing with the headscarf case at the Molenbeek school handed down a judgment worthy of Solomon: it ruled in favor of the administration, but demanded the reinstatement of the expelled student, and allowed her to wear the headscarf at school, under certain conditions. This first case served as precedent for the Muslim Brotherhood, allowing them to advance their agenda on the pretext of preventing conflict and "recognizing" Islam as a Belgian religion.[8]

The Arrival of the Veterans

As such, Belgium is the site of a synergy between militant currents that are in competition elsewhere in Europe. This new form of Islamism was a clear break from others, which did not escape the attention of a Syrian preacher named Bassam Ayachi.

Originally from the city of Hama, he was trained by the Syrian Muslim Brotherhood and settled in Aix-en-Provence in 1968, acquiring French nationality through marriage. In 1996 he settled in Molenbeek. This was a clear choice on his part: he lived for a time in the Paris region, where he considered Islam too difficult to "reform."[9] As soon as he arrived in Molenbeek, he founded the Islamic Center of Belgium and directed his preaching to young people, whom he familiarized with the jihad taking place abroad. He was immediately accused of extremism, but did not take offense, stating to the Belgian media: "Certainly, it [*my Islam*] is radical compared to others who want a secular Islam [*sic*]. Well, it's true: I'm radical, and I don't think it's possible to say 'I am both Muslim and secular.'"[10] Unlike in France, secularism is not a recognized principle in Belgium, which means that Ayachi here is referring to the principle of the separation of politics and religion, mentioned in the Belgian Constitution via the expression "neutrality of the State in religious matters." The Ayachi Institute, at 6 rue des Étangs-Noirs, not far from the municipal square, is located next to one of the largest mosques in Molenbeek. It provides religious education, celebrates "halal" marriages, and encourages its already numerous followers to proselytize to those around them. Several emblematic figures of European jihad have emerged from this Institute.[11] Ayachi's profile is similar to that of other Syrian preachers who were active at the same time, and who all played a decisive role in the incubation of jihadism in their respective regions: Omar Bakri in London, Olivier Corel (known as the White Sheik) in Toulouse, Abu Dahdah in Madrid. Their common feature is that they were all intellectually trained, in part, by the Syrian Muslim Brotherhood, a movement fiercely repressed from the 1970s onwards by the regime of Hafez al-Assad, resulting in the exile of many of its leaders. Saïd Mansour in Copenhagen, of Moroccan origin, also falls within this constellation.

The Ayachi Institute helped to spread Salafi-jihadist ideas in the relatively restricted circles of the municipality; these included members of the Algerian GIA.

Algeria's Black Decade

The 1990s in Algeria are referred to as the "black decade," during which, according to estimates, between 100,000 and 150,000 people disappeared. The root causes of this were the constant deterioration of living conditions, mass unemployment among young people, the sclerosis of the FLN (which had kept a grip on power since independence), and the end of financial aid from the former USSR. The direct causes lay in the interruption of the democratic process by the army in 1992 at the end of the first round of legislative elections, which placed the Islamic Salvation Front (FIS) well in the lead. The coalition was dominated by Brotherhood currents but also included reformist parties. The arrest of the movement's leaders let to uprisings, during which several of its supporters took up arms and targeted the country's power brokers, members of its military, and security officers. The Algerian regime responded with fierce repression, and the country was plunged into a horrific civil war. The wholesale imprisonment of Islamist activists and the indiscriminate use of torture led many to seek refuge abroad, primarily in France, Belgium and Quebec. The vigilance of the French authorities in monitoring Algerian affairs pushed the most radical members of the movement to neighboring countries, particularly Great Britain, Belgium, and to a lesser extent Germany.

Starting in 1993, a split arose in the opposition ranks with the emergence of the Armed Islamic Group (GIA), an organization founded and led by Algerian veterans of the Afghan jihad. Inspired by the harshest ideas in circulation in Peshawar, and having established their own faction in Kandahar, they were distinguished by their excessive use of violence. They aimed to fight not only the forces of the regime but every part of society that showed resistance to their plans. The GIA and their followers are the heirs of a current that drives part of the Algerian Islamist movement and which believes that an Islamic state should have sprung up from the ruins of French colonialism. At the time of independence, this had been very much a minority point of view, with most movements speaking a language of rights and self-determination, and referring to Marxist–Leninist ideals or the principles of non-aligned states at the 1955 Bandung Conference. Islamist references were not absent, but they did not constitute the dominant political register, and contemporary "jihadist" ideas had not yet been theorized. But the GIA leaders, shaped by the Afghan experience, advanced the idea that the "impious" Algerian regime against which they were fighting was nothing more than the illegitimate child of French colonization, which justified jihad against it.

One of these leaders, Seif Allah Jafar al-Afghani, encouraged the fighters to target intellectuals, journalists, and foreigners: "He who fights us with the pen, we will fight him with the sword."[12] The arrival of Djamel Zitouni as emir of the organization in 1994 reinforced this trend. He himself never went to Afghanistan, but was trained by veterans he knew from prison, and gained prominence as the head of the "green battalion," one of the most cruel and sectarian groups of that dark period. Zitouni advocated murdering all those who refused to pay a religious tax to his group or submit to the dress code required by his version of Islam. The resulting mass atrocities caused a rift even within the ranks of international jihadists, some of whom were then living in London.[13] Zitouni prioritized respecting "Islamic" norms over fighting against the Algerian regime.[14] He also sought to extend the conflict to Europe, deliberately targeting France, with the aim of pushing the leaders of the former colonial power to support the regime in order to discredit it. By reawakening anti-French sentiment, the group hoped to gain the possible support that had been denied it because of its massacres. With its attacks in France, it aimed to open a new front directly at the heart of the former empire and to export the seeds of civil war and jihad.

France and the Gia's European Campaign (1994–1996)

On Christmas Eve 1994, Air France flight 8969 from Algiers to Paris was hijacked by four GIA members on the tarmac at Houari Boumedienne Airport. They negotiated with the local security forces and proved their ruthlessness by killing the first hostages. The French authorities authorized the aircraft to take off and enter French airspace. They persuaded the terrorists, who had left the engines running during the negotiations, that their fuel reserves were insufficient to reach Paris. The airbus landed in Marignane, where French counter-terrorism units were standing by. On December 26 these tactical units, sheltered by a runway vehicle, made a high-speed advance on the tarmac. They forced open the front right door of the aircraft and neutralized the hostage-takers, who had initially intended to crash the plane into the Eiffel Tower.

Six months later, in the summer of 1995, the GIA organized the first large-scale jihadist operation on European soil. An explosion in Paris, at the Saint-Michel RER station, killed eight people and injured another 117. The claim for the attack arrived from London. It was led by Rachid Ramda, the head of the group's European networks, who had been granted asylum in Great Britain three years earlier. Ramda followed in the footsteps of the emirs of Londonistan, such as Abu Hamza, Abu Qatada, and Abu Mus'ab al-Souri, who published their propaganda magazine, *Al-Ansar*. Al-Souri, an influential Al-Qaeda strategist who moved to London after living in Granada, Spain, became friends with several of the GIA's founders during the Afghan war. He boasted of having given them the idea of targeting France "in order to lead it to express its public support for the Algerian regime," which he believed would be likely to "unify the Islamic nation around jihad in Algeria as it had been unified in Afghanistan against the Soviet Union."[15]

Al-Ansar was also used to communicate encrypted orders to operatives. Some of the instructions for the 1995 operations were transmitted using coded language in an article in the magazine. Abu Hamza, the man with hooked hands, celebrated the campaign of terror in France during weekly sermons in the presence of several hundred followers, using terms similar to those used twenty years later by ISIS. He declared that "infidels" could be treated like "cows or pigs" and that "non-Muslim women and children could be enslaved."[16] In his opinion, the attacks were "justified on religious grounds and were part of the war being waged by believers against the enemies of Islam." They were also a means of "compensating" for the "failings" of the GIA (the atrocities committed against Algerian civilians).[17] Jean-François Clair, then head of the Direction de la surveillance du territoire, the French domestic intelligence agency, said the following about how the GIA came to establish itself in the international jihadist circles of Londonistan:

We alerted the English quite quickly, and despite the fact that they prioritized fighting the IRA, they took an interest. But it wasn't easy. Rachid Ramda kept changing his name, and the members of the GIA were scattered across what was known as Londonistan, particularly around Abu Hamza's Finsbury Park mosque, and blended in with other leaders who were fairly well known at the time. The Islamists of Londonistan published a publication called *Al-Ansar*, which represented the global Salafist struggle, for whom everything that was happening in Algeria was an example to follow, the achievement of what could be done elsewhere.[18]

Certain of Al-Qaeda's international supporters condemned the ultra-violent methods used by the GIA in Algeria; this was due in part to the fact that the group refused to open its ranks to Bin Laden's non-Algerian fighters.

In addition to its operational networks in London, the GIA benefited from logistical support in the municipalities along the Brussels canal. As Jean-François Clair recalls:

The first operation took place at the beginning of 1995, involving an Algerian network called Zaoui. Belgian investigators found a document showing the Eiffel Tower on fire, scratched out and struck through on the page. Zaoui was not part of the GIA, but GIA members used their accommodations. They also went to Holland, but Belgium was the place where there were people in all these networks.[19]

One element of the Zaoui file that was not made use of at the time was a list contact information for those behind the attacks in the summer of 1995 in France. As an investigator in Brussels explained:

It was during the investigations into the Zaoui case that the identities of the masterminds behind the attacks in France were discovered, notably Boualem Bensaïd and Aït Belkacem, who were the real driving forces [*behind the 1995 attacks*]. We gave all of this to our French colleagues. I remember it very well, it was in a cabinet behind a desk. And every time we went to say hello in France, we would ask them: "Hey guys, have you looked in that cabinet over there?" They would reply: "No, not yet." What we gave them was essentially the warning signs [*of the attacks*]. But don't put words in my mouth: they couldn't have stopped the attacks even if they'd looked in the cabinet.[20]

This information is necessary to understand what was happening in France in the mid-1990s. The attacks, followed by several unsuccessful attempts in the Lyon and Lille areas, were "planned" operations that in many respects anticipated the model used by ISIS twenty years later. They featured the same places of preparation and retreat (Molenbeek and the canal municipalities), the same targets (city dwellers in the heart of Paris), and gave rise to the same type of justifications. They were the result of similar ideological and strategic considerations, produced by the transfer of networks of Afghan veterans into the Euro-Mediterranean area. The GIA sought to exploit the civil war in Algeria in order to impose an Islamic state project that, in their view, should have emerged thirty years earlier, at the time of independence. They used methods to terrorize the local population that were similar to those of ISIS in Syria, in the name of the same ideals of "Islamic purity." Unable to generate support for their ideas and their program, the organization mobilized its contacts in Europe to target France. The colonial dispute, which was still very much alive in relations and memories on both sides of the Mediterranean, allowed them to present their actions as legitimate reprisals. Targeting France also became a means of diverting attention, as Abu Hamza suggests, from the countless acts of violence committed in the name of jihad against other Muslims in Algeria. These methods are reminiscent of ISIS propaganda, which explained that it was attacking Europe to avenge the death of "Syrian civilians," while at the same time its supporters from all over the world were imposing their bloodthirsty order on the same civilians. The presence of certain major GIA figures at the heart of the ISIS machine partly explains the similarity of their *modus operandi*.

This observation should not lead us to overlook the importance of the postcolonial context. The journey of the perpetrator of the 1995 attacks, Khaled Kelkal, illustrates a deep resentment on his part, one that undoubtedly played a role. This resentment led him to see his terrorism as a heroic and redemptive gesture. The path he took to militancy, however, shows that his motivations were once quite different. The interviews he undertook with a German sociologist before his radical-ization show that Kelkal, who was of Algerian origin and grew up in the suburbs of Lyon, was a young man with a real capacity for reflection and even a certain wisdom.[21] During a jail sentence in 1992, he was first introduced to Islamist ideas by a fellow inmate who was a member of the Muslim Brotherhood. Upon his release from prison, he began to attend the Bilal mosque in Vaulx-en-Velin run by the Tablighis; this movement was apolitical, but those who came into contact with it in Europe in the 1990s often ended up being recruited into jihadism. Kelkal began to do some preaching in his neighborhood, alongside a few childhood friends. In 1993, he visited relatives in Mostaganem, Algeria, where he is said to have been in contact with GIA members. Certain of the latter settled in Toulouse at the end of the 1990s and took charge of the religious education of the Clain brothers, who would become leading figures in French jihadism.[22] In 1994, Kelkal "re-entered" the criminal justice system for common crimes. During his second incarceration, he rubbed shoulders with a member of the GIA, who familiarized him with the cause. After his release, he spent time with a relative, Karim Koussa, who had followed a similar path: he had been in Pakistan and was recruited by the same group. Together, they watched videos of the exploits of jihadists, which they now circulated among their friends and family. Kelkal was put in touch with the London operational cell by Safé Bourada, a former activist in the Socialist Party and the 1983 March for Equality and against Racism (known colloquially as the "March of the Arabs"), who would become one of the bomb makers for the 1995 attacks.

Kelkal was ten years ahead of time: an example of ideological transmission between veterans of the Afghan and Algerian jihad and a young European, a pattern of transmission that would mark the rise of the pioneers of European jihadism after 9/11.

In 1996, as a sign that these developments are not solely the effect of the postcolonial relationship between France and Algeria, the "Roubaix gang," linked to jihadist networks established in Bosnia, carried out a series of attacks in the North. The cell was led by converts from the upper middle class: Lionel "Abu Hamza" Dumont and Christophe Caze, a medical student. They claimed to have traveled to the Balkans to do "humanitarian work," an argument that many returnees from Syria would use in court to justify their presence in the Levant. The gang was neutralized in March 1996 following the assault on their hideout in the rue Henri-Carette in Roubaix, a few days before the G7 summit in Lille, which they planned to disrupt with a car bomb.

Even today, the series of attacks perpetrated in France in the mid-1990s continues to be understood as a specifically French phenomenon – the consequence of a weighty and poorly resolved colonial dispute. This explains why France was targeted, but the campaign was above all the product of the relentless progression of the GIA, which saw the attacks as a convenient way to make people forget the horror of its atrocities in the Algerian civil war. The campaign demonstrated the capacity of jihadist organizations to anchor their actions in potentially broad and mobilizing political narratives, and to target the fault lines, whether political or identity-related, that characterized European nations at the end of the twentieth century. From the outset, the terrorist risk they posed to democracies was an extension of their ideological activism, and of the settling of the first veterans in Western capitals.

5

London: *"The New Peshawar of the Islamic Revival"*

After 1995, everything sped up. We began to identify GIA supporters who had gathered several groups around them. There were offshoots in Italy, the Netherlands, Sweden, Denmark and London – everything converged in London. [. . .] *Al-Ansar* [*the GIA newspaper*] began to speak about Egyptian groups. There are Moroccans who said: "Hey, we could do something like that at home." [. . .] There were Tunisian, Moroccan, and Libyan ideologues in London who were trying to set up organizations in their home countries based on the model of the GIA, which is the archetype.[1]

Alain Grignard, who in the mid-1990s was an investigator with the Brussels anti-terrorist squad, here highlights two key changes from that time. The first is the centrality of the GIA, which became a model to be replicated by other terrorist movements in the Mediterranean region. The second is the fact that London became an epicenter, a stronghold of radical militancy.

Contributing to Jihad from London

The Belgian policeman's observation echoes that of Abu Mus'ab al-Souri, a prominent figure in Al-Qaeda, who stated at the same time that London was establishing itself as the "new Peshawar of the Islamic revival, particularly for jihadists." He added: "Being in London puts you at the center of events." In his view, the concentration of extremists gave him "the opportunity to write and make [his] contribution [to jihad] while remaining in London." While there, he ran an "information bureau" for Bin Laden, scheduled interviews for his mentor in Afghanistan with the BBC and CNN, and supervised the publication of *Al-Ansar*, the GIA's propaganda magazine. Ten years later, he would reflect on his time in London in a book, in which he detailed the conditions for a jihadist uprising in Europe, referred to as "the soft underbelly of the West."

Rashad Ali, then a member of Hizb at-Tahrir, but who has since repented, gives an indication of the approximate size of the Islamist ecosystem, which he breaks down as follows:

> In the 1990s, young people probably represented around 50 to 60% of the diaspora originating from the Indian subcontinent. Among them, 90% identified as Muslims, but had little more than a cultural connection to their religion. Of the 10% of young people who were practicing Muslims, I would say that perhaps 10% of them were Islamists. So, we're talking about a very small group, the bare minimum. [. . .] And among the radical Islamists, the jihadists were a very small number, a tiny number.[2]

These groups may have been a tiny minority, but they were marked, according to Ali, by the virulence of their ideology and the rapid spread of their approach:

> The real problem wasn't the numbers, it was the ideas. Because the identity these groups began to develop became the default discourse of other Islamists. Jihadism started to become a more commonplace and everyday idea, and recruitment and radicalization became easier because it became a kind of "acceptable" version of Islam.[3]

In the second half of the 1990s, the entrenchment of the veterans and their comrades in the religious environment became a reality. Omar Bakri was expelled from Hizb at-Tahrir and founded his own organization, Al-Muhajiroun (literally "the emigrants"). It promised to establish an Islamic caliphate directly on British soil and to prevent Muslims from adopting "impious" Western practices – in other words, it more freely assumed Omar Bakri's jihadist orientation. Rashad Ali, who at that point was rising through the ranks of the Hizb at-Tahrir hierarchy, summarized the importance of the emergence of Al-Muhajiroun:

A decisive turning point in radical Islamism in Great Britain came when Omar Bakri was expelled from Hizb at-Tahrir. He left to form a revolutionary group that set itself the goal of imposing Sharia law in the West and establishing a caliphate there. [. . .] That was his approach. He realized that he had more in common with Salafi-jihadist groups. [. . .] For many people, it didn't seem very serious . . . It was like: who are these kids? They even seemed a bit ridiculous when you looked at them.[4]

As Rashad Ali notes here, the project seemed nonsensical, even to radical Islamists. Establishing the caliphate in a territory considered by Islamic tradition as a land of unbelief (*dar al-kufr*), before even making it a land of Islam (*dar al-islam*), appeared absurd. And yet the ambition of Omar Bakri and his students belongs to a specific understanding of Salafist doctrine. The name of the organization, Al-Muhajiroun, refers to those who made the *hegira* – the first Muslims who followed the Prophet in his flight from Mecca to Medina in 622. They were driven out by pagan tribes (including Mohammed's own tribe) who refused to convert to Islam. In Medina, they settled under the protection of non-Muslim populations (including Jews), built an army, and undertook the military conquest of Mecca. This stage opened a century and a half in which Islam spread to the four corners of the known world (*foutouhat*). In Omar Bakri's understanding, this episode was analogous to the situation of Muslims in Great Britain in 1996. London was his Medina, where he was forced to reside after being hunted by various Arab regimes. In his eyes, the entire Muslim world was falling prey to a religious decline (*jahiliyya*) identical to that of Mecca at the time of the Prophet. Only the Salafi-jihadist avant-garde followed the true beliefs of Islam, which they referred to as "true." The militants were the only ones who deserved the title of the faithful. Their struggle against their own regimes was similar to Mohammed's fight against the Meccan tribes, and had to be supported. Bakri saw his status in England as an opportunity to advocate for them, and at the same time to spread the message to the British, in order to convert the unbelievers and awaken the "sleeping" or "misguided" Muslims in the West. The "emigrants" who joined his London organization were to behave in the image of the *"muhajiroun"* of yesteryear and would be rewarded by God in turn.

The movement that took shape in Great Britain would remain very small in size, but would have profound and lasting consequences on the development of European jihadism. Its actions were imitated in neighboring countries, and were seen as an embodiment of what Salafi-jihadism looks like in Europe "at low tide."

Like Omar Bakri, the emirs of Londonistan had their own organizations, funding networks, and propaganda channels. Abu Hamza has also created his own group: Supporters of Shariah (SOS). Abu Qatada, meanwhile, established himself as an ideological figurehead of choice for global jihadist movements, from the Algerians of the GIA to the first Al-Qaeda networks in Europe.

Bakri also founded a company, Info 2000, based in Tottenham Hale, an incubator designed to help companies specializing in services and new technology. He set up his own printing company and a publishing company, Al-Khilafah Publications. Similarly, a company linked to Omar Bakri and Abu Hamza was set up, Sakina ("serenity") Security, whose purpose was to train young Muslims in self-defense. They explained that the company was needed because the government wanted to turn citizens against believers, and to "compete with the Islamists where the social integration of young Muslims was concerned"; this, in their view, fell to them, not to the government.

In this way, the emirs of Londonistan acquired an organizational autonomy in the mid-1990s that allowed them to maneuver in militant spheres and act as a small but virulent Islamist counter-community. They were now able challenge movements of traditional Islam or the radical currents, which were more numerous or better established, starting with the Salafists or Hizb at-Tahrir.

The War of the Mosques

In 1996, the Finsbury Park Mosque, the second largest in London, became the object of a struggle between Omar Bakri, Abu Qatada, and Abu Hamza, which eventually turned to the advantage of the latter. The veteran with hooked hands relied on local thugs or activists with links to jihadist strongholds abroad. Power was seized through a mixture of physical intimidation of, and religious pressure on, those of the faithful who resisted him. The Finsbury Park Mosque, with a capacity of two thousand, became the headquarters of SOS. The name played on the international distress signal, wherein SOS means "Save Our Souls," but in this context it meant Supporters of Shariah. Its Arabic translation, *Ansar al-Sharia*, refers to the *ansar*, the companions of the Prophet, those pious Muslims of the beginnings of Islam who served as role models, particularly for Salafists. The organization sent dozens of fighters to participate in jihad abroad, and prepared attacks, first in the Middle East and then in the United States and Europe. Other mosques throughout the city were taken over using similar methods, in Turnpike Lane (north) and Shepherd's Bush (west), where Omar Bakri regularly preaches; Abu Qatada did the same in gyms in Paddington. The mosque in Brixton (south), until then dominated by a mystical branch of Islam, Sufism, was taken over by Salafists. Usama Hasan, who took part in these operations, said the following:

> Our group took control of some fairly large mosques, like the one in Brixton and others in this Afro-Caribbean neighborhood. We had it for many years after taking it from the Sufis; today [2022] it remains a Salafist mosque.[5]

Abdullah al-Faisal, a converted preacher of Jamaican descent, often viewed as the fourth emir of Londonistan, was allowed to preach there. He was expelled in the mid-1990s because of remarks deemed too compromising. Usama Hasan explains:

> I saw that Abdullah al-Faisal was preaching there. The guy spent a year in Saudi Arabia but he preached as if he were a religious authority! [. . .] I realized from the start that he was an extremist and that he was recruiting a lot of Salafists. Later he became a full-blown jihadist.[6]

After he was ousted, Al-Faisal settled in the Brick Lane neighborhood (east), where he recorded virulent sermons in praise of the global jihadist struggle. He encouraged Muslim women to raise their children in this ideology, and to have them participate in the sacred struggle from the age of fifteen.[7] Several members of the 9/11 commando, including Zacarias Moussaoui from Toulouse, who was ultimately not selected for the operations, followed his teachings closely.

The extremists looked with envy upon the largest mosque in London, the one in Regent's Park (center). Its large size (it has a capacity of nearly ten thousand) protects it from the assaults of preachers, but their supporters proselytize outside, especially after Friday prayer.

Control of these spaces is a means of securing resources, gathering supporters, and conducting external actions. In 1996, Omar Bakri published a book, *The Role of the Mosque*,[8] in which he criticized the "apolitical" places of worship managed by the authorities of British Islam. In his view, the mosque should be an essential part of preaching activity, and establish itself as a kind of embassy of Salafist proselytizing, so that it could transform the religious sphere. It should host "political activities defined by a guide with religious knowledge," an imam responsible for defining the doctrinal and educational line and for providing a window onto the international situation.[9] A cultural center should be attached to it, for the organization of meetings and events. It should provide religious education for older children and Arabic language and Qur'anic studies for younger children (a *madrassa*, in other words); it should also offer introductions to IT. Finally, it should be a place for social support, offering meals to the poor and even a guest house for travelers and those in need. This is all reminiscent of the missions carried out by the Services Bureau in Peshawar ten years earlier, and the functioning of the Finsbury Park mosque under the leadership of Abu Hamza.

A radical, vast and diverse ecosystem took shape in certain London neighborhoods. The movements in question, from the political activities of the Muslim Brotherhood to Salafi-jihadism, were far from united, and did not always share the same interpretations of Muslim dogma. Several witnesses and actors of this period have spoken of the recurrent clashes between the various currents. The disagreements, whether between people or doctrines, were not always clear or important for those flocking to mosques, who sometimes went back and forth between different influences. Usama Hasan, at the head of a Salafist movement in conflict with the emirs of Londonistan, provides an example:

> Many ordinary Muslims were fed up with the arguments, and the rivalries were driving people away. But, on the other hand, it was bringing the members of the different groups together. One of the strangest things I saw was people attending the sermons of two groups that were at opposite poles [*of the Islamist spectrum*]. One of these people told me that he loved listening to the Tabligh and the Hizb at-Tahrir . . . I thought for a moment about it

and said to him "Wait . . . that doesn't make any sense!" And then I realized that for him it was complementary: the first group only talked to him about spirituality and piety, never about politics, while the second group talked to him all the time about politics and almost never about spirituality. For him, it was complementary: it all went together in his head . . . ![10]

As was clear in the case of this young man, the competition generated dynamics that were impossible to control, and went far beyond partisan frameworks. This meant that, while the number of militants active in Londonistan remained low (a few hundred individuals), their ideas spread to a second circle of followers, which was much larger. Similarly, the Londonistan scene "radiated" outward, depending on the movements of the various actors. Al-Muhajiroun had branches in Luton, Manchester, Birmingham, Leicester, and Leeds, and sent a team of scouts to Pakistan, made up, as Bakri told the *Guardian,* "of a branch for preaching and a branch for jihad."[11] He also sent students to canvass in Scandinavia. Abu Qatada and Abu Hamza also maintained links with Saïd Mansour, based in Denmark, a loyal supporter of the GIA, whose publishing house stocked the shelves of radical bookshops in Madrid and Brussels.

The organizations in question diversified their communication channels (magazines, interviews, lectures, etc.) at a time when connections made over the internet began to develop. In 1996, a British student of Pakistani origin, Ahmad Babar, founded the first website dedicated to jihadist content. The young man traveled back and forth several times to Bosnia before enrolling in a prestigious technology program at Imperial College London. He launched the website "azzam.com" on the university's server without the knowledge of the administration. This site, which paid tribute to the father of contemporary jihadism, described itself as a branch of "independent media" promoting reliable information produced by committed reporters. The site featured photographs, videos of training or fighting, and hagiographies of "martyrs" sent from various regions of the world. Ten years before the existence of social networks, the site became a platform allowing for contact between fans of the movement and budding jihadists. Imitating the initiative, Al-Muhajiroun and SOS created their own website, publishing the sermons and religious opinions of their respective leaders. Omar Bakri sent regular newsletters to the entire British press, exploiting the 850,000 e-mail addresses that had been hacked by his followers.[12]

6

The Afghanistan Emirate and September 11

In 1996, the Bosnian War ended with a ceasefire and an international settlement, overseen by the UN.[1] In Algeria, Zitouni, the head of the GIA, was killed in what was probably an internal settling of scores. The group intensified its policy of terror, ushering in the "era of massacres" during which entire villages were massacred, as in Bentalha. The unpopularity of these acts of violence allowed the Algerian regime to emerge victorious at the end of the decade, establishing what it called a "civil concord." This lull, however, did little more than mask a broader change that was taking place. The first step of this change was the arrival of the Taliban in Afghanistan, which revitalized the activities of jihadist groups until the high point of this first cycle: September 11, 2001.

The Taliban, Heart of Global Jihad

The Taliban's conquest of Kabul on September 27, 1996 brought about profound changes in jihadist spheres. After four years of clashes between the various factions that had defeated the Soviets, the Taliban entered the Afghan capital and proclaimed an "Islamic Emirate of Afghanistan." The movement, whose name means "students," took shape in 1994, spurred by young people from religious schools (*madrassas*) located along the Pakistani border. They gained the supported of the country and rallied by the militias of the radical Afghan mujahedeen, such as the Haqqani network.

Although they promised to "pacify" the country, the Taliban made the establishment of their strict interpretations of Islamic law their top priority. Fundamental freedoms were abolished. Women, prohibited from school and professional life, were the most severely affected. Everything they did had to be approved by a *mahram*, a male guardian, usually a husband or a close relative. Wearing the full veil of this region, the *chadri* or the *burka* – which covered women from head to toe and concealed their eyes behind a grid of fabric – was required from a very young age. For men, shaving was forbidden. Leisure, cultural and sporting activities, cinema, television, and music were all banned. Musical instruments were destroyed and singing, aside from religious chants (*nashid*), was prohibited. Depictions of living beings were eradicated, from dolls to the monumental Buddhas of Bamiyan, destroyed in 2001. Where morality was concerned, Islamic punishment (*hudud*) was strictly applied: the Taliban reinstated beheadings, hangings, and amputations for acts ranging from theft to more serious crimes. Flogging was the penalty for adultery, and public stoning was instituted for repeat offenders, with onlookers being encouraged to throw the first stone. Homosexuals were executed. The Taliban regime was ostracized by the international community, as deteriorating living conditions, daily violence, and poppy cultivation turned Afghanistan into the world's most sinister narco-state.[2]

In 1996, Osama bin Laden pledged allegiance to the Taliban leader, Mullah Omar, who hosted Al-Qaeda's leadership in the country. The Saudi billionaire provided the regime with much-needed financial support, and a network of supporters of their cause from London to Indonesia. In return, he was granted a huge swath of remote territory, difficult for foreign agents to access, thus enabling him to carry out his projects on a global scale.

In August 1996, he issued a religious edict (*fatwa*) declaring that "killing American citizens and their allies, civilian or military, is a personal obligation for every Muslim who is able to carry this out, wherever he may be." Two years later, in February 1998, he launched a so-called "global front for holy war against Jews and Crusaders."[3] The United States is accused of occupying the three holy places of Islam: Jerusalem, through their support for the state of Israel, and Medina and Mecca, due to their stationing of troops in Saudi Arabia as part of the liberation of Kuwait (1991). These declarations are commonly thought of as enacting the transition to global jihad. Starting from this point,

Al-Qaeda took as its objective to conduct attacks against American and Western interests all over the world. Afghanistan once again became the space in which the international movement was defined.

Afghanistan, Global Terrorist Factory

Starting in the fall of 1996, calls to join the Taliban emirate went out in Salafi-jihadist circles. According to a veteran from Saudi Arabia interviewed in the December 1, 2001 edition of *Al-Hayat*, more than a thousand Saudis, five hundred Yemenis, and around sixty Kuwaitis are said to have served in the units aiming to take the north of the country back from the alliance led by Commander Massoud. Routes via Pakistan were re-opened. Training and indoctrination camps sprang up in the tribal areas, extending the Peshawar model across the entire country.

Some of the former Arab-Afghans in exile returned and settled in Kabul, such as Abu Mus'ab al-Souri, who had been in England. The most motivated disciples of the emirs of Londonistan benefited from recommendations (*tazkiyya*) from their contacts. Abu Hamza and Abu Qatada also redirected some orphaned GIA members toward Afghanistan. The British were among the first Europeans to take the new road to Peshawar. As Rashad Ali recalls:

> There were a lot of young people, seventeen, eighteen years old, who saw the arrival of the Taliban as an opportunity to satisfy their desire for martyrdom. They joined the jihad being waged by a group that, from their point of view, was committed to following the road toward truth.[4]

Many of these young fighters soon turned back, unable to meet the demands of the profession of jihad that was then becoming standard on Al-Qaeda bases. Rashad Ali met some of them:

> They had been indoctrinated at a time when the British authorities believed there would be no consequences. People I knew [from Sheffield] were sent home because they couldn't fight and were a burden to the jihadist groups in Afghanistan. They came back with the same mindset: the West was the enemy. You know what happened next, 9/11 and all that.[5]

Figures released by British intelligence in 2001 give an idea of the scale of the movement, which reached its peak at the turn of the millennium. Nine hundred people are said to have left the country each year to train with jihadist groups in the region (including in Kashmir).[6] There were also departures from Brussels, to a much lesser degree. Mustafa Kastit, a revered Salafist imam in Brussels, noted this in an interview in the fall of 2016:

> Before September 11, there were already departures for Afghanistan, and afterwards for Iraq.[7]

Alain Grignard, the investigator from the anti-terrorist unit of the Brussels police, confirmed this:

> We do not know of any individuals from Belgium who went to fight against the Soviets. The generation of people who went to fight in Afghanistan did so starting with the Taliban.[8]

In Germany, several people who had already been in Bosnia also went to Afghanistan. Christian Ganczarski, who supplied Osama bin Laden with insulin to treat his diabetes and would later be involved in attacks, is one example.

The Emirate's European Representatives

On September 8, 1996, a few days before the Taliban took Kabul, Al-Muhajiroun organized an international conference at the London Arena. Omar Bakri promised to broadcast Bin Laden's call for jihad against the United States, recorded a few days earlier. The "Rally for Revival" was modeled on the 1994 demonstration at Wembley Stadium.[9] This time, the conference aimed to "find solutions to unite the Muslim community and address the issue of young Muslims living in Western societies."[10] In addition to the message from the leader of Al-Qaeda, Omar Bakri intended to advertise a sermon by the blind sheikh, sentenced to life imprisonment and solitary confinement for the 1993 World Trade Center attacks.[11] Five thousand participants were expected from all over the world. The governments of Egypt and Algeria asked their British counterparts to cancel the event so that "London would not become the world capital of Islamist terrorism." The authorities initially refused, on the grounds that there was no legal evidence that the speeches would "incite violence and racial hatred." Various associations swung into action, denouncing in particular the anti-Semitism and homophobia of the preachers. Two days before it was to take place, the rally was finally banned, officially for "security reasons."

The Taliban were presented by the emirs of Londonistan as a movement of idealistic young people with enlightened ideas, who had managed to restore order and Islamic morality to a country riddled with divisions and spiritual corruption. For them, the emirate was proof that their own utopian vision – the seizure of power and the return of sharia, which would both serve as preludes to the establishment of a caliphate that would rule the world – could be embodied in a concrete political program. The SOS publishing house released a brochure entitled *An Exemplary Rule of an Exemplary State*,[12] penned by one of Mullah Omar's spiritual mentors, which praised the effectiveness of the Taliban. The website azzam.com celebrated the Afghan model of government, arguing that it should encourage Muslims from all over the world to emigrate to the country in order to live under the laws of God. Media coverage was presented as Western propaganda aiming to prevent any alternative from emerging. Al-Muhajiroun embraced the cause and cast itself as its extension in Europe. As Rashad Ali notes:

> Omar Bakri espoused the views of Al-Qaeda and publicly declared that he was drawn not only to the Taliban regime but also to Bin Laden . . . We found ourselves in a strange situation where you had a group formed in the United Kingdom, Al-Muhajiroun, which began to affiliate with various jihadist groups in the Middle East, Afghanistan, North Africa . . .[13]

In Britain, the scale of these developments was beginning to cause concern. In September 1998, the *Criminal Justice Act* was passed in Westminster; this was the first step of a legal response. The measure authorized the prosecution of British residents who were responsible for terrorist acts abroad. It followed two years of parliamentary debate during which similar proposals were tweaked by the majority, which made it impossible to distinguish, *de jure*, between jihadists carrying out operations on behalf of Al-Qaeda abroad and political opponents and refugees. In 2000, Parliament enacted the *Terrorism Act*, according to which "any person connected with any terrorist organization, including one based outside the country, is liable to be arrested and questioned." The emirs of Londonistan were now liable to prosecution in the United Kingdom. They did not take long to react. On the one hand, they played up their victimization. Omar Bakri, for example, was outraged that parliamentarians were confusing "jihadists and terrorists." Those around Abu Hamza denounced the "racism" of the political class, following the familiar pattern of claiming that the new law targeted all Muslims.[14]

On the other hand, the emirs of Londonistan, feeling the noose tighten, doubled down on their invective and now became threatening. Omar Bakri called on Muslims not to respect British law, so as to show solidarity with those "who are fighting the infidels to liberate their territory." He warned the faithful not to participate in legislative elections, on pain of apostasy – the punishment for which is death, according to Salafi-jihadist interpretations.[15] In 1999, the first member of Al-Muhajiroun was convicted of plotting an attack on a military base in London.

September 11 as Culmination

In the final years of the twentieth century, Al-Qaeda's jihad manifested itself as an increase in operations against American interests in various locations around the world.

In 1998, the US embassies in Tanzania and Kenya were targeted, and these attacks – publicly applauded by Omar Bakri – resulted in dozens of deaths among the local populations. Five members of Supporters of Shariah were charged in England, including the son of Abu Hamza, who oversaw, from London, the establishment of a jihadist camp in Oregon. In 2000, the destroyer *USS Cole*, anchored in the port of Aden, Yemen, sustained a suicide attack.

At the same time, the 9/11 commando unit was making its final preparations. Its members met in a Salafist mosque in Hamburg, from which they had access, via a short flight or train journey, to various representatives of the movement. Mohammed Atta, the engineer who directed the operations, traveled to London several times, where he collected funds sent to him from Madrid and moved in the circle of Abu Qatada.

In the meantime, members of the GIA were remobilized by Al-Qaeda. In 1999, one of them was arrested in California, where he was planning an attack on Los Angeles International Airport at the turn of the millennium.

In 2000, another former GIA member, Abu Doha, plotted an attack on the cathedral and Christmas market in Strasbourg, eighteen years before a similar plot orchestrated by ISIS. One of the perpetrators, scouting the area with a camera in hand, filmed Christmas shoppers in the city's historic center, delighting in what he had in store for them.[16] He was arrested following the dismantling of a cell in Frankfurt, along with militants in Brussels and London.

In August 2001, the Hamburg unit met for the last time in Tarragona, Spain. They drew up the flight plans and the final list of targets in New York and Washington, and set the date of the operations for the morning of September 11, 2001. A few days later, Djamel Beghal, another former GIA supporter, was arrested in Dubai while planning an attack on the American embassy in Paris. He was working with a former Tunisian international footballer residing in Molenbeek, Nizar Trabelsi, who wanted to attack a NATO base in Uccle, Belgium.

Ten years after the end of the Soviet occupation of Afghanistan, the proliferation of terrorist projects revealed the different dynamics running through global jihad. First there was Al-Qaeda, which sought to act on Bin Laden's obsession with striking American interests and Jewish targets in the West, and had a number of cells set up specifically for this purpose in Western Europe, which were connected to a greater or lesser degree to the ecosystems established by Afghan veterans.

Second, the former GIA cells, reconstituted on Al-Qaeda's coattails, which extended their targets to include their European neighbors. Just as the militants present in Peshawar had stepped up their activities after the withdrawal of the Red Army, when their original raison d'être had disappeared, the former GIA networks embraced this shift as the civil war in Algeria came to an end. The plans put in place between 1994 and 1996 to strike France, accused of supporting the Algerian regime, were thereby extended to other European democracies. Militants now justified their murderous designs in Belgium or Germany on the simple grounds that the citizens of these countries are essentially "enemies" of Islam, for the simple fact of being "infidels." The same shift, with the same consequences, took place with certain returnees from Bosnia, such as the Roubaix gang.

Indeed, alongside Bin Laden's calls to action, a current within the jihadism that was brought to Europe was beginning to assert itself. Before 9/11, it targeted Western European societies. Usama Hasan, a well-established figure in London's Salafist circles and, at the time, a supporter of jihad abroad, noted the emergence of this trend in GIA circles twenty-five years on:

A large number of Algerians settled in London in the 1990s because of the civil war. The Algerians [of the GIA] had a different mindset. They said they considered Europe to be the enemy, a colonial occupier. That's the history of Algeria, of France. But for many Pakistanis in Britain, the West was our home. We were against Western influence, we had anti-Western ideas, but we never thought about carrying out terrorist acts here. It was insane. If you wanted to join the jihad, you traveled thousands of kilometers to a real border, Afghanistan or Bosnia for example. Those were legitimate wars and you could take part in them without any problems, that's how we understood jihad. That's what started to happen in the 1990s. [. . .] I didn't understand that mindset and those ideas, and I didn't take them seriously at the time. I said to myself: "No Islamist will ever attack England." But looking back now, I realize that I was naive. Europe wasn't really a target yet, but that changed after 9/11.[17]

Thinking about the several large-scale terrorist projects that were planned and mostly thwarted allows us to see the September 11 attacks in the general context of a rising tide. Operationally, they were the culmination of a decade of planning. As in 1993, they targeted the World Trade Center, and they involved the hijacking of airplanes, inspired by the episode of the Algiers–Paris flight that was supposed to hit the Eiffel Tower in 1994.

On the morning of September 11, nineteen hijackers seized control of four commercial aircraft and charted a course for the symbols of American superpower: financial superpower in New York (the Twin Towers), military in Virginia (the Pentagon), and political in Washington

D.C. (the Capitol or the White House). The last objective was not achieved: the Boeing crashed in a field in Pennsylvania after passengers resisted. Nearly three thousand people were killed in this major event, whose many chain reactions continue to affect the geopolitical situation throughout the Euro-Mediterranean zone.

II

THE PIONEERS –
THE 2000s

I'm ashamed to admit it today, but I celebrated on September 11 . . . I was in my twenties, I was the leader of a group that had taken part in jihad, and I had recruited people for jihad. That day, I was overjoyed . . . It was a great victory for the Islamists. In fact, they still celebrate it. September 11 was a consecration. America had been hit.[1]

The words, spoken by Usama Hasan, a British man who traveled to Afghanistan ten years before the September 11 attacks and has now repented, show that these attacks are perceived as a spectacular accomplishment and a paradigm shift in jihadist circles. This date marks the beginning of the twenty-first century, and is the starting point of jihadism as a fully-fledged European phenomenon.

1

The War on Terror

In the aftermath of the attacks, American leaders demanded the surrender of Osama bin Laden and the leaders of Al-Qaeda. Mullah Omar rejected the demand, which triggered the American intervention in Afghanistan, under the umbrella of the United Nations, on October 7. Three weeks later, the Taliban were driven out of Kabul and took refuge in the mountains and tribal areas, promising the GIs and their allies the same fate as the soldiers of the Red Army. The hunt for the Al-Qaeda commander began, and would last ten years.

The Bush administration responded to fear by declaring "the war on terror." In the view of the president and the neoconservatives around him, the moral struggle was a battle between a good side and the evil entity that opposed it, composed of "rogue states" that supported terrorism. In addition to the regime of Mullah Omar, an abhorrent "axis" was drawn up, which included North Korea, Iran, and Saddam Hussein's Iraq. Bruce Riedel, a CIA analyst, described how the initial discussions in the White House shaped the contours of the American response:

On September 13, I'm invited to the Oval Office for a meeting with the president [George W. Bush], the secretary of state, Colin Powell, and the president's communications director. The purpose of the meeting is to help the president prepare a speech in which he will outline the American strategy for the "war on terror." During the meeting, I spoke up and said, "Mr. President, I think this is a mistake. Terrorism is a tactic, not an organization. Terrorists have existed since Roman times; the British considered George Washington a terrorist; Israel was founded by an organization that

85

used terrorist methods . . . Instead, we should call it 'the war on Al-Qaeda.'"
And the president's communications officers said, "No, impossible, no one
in the United States knows what Al-Qaeda is, they don't even know how to
pronounce the word correctly. We need a target that's easy for Americans to
understand." And that's how we ended up with the war on terror as our only
communication tool.[1]

In the minds of the president's advisors, the specific threat of jihadism
was a mere geopolitical hazard and hence relegated to the background:
ease of communication took precedence over strategic clarity. At the
same time, republicans on Capitol Hill were demanding a change in the
American approach to the Arab world, and re-examining the geopolitical
priorities of the world's leading power. As 15 of the 19 hijackers were
Saudis, the Gulf petro-monarchs were accused of fomenting anti-
Americanism in the region and supporting radical Islamism throughout
the world. The uncertainty prevalent in George W. Bush's entourage
was exploited by the hawks gathered around the vice-president, Dick
Cheney, who presented a plan for a "new Middle East" that had been
sketched out ten years earlier. The project depended on the emergence
of a liberal and pro-American regime in the heart of the Arab Middle
East. According to this view, the overthrow of Saddam Hussein, within
the general framework of regime change, would lead to a peace deal with
Israel and initiate a process of democratization in the region. Iraq's oil
reserves would compensate for Saudi Arabia's relegation in the hierarchy
of regional partners. Post-Saddam Iraq would be a model of successful
transition, making those dictatorships resisting peace with Israel, such
as Syria, look out of touch, and injecting new life into anti-Khomeini
revolt in Iran . . . In fact, the entire initiative led to a disastrous military
stalemate and buried Iraq under the rubble of a decade of civil war, one
with immeasurable consequences.

No Transition: From Afghanistan to Iraq

In 2002, the Iraqi head of state was accused, through a campaign of
disinformation orchestrated by the Bush administration, of possessing
weapons of mass destruction and seeking to make them available to
terrorist organizations.

With the exception of Tony Blair's government in the United Kingdom, American allies refused to follow the White House's lead. Nearly 3,000 demonstrations took place in the first months of 2003, involving nearly 35 million people across the globe. The largest gatherings took place in Europe. Three million people came out in Rome; this remains the largest peaceful march in history.[2] At the UN Security Council, France expressed its opposition, supported by Russia and Germany.

Military intervention, however, was still becoming more and more likely, and this did not escape the attention of the jihadist leaders, particularly Abu Mus'ab al-Zarqawi. Unlike the well-heeled Al-Qaeda leaders, such as Osama bin Laden, son of a Saudi billionaire, or Ayman al-Zawahiri, scion of a line of doctors, Zarqawi came from a working class background. Jordanian by birth, originally from the industrial city of Zarqa (population 850,000), he turned to a life of crime at an early age, getting involved in drugs and pimping. He became a jihadist after serving time for arms trafficking. In prison, he rubbed shoulders with one of the most renowned Jordanian ideologues, Al-Maqdissi, who had been imprisoned since his return from Peshawar in 1992. Upon meeting him, Zarqawi threw himself body and soul into learning the doctrine. His numerous tattoos, which were respectable in criminal circles, became a reminder of the indelibility of a life spent in sin. Outlawed by Salafist ideology, which considers them an alteration of the body bequeathed by Allah, they had to go. He used a razor blade that he obtained in prison to cut away these residual impurities. Covered in scars, he bore his commitment to the dogma on his very flesh. Upon his liberation in 1999, he returned to Afghanistan, on his mentor Al-Maqdissi's recommendation. He underwent military training there, but struggled to break into the inner circles, which led him to rethink his plans. The inevitability of the invasion of Iraq came to appear to him as an invaluable opportunity to set up a brigade there.

Shock and Awe

On March 20, 2003, at 5:32 a.m., the United Nations Charter was trampled by the world's leading power, which launched Operation Shock and Awe. Several European countries took part, such as Great Britain, Belgium, Spain, Italy, Denmark, the Netherlands, and Portugal. As in

Afghanistan, the deluge of force that rained down on Iraq settled the military question in three weeks. Saddam Hussein was deposed. This is the point at which things got difficult for the occupying forces. The stabilization of the country rested on prerequisites that were never met. First, Iran managed to gain a foothold in Iraq, contrary to what the Pentagon had hoped. Second, the banning of all civil servants affiliated with the Ba'ath party, which had been in power until then, deprived the administration of the resources necessary to govern. The massive layoffs in the civil service, the only sector offering a stable income at a time when the economy was collapsing, encouraged senior Sunni officials to join the resistance. Twelve years later, ISIS's High Strategic and Military Council would be a sinister by-product of this, as it was largely composed of Saddam Hussein's former intelligence officers.[3]

The horizon darkened on August 19, 2003. A booby-trapped truck was driven into the United Nations headquarters in Baghdad, which was in charge of reconstruction. This was the most violent attack in the history of the UN. It led to 22 deaths, including special representative Sergio Vieira de Mello, and hundreds of injuries. A second attack took place on March 2, 2004, the day on which the Shiite religious festival of Ashura was celebrated. A series of detonations in the holy city of Karbala and in a mosque in Baghdad resulted in the deaths of 170 worshippers and injured more than 550. On the first anniversary of the overthrow of the dictator, Iraq disintegrated into a civil war that took on an increasingly sectarian hue, giving rise to acts of violence of unprecedented brutality.

The attacks were perpetrated by the organization founded by Abu Mus'ab al-Zarqawi, Al-Tawhid, renamed Al-Qaeda in Mesopotamia (2003–2006) and then the Islamic State of Iraq (2006–2010). It would serve as a prototype for ISIS. Their objective was to destroy the slim hopes for peace on which the American strategy was based by lighting the powderkeg that intercommunal relations had become. At the time, almost two-thirds of the population were Shiite, a quarter were Sunni, and just under ten percent were Christian. Since the creation of the modern Iraqi state following the 1916 Sykes-Picot Agreement, the Sunni minority had feared political subjugation by the Shiite majority. The Ba'ath Party dictatorship, though its objectives were "secularist," had the specific trait of being led by Saddam Hussein, a Sunni from Tikrit, who held the political, religious, and cultural influence of the Shiites in an iron grip.

The jihadist attacks during religious festivals, and in the holy cities of Shiism, aimed to create the conditions for a sectarian clash, which would allow Zarqawi to justify his presence in Iraq – after all, he was "defending" the Sunni minority. This strategy of chaos was the subject of public disagreements expressed by the central command of Al-Qaeda, led by Bin Laden, the effects of which would manifest themselves ten years later in Syria.

In March 2004, four soldiers from Blackwater, the private security force employed by the US government, were killed in Fallujah, the capital of the predominantly Sunni province of Western Iraq. Their mutilated bodies were displayed by the insurgents who controlled the city, in which most of the jihadist rebels, and their leader, Zarqawi, were living. In November 2004, the American, British and Iraqi armies laid siege to the city and slowly recaptured it, street by street, over more than a month. The battle, considered to be the worst of the decade, provided justification for the nascent jihad in Iraq. Several Europeans distinguished themselves in this jihad, including a Frenchman and a Belgian, who inspired, respectively, the January and November 2015 attacks in Paris.

The missteps of the neoconservatives in Iraq had a knock-on effect in Afghanistan. Bruce Riedel explains the interaction between the two zones:

I think historians and psychologists will debate for centuries what made George Bush decide to invade Iraq. The truth is, we don't know. The result, however, is undeniable. As soon as the decision to pivot to Iraq was made, the CIA's best and brightest agents, the Arabic speakers, the operatives deployed in Afghanistan, were sent to the Middle East. The head of operations for fighting Al-Qaeda within the CIA was transferred from Afghanistan to Iraq. The same thing happened with the U.S. military. The mission in Afghanistan then became severely underfunded and lacked essential skills. The construction of the Afghan state to replace the Taliban, which in itself required a monumental effort, was now being done with shoestring resources. The result was predictable.[4]

2

Europe, Caught in the Middle

Two trends emerged at the beginning of the 2000s. The first was the acceleration of the spread of Salafism within European Islam. The second was the emergence of new jihadist actors in the west of the continent: the pioneers, who took over from the veterans.

The Saudi Response: Strengthen Salafism in Europe

The spread of Salafism within European Islam is undoubtedly the least understood but most important ideological revolution since the beginning of the twenty-first century. It was facilitated by the fact that Muslim populations are more likely than others to experience economic, social, political, and cultural marginalization; this was made even worse by the economic and financial crisis of 2007–2008. It was also provoked by exogenous factors, starting with the Iraq crisis. The deterioration of the public debate on issues related to immigration and European identity facilitated the victimizing discourses and feelings of rejection on which Salafism feeds. The rise of European Islamist movements independent of foreign authorities is also important. A final factor is the role played by certain state and private actors, particularly from the Gulf countries.

Since the last quarter of the twentieth century, support for Salafist movements around the world has been one of the main levers of Saudi soft power abroad. It is used as a tool to rally diverse Muslim communities to the Gulf petro-monarchies. In the 1990s, Saudi interest in Islam in the West was partly a reaction to the Gulf War. The invasion of

Kuwait by Saddam Hussein's troops in 1991 sparked unexpected enthusiasm among Muslims living in Western Europe. This came to the Gulf States because the survival of Kuwait was at stake. As a result, the leaders of Saudi Arabia, Qatar, and the United Arab Emirates became increasingly aware of their extreme vulnerability, and set about remedying it by forging new alliances.[1] The result was a series of extensive diversification programs in the economic, cultural, and sports sectors, as well as the establishment of museums with "high global visibility," such as the Louvre and the Guggenheim in Abu Dhabi. Al Jazeera was founded in 1996 in Qatar, while the ruling families took aim at gaining a foothold among the most prestigious teams in world football. Investments were a means for regimes to multiply their anchors with a global elite that was no longer confined to military-industrial circles. The spread of Salafism within European Islam fits within this context and responds to similar issues, though it is rarely considered in this way. The dissemination of Salafist doctrine, whose leading scholars sang the praises of the Saudi monarchy, was effective at spreading religious discourse that favored the interests of the kingdom. The problem was that this current shared many elements of its dogma with jihadism, such as the rejection of any form of sovereignty that does not emanate from Allah (such as democracy), intolerance towards other religions, and the claim to represent "true" Islam.

After 9/11, the Gulf countries' support for the expansion of Salafism in Europe was refocused to meet other imperatives. The aim is no longer to co-opt religious circles for political gain, but to contain the jihadist excesses that are leading Saudi Arabia to come under fire in Washington. In Saudi logic, promoting Salafism in its "quietist" or apolitical version in Europe is a way of curbing deviance and providing an antidote to jihadism. It also protects the country against accusations of passivity or complacency toward terrorists. The risks remain the same, and given the compatibility between Salafism and jihadism, this strategy could prove counterproductive, increasing the possibilities of ideological combustion. Salafism, after all, tends to increase the desire, on the part of European Muslims, to break with Western society. The accession to power of Crown Prince Mohammed bin Salman in Saudi Arabia in 2016 has resulted in an official renunciation of this policy in Europe.

The Decline and Resilience of Londonistan: The Subversion of Open Societies

Between 2001 and 2004, most Western European countries strengthened their legal arsenal against a backdrop of security threats. On December 22, 2001, a British convert and sympathizer of Al-Muhajiroun in Ilford, tried to detonate his shoes, packed with explosives, on a Paris-Miami flight, before being overpowered by other passengers. In 2003, several militants were arrested while preparing a ricin attack on the London Underground. Attempts failed in Germany, Belgium and France. Several senior Al-Qaeda leaders were also arrested or killed in Central Asia. The "mastermind" of 9/11, Khaled Sheikh Mohammed, was kidnapped by the CIA in Pakistan in 2003. Throughout Western Europe, police services dismantled networks formed during the previous decade, and the international movement and its European component shrank.

In England, the situation grew more complicated for the preachers of Londonistan. Peter Clarke, head of the anti-terrorist unit at Scotland Yard from 2002 to 2008, described the prevailing mindset in the ranks of the London Metropolitan Police when he took up his post:

> I know it sounds a bit like a cliché, but 9/11 really changed everything. Threats changed, as did the ways to protect against them, and we had to rethink our modus operandi. The first thing was to find out whether the many Islamist groups in our country were a threat to the United Kingdom. [. . .] We then developed a two-pronged approach: we targeted individuals who spread hate and terrorists who wanted to commit attacks.[2]

The Jordanian Abu Qatada, described by Tony Blair's Home Secretary as "the most important radical preacher in the United Kingdom" and by the police as "the spiritual leader of Al-Qaeda in Europe," was given a great deal of attention. His name appeared at the top of reports from the various investigative services working in Western Europe. In addition to references to his religious opinions (*fatwa*) legitimizing the abuses of the GIA, he appeared to be a privileged contact of the Hamburg cell, which planned 9/11, and of Abu Dahdah, arrested in Madrid and extradited to the United States for his role in financing the operation. In an interview published by *Al-Hayat* on December 13, 2001, Abu Qatada described the anti-terrorism legislation as a "racist law directed against foreigners." He denied belonging to any organization, but lent his support to the Taliban regime, which was "oppressed" by the American intervention, and refused to condemn the World Trade Center attacks, questioning the idea that the victims were "innocent civilians."[3] After ten months on the run, he was finally found in a council estate in south London and imprisoned at the end of 2002. His arrest caused turmoil among sympathizers: demonstrations broke out calling for the Sheikh's release, and threats were made against Belmarsh Prison, where he was held. After years of difficult legal proceedings, during which he alternated between imprisonment and house arrest, Abu Qatada was deported to Jordan, where he has resided ever since.

While he was still in England, Abu Hamza was at the eye of a storm. He received notification of a preaching ban, which he ignored, continuing his weekly service at Finsbury Park mosque. On January 20, 2003, at 2 a.m., 150 Scotland Yard police officers raided the building as part of a counter-terrorism investigation. The then-head of operations, Peter Clarke, looked back on how it unfolded:

> At first, we were following a trail of forged documents in Norfolk. [. . .] As the investigation progressed, we came across a recipe for making ricin [a highly toxic agent] and a plan to attack the subway. The investigation led us to the Finsbury Park mosque, run by Abu Hamza. [. . .] I remember the raid . . . it was quite extraordinary. There was paramilitary equipment, gas masks, bulletproof vests, fake firearms, wooden pistols . . . We started to lift the ceiling tiles, and then a shower of credit cards, passports, and checkbooks fell on us. It didn't look like a place of worship. It probably was for many people, but clearly not for Abu Hamza. It was the base from which he ran all his operations.
>
> If you look at the profiles of the people who found refuge there, people like Kamel Bourgass [who was behind the ricin attack plot and who had killed a police officer a few days earlier], it's obvious what was going on in that place.[4]

In the days that followed, the mosque was temporarily closed. For more than a year, Abu Hamza delivered his weekly sermon in the street, in front of an audience of the faithful who blocked traffic. His home was searched repeatedly, and his rhetoric against Great Britain became increasingly explicit. In 2004, his involvement in several plots was proven, and he was arrested and imprisoned for seven years before being deported to the United States. There he was convicted on eleven counts of terrorism, including organizing a jihadist cell in Oregon and overseeing a hostage-taking in Yemen that killed three Westerners. During his trial, the veteran mocked the American justice system, minimized his actions, and expressed his admiration for Bin Laden and his approval of the World Trade Center attacks.[5] In 2014, he was sentenced to life imprisonment by a New York court located a few blocks from Ground Zero and the September 11 memorial. Since then, he has been held in a high-security ward at ADX Florence, a supermax prison in Colorado described as the "Alcatraz of the Rockies."

Omar Bakri was the last to be investigated. He was first targeted financially, to which he responded, like the others, by upping the ante. On September 11, 2002, in the Finsbury Park Mosque, he organized a conference entitled "The Magnificent 19," a reference to the New York and Washington hijackers. Stickers distributed at the event were marked by their black humour: "9/11, A Towering Day in World History." The event was attended by 150 people; one of its organizers would later become an ISIS executioner.[6]

The little information provided on the event poster offers a condensed version of how Salafi-jihadist groups flout the law and spread their message of hate. The hijackers are recognized as "martyrs" (*shouhada*), one of the most important honours in the Islamic tradition. Paradise and its carnal and spiritual rewards are offered to them for eternity. The American, Israeli, and British heads of state, by contrast, are referred to as "terrorists," a modern political category that does not refer to any Islamic concept. They are also said to have "the blood of Muslims on their hands," which means, according to the Salafist interpretation of religious jurisprudence, that they should be put to death. It also implies that any act of "revenge" against the citizens who elected them is legitimate, and thus (reading between the lines) that the operations of September 11 are in accordance with Islam. Finally, certain Muslim leaders are represented: the Pakistani and Afghan presidents, Pervez Musharraf and Hamid Karzai; King Fahd of Saudi Arabia; and the Palestinian leader Yasser Arafat. They are described as "apostates" (*murtaddin*), one of the worst

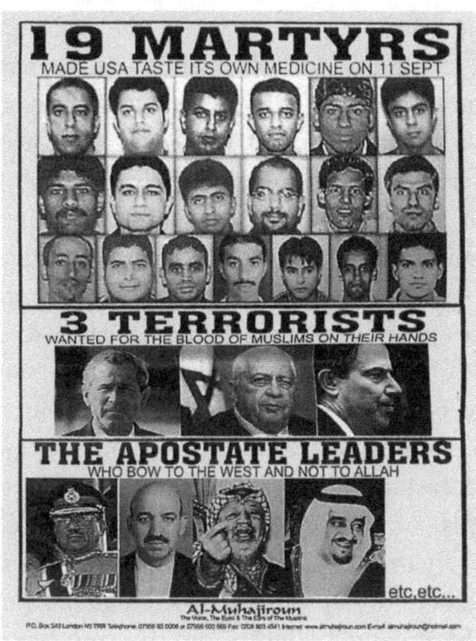

Poster for the September 11, 2002 Al-Muhajiroun conference, in the east of London.

categories of humanity according to medieval Islamic jurisprudence, which decrees that shedding their "blood" becomes "lawful" (*dam halal*), meaning that any believer who takes their life will be rewarded by Allah. In fact, this accusation, which aims to strip a Muslim of his status as a believer because of actions contrary to divine law, is extremely serious. In principle, it is the sole prerogative of a Muslim sovereign, but the Salafi-jihadists have appropriated it and use it extensively, earning them the pejorative title of *takfiri*, literally "those who excommunicate." On this poster, a single line serves as justification: the aforementioned leaders have decided to "bow to the West and not to Allah." In other words, through their policy of alliance with the United States, they flout the principle of "loyalty and disavowal" that is fundamental for the Salafi-jihadists, as we have seen. The "etc, etc" where the fifth photo should be invites the observer to reflect on "apostates" of the same ilk who are all around him, and on how best to restore justice . . .

The poster leaves no doubt as to the orientation of the event organizers for anyone with even a very basic understanding of the references. The justification of terrorism, the legitimation of violence against Western civilians, and the call to assassinate apostates and leaders of the Arab world are all very explicit. They are not, however, objectionable within the legal framework of European countries, because they refer to categories established by religious jurisprudence (medieval, in this case), which these activists hold up as the only form of legitimate legislation on earth. Indeed, the organizers played on the ambiguity of their position. Journalists, who were not allowed to attend the debates, were invited to a press conference in a room called "Ground Zero." One of Omar Bakri's associates said the following: "It may not have been the smartest thing to do, but it was legitimate [from a religious standpoint], yes. An eye for an eye, a tooth for a tooth, as the Old Testament says . . . But in this case it was just one eye for a hundred eyes . . . there is still so much to be done." The website of Omar Bakri's organization refers on the page for the event to "the positive consequences of September 11, such as the clear crystallization of two camps: Islam and believers on the one hand, and *kufr* [the impious] and hypocrites [Muslims who refuse to recognize this binary distinction] on the other."[7]

This detour allows us to understand how Salafi-jihadist preachers often existed in a "gray area" after September 11. They disseminated the intellectual framework that would allow their interlocutors to think within a jihadist logic, but took care not to make statements that would fall under the scope of anti-terrorist measures. In this way, they set a trap for democracies that were trying to reduce their influence. When these democracies expanded their legal frameworks in order to prosecute militants, they ran the risk of moving away from the rule of law, and creating "crimes of opinion" incompatible with the values and functioning of democratic societies. Many regimes in North Africa and the Middle East did something similar (though not identical) in the 1980s and 1990s, strengthening their authoritarianism in response to security threats, thus dashing any hope of transitioning to a model based on the rule of law. At the same time, doing nothing meant giving these movements free rein, allowing them to retain full latitude to act within democratic frameworks and spread the very ideological content that compromises security, the future of Islam in the West, and Europe's political equilibrium.

The skill of the emirs of Londonistan in subverting liberal values as far as possible served as a model for several other movements. This skill explains why investigations into them took such a long time, but it also, paradoxically, led them to underestimate the juricial response on the part of the state. Abdullah Anas, son-in-law of London-based Abdullah Azzam, explains that these preachers ended up thinking they were out of reach, convinced that they would escape prosecution:

> These people did not see that the authorities, all of a sudden [after September 11], took things very seriously. I still remember, they [the triumvirate of Londonistan] always said that nothing would happen to them, that they didn't need to be concerned. Omar Bakri was asking people to go and wage jihad, and so was Abu Qatada. Until they realized that it wasn't going to happen like that. They didn't expect the [British] democracy to be able to react quickly. And by the time they realized things were going to get serious for them, well, they were already in Belmarsh [Prison] with an extradition request being processed. The British authorities underestimated them for a long time, but they did the same thing, they really underestimated democracy.[8]

The various investigations into the emirs of Londonistan show just how incompetent the British approach was in the 1990s. The trial hearings reveal, for example, that Abu Qatada, in conversations with MI5, had promised not to "bite the hand that fed him," and to use his religious influence with the Algerian community in London in positive ways. He also received 1,600 pounds a month as a housing benefit and for his "inability to work." Abu Hamza, meanwhile, received a disability pension for the hands he had lost handling bombs, and his London home was renovated at the Crown's expense. While he denounced British "immorality" and the way Muslims were trampled on in the UK, one of his wives received 4,000 pounds per month in social assistance. Omar Bakri is said to have received almost half a million pounds from public insurance funds, but this did not prevent him from describing the British Isles as the worst place on earth to practice Islam, or from calling for the Prime Minister to be killed. After their arrest, all three would explain that the government was waging a "war on Muslims" of which they were the first victims, and said they would applaud any and all attacks.[9]

Awlaqi, the New Face of Western Jihad

The London ecosystem had grown increasingly complex over the course of a decade, which meant that it would not disappear in just a few months. Between 2002 and 2004, there were even new preachers who appeared on the scene. The Yemeni-American Anwar al-Awlaqi, mentor of two of the 9/11 terrorists, is one example. In 2003, he toured the UK, participated in rallies organized by Omar Bakri's group, and became a star preacher in British Salafism. That summer, the Muslim Association of Britain, dominated by the Muslim Brotherhood (of which Awlaqi was a member), organized a lecture tour for him, bringing him as far as Aberdeen, Scotland.[10] As part of a day co-organized with the Muslim student unions of prestigious universities,[11] he presented his vision of "renouncement" and insisted on the importance of preaching in the field. The tour, entitled "To be a Muslim, think globally and act locally," sparked public outrage. Rashad Ali, at the time a member of an Islamist group, attended several of these events. He recalls how Awlaqi brought up extremely contentious subjects and generated a great deal of excitement:

> Awlaqi was an extremely popular preacher. He was American, he knew how to speak in public and interact with young people. He wasn't sectarian like the Salafists; he didn't care which faction you belonged to. The only thing that interested him was giving an overview of global jihad. [. . .] In 2003, he came to give lectures. In some of his speeches, he was careful about what he said and only hinted at a few radical aspects in the middle of a narrative in which he spoke about the life of the Prophet. He subtly introduced key concepts: the sole source of sovereignty is Sharia law, democracy must be rejected, and participating in elections is forbidden. In other lectures, dedicated specifically to jihad, he was very, very explicit. [. . .] He said that suicide bombings were legitimate, that we had to support the jihadists in Iraq, raise funds for them and fight [. . .], things that only Al-Qaeda people were saying at the time.[12]

Awlaqi's visit took place at a pivotal moment, when the first European militants were beginning to emancipate themselves from the tutelage of the veterans, and planning to take action against their countries. The politicization of the jihadist discourse proposed by Awlaqi, through a brutal denunciation of Western democracies, provided them with the justification they needed. Rashad Ali says the following about this:

> Awlaqi's ideas appealed to young people because he offered them a worldview. People look at the world and see problems everywhere, horrors, political failures, conflict zones, and the injustice of it all. This was an environment that was ready to absorb his ideas intravenously.[13]

In 2004, Awlaqi left Europe for Yemen, where he would later become the regional emir of Al-Qaeda and modernize jihadist communication online. In the first half of the 1990s, the environment of Peshawar had given birth to Al-Qaeda's global jihad just as the veterans began to leave the city. Ten years later, the dismantling of Londonistan occurred at the same time as new theories of action were emerging, theories that insisted on the need to wage guerrilla jihad in Europe. Abu Mus'ab al-Suri, Bin Laden's media advisor, who lived in London until 1997, provides an example. At the same time Awlaqi flew to Yemen, he posted a 1,400-page volume online entitled *The Global Islamic Resistance Call* (*Dawa al-muqawama al-islamiyya al-alamia*). In it, he set forth the idea of a jihad based on numerous unsophisticated individual attacks against Western countries with large Muslim communities. He specifically identified Western Europe, which he knew well, as a weak link, and made it a preferred target over the United States, in contrast to Bin Laden. The objective of the jihadist guerrilla, he argued, was to continually harass democratic societies, which would lead the latter, he believed, to turn against all Muslims without distinction. Confronted by growing distrust by their own societies, these Muslims would have no choice but to join, en masse, the holy war, leading to a civil war in which they would emerge victorious.[14] His work enjoyed relative success, but the partial materialization of his theories in jihadist circles would occur only ten years later, with the advent of ISIS and the exploitation of new means of communication in the framework of Jihad 2.0.

3

From Ulm to Toulouse: Passing the Baton to the Pioneers

The early 2000s were marked by a Europeanization of jihadism that was not perceived as such. Arresting the veterans or driving them away destroyed their cells, but did not put a stop to the preaching machines they had established. In these still embryonic circles, a transition was taking place from one form of transplanted jihad to another; the figureheads of the new form were the pioneers. Besides London, two archetypal territories illustrate this phenomenon: Ulm in Germany and Toulouse in France.

The German Model

The place of Islam in Germany can be thought at the intersection of the English, French and Belgian cases. Like Belgium, the country has no colonial past in the Arab-Muslim countries, and like England and France, it is home to a large immigrant population, estimated at 3.8 million people in the early 2000s (5.3 million in 2021).[1] The presence of Islam is mainly linked to the guest workers (*Gastarbeiter*) who came from Turkey, and to a lesser extent Morocco and Tunisia. During the postwar economic boom, they traveled to the industrial belts and mines of West Germany, which lacked manpower, and then to Berlin after reunification. This immigration, which was initially male and temporary, came to a standstill with the economic crisis of the 1980s. It then became more feminine and was made permanent by family reunification mechanisms. The Turkish communities in Germany are large and reflect the political and religious spectrum of the country of origin,

100

from secularizing movements (the "Kemalist" parties, inspired by the founder of the Turkish nation, Mustafa Kemal Atatürk) to conservative Islamist movements. Historically, the organization of worship was handled by the Turkish State through its Ministry of Religious Affairs. For all these reasons, Turkish communities in Germany have tended to be swept up in the same transformations as those taking place in Turkey itself. Secularizing tendencies, which were still dominant in the 1990s, have given way to Islamist currents. Milli Görüş, a group close to the Muslim Brotherhood, whose emblem depicts a white crescent moon on a green background outlining Europe, has been the most active in the re-Islamization of young people of immigrant descent. It has enjoyed growing support from the authorities since the election of Recep Tayyip Erdoğan, to the point that its activities now tend to merge with those of state networks.

For immigrants from the Arab countries and their descendants, institutional and religious structure took shape at the end of the twentieth century around student groups. The presence of the Muslim Brotherhood is perceptible in ways that are comparable to neighboring countries. Similarly, Saudi investments have followed trends similar to those of Belgium or Switzerland. Starting in the 1990s, this had led to the construction of several religious institutes, notably in Freiburg, Berlin and Aachen. One of the best Salafist examples is the King Fahd Academy, which opened with great fanfare in Bonn in 1995 in a diplomatic gesture worthy of the coat of arms of the former West German capital. In 2003, the German security services discovered that one of its imams was urging his followers to wage jihad, and that children studying there were being taught to hate Jews and Christians, and instructed in the value of the supreme sacrifice for the advent of a world dominated by Islam. Beyond these examples, the Salafists were able to reach converts and children of Turkish descent through sermons in German. This partly explains the over-representation of the former in jihadist networks, and the change in the latter, who previously had little involvement in extremism.[2]

In the early 2000s, the discovery of the Hamburg cell responsible for 9/11 sent shockwaves through the region. Until then, a few Salafi-jihadist veterans had appeared from time to time in Germany, but not to the same degree as in its European neighbors. This changed in the 2000s, and the starting point of this transformation was the peaceful conurbation of Ulm and Neu-Ulm.

The Other Battle of Ulm

The city of Ulm became famous in the fall of 1805 for being the site of one of Napoleon's greatest military demonstrations. The Emperor, defying Europe, seized the city thanks to a series of deft maneuvers. With few human losses and little bloodshed, he surrounded the city, obtained the surrender of the Austrian forces, and paved the way for the conquest of Vienna, which fell a month later. The Ulm campaign gave its name to the street in Paris where the École normale supérieure is located. The city is far less recognized for its role in the history of European jihadism, which concerns not Napoleon but a discreet man named Doctor Youssouf.

In the early 2000s, Ulm had a population of 120,000, while Neu-Ulm (literally New Ulm), its outgrowth, had 50,000 inhabitants. Together, the two cities gave birth to the first entirely German jihadist cell, known as the Sauerland Cell. No one could have predicted this, because Ulm and Neu-Ulm are in many respects the anti-Molenbeek. The conurbation is located in the heart of the "tech belt" of Southern Germany. There is barely any crime, and there were no incidents against the Muslim community splashed across the local news. The cities did not experience the economic austerity that disrupted lifestyles in the East after reunification, or sociological transformations comparable to those in Berlin or the major cities of the West. The conurbation boasts a rich student life, a renowned university, and a dense network of small- and medium-sized businesses specializing in cutting-edge sectors.

However, they share two features with places where the veterans have tended to settle (though these features do not necessarily explain their presence in these cities). First, they form a regional communications hub: they are located halfway between two metropolises, Munich and Stuttgart, and at the heart of a motorway junction providing links to every corner of the country. Second, unlike Peshawar, they form a unique "border area": though they are separated only by an arm of the Danube that is about 50 meters wide, and connected by a bridge, they belong to two different *Länder*, and therefore to two different federal jurisdictions:

Baden-Wuerttemberg for Ulm, and Bavaria for Neu-Ulm. This administrative specificity largely determined the nature of the local preaching machine.

The first Salafists appeared in 1996, at the time of the attacks by the Roubaix gang in France. About forty of them, having arrived by way of Duisburg, Freiburg, or Aachen, founded the Multicultural House (MKH) in Neu-Ulm. This was a religious complex comprising a community food store, a well-stocked Islamic library, accommodation to welcome visitors, and several classrooms and prayer rooms. The center offered courses in religion and Koranic Arabic, and corresponded in every respect to the "preaching embassies" that Omar Bakri was theorizing at that very moment in Londonistan. The MKH held the first Salafist gatherings in the region, hosted seminars for Muslim converts, and sought to "raise awareness" of Wahhabi orthodoxy among young people of Turkish origin.

Among the founding members of the MKH was an Egyptian jihadist who was a member of the Gamaa Islamiyya and rubbed shoulders with the leader of the Hamburg cell. He was also close to a German-based financier of Osama bin Laden who was later extradited to the United States for his involvement in the attacks on the American embassies in Tanzania and Kenya.

In 1999, MKH associates inaugurated the Islamic Information Center (IIZ), which had a clear Salafi-jihadist orientation, just across the bridge in Ulm. So as to represent the diversity of local Islam, the association named a Turkish president, a vice-president of Arab origin, and a secretary who was a German convert – at the time a high school student and a minor. The secretary was later sent to study at the University of Medina, and upon his return, 9/11, he became a teacher . . . at the MKH. There, he published German translations of Saudi pamphlets which promoted the concepts of loyalty and disavowal, and championed Abdullah Azzam's version of jihad. In his sermons, he rejected democratic values, and defended the assassination of Muslim "apostates," the stoning of unfaithful women, and crude forms of physical punishment – all against a backdrop of unbridled anti-Semitism.[3] The eight other people working in the IIZ office included a convert who would die in Chechnya, and three others who would train in Afghan camps. Herbert Müller, who was then head of the "Islamism" unit within the Federal Office for the

Protection of the Constitution (the German intelligence services) for the *Land* of Baden-Württemberg, said this of the center:

> The IIZ was a little shop. You could look right inside to the meeting rooms. In the window there were books with an Islamist orientation. [. . .] The alarm bell sounded with the Chechen war [1999–2002], when it was discovered that a young convert had been killed by Russian troops. There were many others after that, but these were the first indications.[4]

Even though they arose from the same militant environment, the MKH and the IIZ were two legally distinct institutions, located in two cities that belonged to two different jurisdictions. This administrative peculiarity was exploited by the Salafists: the members of the MKH, based in Neu-Ulm, carried out their operations in Ulm, while the IIZ did the same in Neu-Ulm. This complicated legal proceedings and surveillance: police on either side could go no further than the bridge separating the two *Länder*.

The development of a terrorist cell within this ideal ideological microsystem occurred in the first half of the 2000s. Shortly after 9/11, the MKH welcomed a new imam, Dr. Youssouf. Of Egyptian origin, he was involved in building a pipeline of fighters to Bosnia, even though he came across as entirely respectable. As Herbert Müller states:

> If at the time we had portrayed this person as a demagogue, as a promoter of terrorism, I think we would have been seen as mad or deranged. Because this man was a highly trained doctor, a researcher whose work had won an award. He had engaged in interfaith dialogue with non-Muslims, as Islamists often do. He had constructed a perfect intercultural facade. Despite his long beard and his appearance, no one saw him as an Islamist or an extremist. We realized later that he had been involved in a pipeline to Bosnia. Since he was intelligent, he had done this from a very small town in the middle of the Black Forest. [. . .] This kind of unimaginable thing is obviously very difficult for the authorities to control. He had a good front, he camouflaged himself well, and it was not easy to find traces of his activities.[5]

Dr. Youssouf arrived at the MKH in 2001. That same year, his son, who was a minor at the time, made his way to the jihadist camps in Pakistan.

He was arrested on his return, found to be carrying manuals on how to make explosive devices in his luggage. Shortly thereafter, Youssouf hosted one of his protégés, Reda Seyam, whom he had sent to Bosnia in the 1990s. In the meantime, Seyam had rubbed shoulders with Al-Qaeda members and was suspected of having helped finance the Bali bombings in 2002. Arrested on his return to Germany, he was placed under house arrest in Ulm. He would later become one of the most senior Europeans in ISIS. The German services noted at the time that Ulm and Neu-Ulm "have become a focal point for extremist Islamism."[6]

The young people who sprouted from the terrain of the seasoned veterans included a convert, Fritz Gelowicz, and a German of Turkish origin named Attila Selek. The first, a resident of Neu-Ulm, turned to Islam at the age of fifteen, in 1995. Reiner Nübel, a local journalist who met him, described the impression the young man left on him:

> Fritz Gelowicz, who is considered the leader of the Sauerland terrorists, grew up here. His mother is a doctor, his father a well-established businessman. He used to walk around in American clothes, wearing a baseball cap, ordinary things, until he converted and became radicalized. This may be linked to his parents' divorce, as the psychologists suggested during their assessment, but that is pure speculation. This is someone who studied economics, who was fully integrated, and who became radicalized. It is a paradigm shift that is difficult to understand.[7]

Along with his new friend Attila Selek, Fritz Gelowicz took part in the activities of the MKH and was one of the founders of the IIZ. Their Salafist activities took a more bellicose turn starting in 2001. In 2004, the authorities, concerned about increasing radicalization, launched a police investigation into the MKH. The veterans took flight: Dr. Youssouf went to Egypt, while Reda Seyam headed for Berlin. There he took up a post as imam in the Charlottenburg district, from which several jihadists would depart for Iraq.

In Ulm, the pioneers Gelowicz and Selek took charge of the local preaching machine and followed in the footsteps of their elders, as evidenced by a search conducted by the services of the two *Länder* at the MKH, and in a half dozen apartments, in 2005. Despite attempts to quickly destroy evidence, they found CDs and VHS cassettes glorifying jihad, and copies of the magazine *Denk mal islamisch!* ("Think Islamically!"), founded by Gelowicz. The MKH was closed by court order. The pioneers, for their part, set off for Afghanistan. They returned to carry out terrorist acts.

Toulouse, Brussels, Cairo: The Wanderings and Emancipation of the Pioneers

The Toulouse region provides another example of the successful passing of the baton from veterans to pioneers. I have discussed the centrality of this area in previous work.[8] The first seeds of Salafi-jihadism in southern France were sown after the arrival of a Syrian preacher in the 1970s, who took French citizenship under the name of Olivier Corel, and was known by the nickname "the white emir." It it likely that he took part in jihad in Afghanistan; what is certain is that he established a closed community of "veterans" in the heart of the Ariège countryside at the end of the 1980s. He lived in Artigat, in a rural hamlet of a few dozen people, but paid close attention to the civil war in Algeria, where some of his in-laws are from. He tried to obtain a post as a preacher in various places of worship in Toulouse. At the turn of the millennium, a handful of GIA militants became involved in the Grand-Mirail districts, where the previous presence of the Muslim Brotherhood and the Tablighi Jamaat was viewed as having developed a "breeding ground" to be exploited. Once there, the jihadists relied on a family of converts, the Clains, who were also closely supervised by the white emir. After 2001, Fabien and Jean-Michel Clain, who would become prominent members of ISIS in Syria, began preaching, filling the vacuum created by the dispersal of their GIA mentors. They organized religious seminars in their apartments and established themselves as visible embodiments of the fledgling Salafism. Their zeal bore fruit among a small number of people. To a much smaller extent than in London, but following similar patterns, the dozen or so militants around them went from door to door and ran stalls selling Islamic artefacts in the Saint-Sernin and Reynerie markets in Toulouse. In council housing estates, they issued "Islamic reminders" (*tadhkir*) to warn against the dangers of assimilation into "infidel" society, the main features of which were a failure to respect moral prohibitions and an absence of ostensible practice.

In the mid-2000s, they set up associations under the 1901 law, thanks to which they organized seminars and welcomed imams who were well known in radical circles in Brussels. A preaching machine took shape and spread locally like a tiny ultra-conservative counter-society. It became more complex as others took part in proselytizing, joined sports clubs and mutual aid associations, and tightened social and religious control over those around them.

The desire to "learn their religion" led the pioneers to continue their indoctrination abroad. Fabien Clain, his wife, and a few of their friends settled in the Brussels canal municipalities, where they marveled at the intensity of religious life. They were prosecuted there for links with a network that transported jihadists to Iraq. Another part of the family, centered around Jean-Michel, went to the Salafist enclaves of Cairo, which became, at the end of the decade, the favorite location for religious training for the European Salafi-jihadist movement.

Preaching Machines Behind Bars

In addition to the emancipation of the pioneers, the spread of jihadist ideas to the prisons where the veterans ended up was another unexpected phenomenon. The case of Khaled Kelkal, recruited by the GIA while in detention ten years earlier, shows that this dynamic is not new. In the early 2000s, the number of imprisoned militants remained low – just a few dozen in Europe. But the 9/11 attacks gave these militants a new stature in prison. The director of the French prison administration, Laurent Ridel, then head of the department of prison security staff, explained:

> At the time, the risk was beginning to form, and may not have been taken seriously enough. [. . .] We were picking up weak signals, but they weren't perceived as an absolute priority. [. . .] Maybe something was missed. I think there was the same weaknesses in analyzing radicalization in prison as in the rest of society.[9]

Prisons assess the danger level of any nascent group on the basis of its potential to disturb the relative peace and quiet of the prison environment. Based on this approach, prison authorities have crushed groups such as the Corsican mafia, Basque separatists, skinheads, and violent ultra-left organizations. The confidence that many decision-makers have in the institution makes it futile to explore the specificities of "Islamist" proselytizing and the conditions of its development among prisoners. One need only glance at French penitentiary history to realize that incarceration does little to prepare for release (rates of recidivism are 40% on average). It is true, however, that the system is successful in "breaking" criminal organizations.[10] As a result, and despite the fact that discussions about this approach continue, relativism reigns in most of the French prison administration.

The evolution of two veterans mentioned previously, Abu Doha and Djamel Beghal, illustrates the dynamics that were taking shape at the time. Both supported the GIA and set up camps in Afghanistan, where they allegedly had contact with Bin Laden. Abu Doha supervised the Frankfurt cell, which was responsible for the foiled attacks in Strasbourg and Los Angeles. He was arrested while using a false identity in February 2001 at Heathrow Airport in London. Beghal was arrested in Dubai six months later while drawing up plans to target the American Embassy in Paris.

Abu Doha was incarcerated at Belmarsh Prison in England, where he was welcomed with open arms by Rachid Ramda, the emir of the GIA in Europe and organizer of the 1995 attacks in France. Abu Doha spoke about how important this was:

> Seeing brothers like him [Rachid Ramda] who had been in Belmarsh for several years inspired me. I couldn't feel weak. [. . .] If I needed courage or felt that my life had taken a wrong turn, I thought of him and his advice. Rachid was a symbol of love, a brother when I was having a hard time . . . If there are people who are better than angels, then he is one of them.[11]

Abu Doha became friends with other prisoners who were the object of general suspicion. As a fellow inmate who had previously worked as a bookseller at the Finsbury Park mosque recalled:

> In the beginning, it was very hard. [. . .] Even the other prisoners were afraid of us because the administration [of the prison] had told them that we were very dangerous and that they should not get involved with us.[12]

Nonetheless, Abu Doha gradually found his feet, and became an outstanding proselyte until the end of his sentence in 2005. In the meantime, he became aware of the possibility of spreading Salafi-jihadist ideas among his fellow inmates. As soon as he was released, he trained to become a prison "listener" – these are volunteers who visit inmates in distress. He trained with a suicide prevention organization, The Samaritans, founded in the 1950s by an Anglican priest, and was accredited by Her Majesty's Prison Service. Once convicted for planning several major attacks and recruiting fighters for jihadist camps in Chechnya and Afghanistan, Abu Doha was now authorized to counsel prisoners in despair.

Imprisoned at Fleury-Mérogis, Djamel Beghal also proved to be a skilled advocate for his cause. His reputation, partially fabricated, as "Ben Laden's favorite Frenchman" granted him great respectability in criminal circles. In the mid-2000s, he took the prisoners Chérif Kouachi and Amedy Coulibaly under his wing. The former would go on to carry out the *Charlie Hebdo* massacre with his brother on January 7, 2015, while the latter would murder a policewoman in Montrouge and customers at the Hyper Cacher supermarket at the Porte de Vincennes in Paris in the days that followed. François Molins, a former state prosecutor in Paris (2012–2018), spoke about the convergence that occurred in prison circles at the time:

> At that time, prisons were the place where three different factors converged. The first was the arrival in prison of veterans, ultra-radicalized people such as Djamel Beghal and Saïd Aït Belkacem [who built the bombs for the 1995 attacks in Paris]. I could name others – they were often veterans of the GIA or the Afghan conflict. The second factor was the arrival of new radicals [the pioneers]. They were the result of all the work that had been done in certain neighbourhoods or through certain associations, work that led to the emergence of a new jihadist population. And the third was the robbers, violent offenders such as the Kouachi brothers, Amedy Coulibaly, or Mohammed Merah [responsible for the 2012 attacks in Toulouse and Montauban], and all the jihadists who would take part in the November 13 [2015] attacks.[13]

Beghal, like Abu Doha, raised awareness among those around him in detention. He exerted a great deal of influence among many different kinds of people, especially the most fragile, as evidenced by a letter, which we were able to obtain, from an inmate to the person in charge of monitoring him within the prison administration. The awkward spelling is matched by the very approximate knowledge he exhibits of the teachings of his mentor, as is clear to anyone familiar with these teachings. Still, the letter gives an indication of the type of relationship that someone of Beghal's caliber was able to form with his fellow inmates:

> Dear Sir, Hello, Let me Give you some Of my News, what's happened During this times, a lot Of thinggs have happened for mee, I Met someoone who completely changedme and Gaveme another Way Of seeing Thinggs, here we practice TAKIKA I've been doing it For 2 years hiddin Religion I convertedto islam, I have a <u>Mentor JAMeL BhégAL</u> butt I can't talked to You About him, he taut me many Thinggs butt there is people who …

Other examples in France show that prisons are rarely places where the veterans of the 1990s renounce their previous views. In one Lille establishment, Lionel "Abu Hamza" Dumont, leader of the Roubaix gang, became a religious figurehead for his fellow inmates. Safé Bourada, convicted of recruiting Khaled Kelkal for the 1995 attacks, was released in 2003. He was said to have supervised a criminal and prostitution network and to have established indirect contacts with the Al-Qaeda branch in Iraq led by Zarqawi. He was arrested in 2005 while his group was planning a triple attack on Orly airport, the Paris metro, and the headquarters of the Direction de la surveillance du territoire (the French domestic intelligence agency).

In Denmark, the prison situation is very different and the number of individuals concerned is very low compared to France and Great Britain, but similar issues have emerged. Bo Yde Sørensen, the representative of the leading Danish prison union, shared these observations:

> There are well-known Islamists here in Denmark, such as Saïd Mansour, and they have always attracted attention. But the main challenge is offenders who become radicalized in prison. They are the ones who then cause problems. They don't have a "name," we don't pay attention to them, we don't notice them when they arrive. And therein lies the difficulty: when a street offender

embraces Islamist ideology and becomes radicalized in prison. This problem began to take shape in 2004–2005.[14]

Prisons reproduce certain dynamics that are also observable on the outside. They are gradually forming a third space of "glocal" militancy, halfway between local dynamics and the fronts of global jihad, where some prisoners will go after serving their sentences, if they are not already returning from these places. One sign of the fluidity and multi-directionality of the movement between these three spaces: in 2004, Al-Qaeda published a leaflet in which it encouraged its minions to recruit in European penitentiary establishments.[15]

4

The Fuse of European Terrorism

There was never a "European" branch of Al-Qaeda,[1] unlike in most of the regions where the group was active, because the continent is not perceived as a "land of Islam" to be defended. But this logic was undermined by the assertions of the pioneers, who are European nationals.

Madrid, March 11, 2004

On March 11, 2004, while Iraq was sinking into terrorist violence, Madrid fell prey to Europe's deadliest jihadist attack.

At the height of morning rush hour, two and a half years to the day after the attacks on the twin towers, terrorists placed a dozen bombs on four commuter trains at the Alcalá de Henares station, north of the capital. Set to go off at the scheduled time of arrival at the Atocha station, the detonations killed 191 people and injured 1,800. One of the trains, running two minutes late, exploded shortly before the final stop. Had it arrived at its destination, the station roof would have collapsed and caused an even greater number of deaths. After the attacks, the seven perpetrators retreated to an apartment in Leganés, in the southwestern suburbs of the metropolis.

They were located three weeks later, on April 4, 2004, as they were preparing an operation against a synagogue and several Jewish schools, based on a model that had been thought up elsewhere. Besieged by the police forces, the jihadists said goodbye to their loved ones on the phone, and contacted an imam to inquire about the lawfulness of a kamikaze mission. Reassured by the preacher, the men seized the stock of explosives at their disposal, chanting verses from the Koran in unison, and blew up the apartment, killing a policeman from the special forces and injuring eleven others in what was the first Islamist suicide bombing in Europe.

At the time, most observers linked the event to the legislative elections in Spain, held three days later. The reason for this was the disastrous management of the crisis by the outgoing government of José María Aznar's conservative party. Fearing defeat, it tried to make the public believe that the Basque independence organization ETA was responsible for the tragedy, before it was compelled to recognize the involvement of jihadists. The state lie led to a political scandal, the defeat of the executive in the elections, and the withdrawal of the Spanish contingent in Iraq. It offered an unprecedented opportunity for jihadists to claim to have influenced a democratic ballot, and forced a military decision through the use of violence in the country of origin, an ambition absent from the claim for the attack released by an Al-Qaeda spokesman on March 13.[2]

But the Madrid attacks stem more from the prolongation of the second jihadist cycle in Europe than the deterioration of the situation in Iraq. It is true that the operation was endorsed by Bin Laden's organization, but it derived from the Moroccan Islamic Combatant Group (GICM). Founded in 1993 in Peshawar, the entity saw itself as a Moroccan offshoot of the Algerian GIA and shared many of the latter's characteristics, including intertwining networks and the spread of cells across several Western countries. One of commando members was himself an Algerian from the GIA who lived in Valencia. Copies of the GICM manifesto – calling for the overthrow of the monarchy and the killing of Jews, Christians, and the kingdom's soldiers – were found in the apartments of GIA members in Brussels and Italy. The headquarters of the GICM is located in the municipality of Maaseik, in Flanders, the town where Muriel Degauque, a Belgian convert, is from. She is the only European to have carried out a suicide operation against American forces in Iraq. Group members were also active in Amsterdam and The Hague, where some worked as educators in rough neighborhoods. The group also had contacts in Molenbeek through the Al-Haski brothers, Salafists well known in the local area who were involved in the attacks in Casablanca and Marrakech in 2003.

As with the GIA, the financing of GICM activities in Europe was largely based on vehicle smuggling and other illicit activities, such as hashish trafficking between Morocco and Northern Europe. This partly explains the locations of their attacks: the Madrid-The Hague axis, which passes through Brussels, and its extensions – in the south, towards Gibraltar, and in the north, towards Germany and Scandinavia – is one of Europe's "hash highways." The March 11 commando unit was representative of the cross-breeding of Salafism and crime. Indeed, the explosives and detonators for the Madrid operation were supplied by a drug addict who had nothing to do with the attacks, and who was rewarded with 25 kilos of hashish and a stolen Toyota Corolla.[3]

These criminal activities should not mask the unit's adherence to hard-line Salafi-jihadism. The mixture of crime and religion, which may seem paradoxical, is actually understandable within the logic of "disavowal." Once criminals begin to serve the jihadist cause and fight against the godless order, their misdeeds become lawful in view of their interpretation of religious morality.[4]

The investigation's analysis of the unit's computer equipment turned up many of the classic texts of jihadist ideology, including the foundational texts of Ibn Taymiyyah, Ibn Abd al-Wahhab, Sayyid Qutb and Abdullah Azzam. The audiovisual media gave pride of place to speeches by Bin Laden, Abu Qatada, and Abu Mohamed al-Maqdissi. The group, which constantly sought new content, was in contact with Saïd Mansour, the Moroccan preacher residing in Denmark, whose publishing house in Copenhagen offered one of the largest catalogues of extremist material.

Ideologically, the choice of Spain was justified by the Spanish presence in Iraq, but also by the unique place the country occupies in Muslim history. Spain, by way of Al-Andalus and the Caliphate of Córdoba, is the only part of Western Europe to have been considered a land of Islam (from the eighth to the fifteenth centuries). From the standpoint of Islamism, this means that it is a former province of the Muslim Empire that was stolen and must be recovered.

The inspiration behind the Salafi-jihadist preaching machine in Madrid was Abu Dahdah, a former Syrian Muslim Brother and Afghanistan veteran who was arrested after 9/11 for his role in financing the activities of the Hamburg cell. He played a key role in raising awareness among a small circle of followers at the M-30 mosque (founded in 1992 with Saudi funding), where he preached, and at the Abu Bakr prayer hall in the Estrecho district. Abu Dahdah would chat with his group during evening classes in apartments on Virgen del Coro Street, and had participated in a network sending fighters to Bosnia and then Chechnya. Some followers visited friends who were active in Islamist circles in Barcelona (Raval district) and Valencia.

These dynamics took shape in the 1990s, before the participation of Spanish troops in the Iraq War. The Madrid attacks were the first manifestation of a trend towards the Europeanization of terrorism targeting Europe.

The Dutch Error, November 2, 2004

A few months after the atrocities in Madrid, Theo van Gogh was murdered in the heart of Amsterdam. The consequences of this act continue to haunt European public debates in the 2020s.

The assailant, Mohammed Bouyeri, was a 27-year-old Dutchman of Moroccan origin, close to the GICM and several figures of Moroccan jihadism in Spain and London. He belonged to the "The Hague Cell," several members of which were linked, by marriage or friendship, to the network responsible for the Madrid attack and their contacts in Brussels and elsewhere. Some of them attended Abu Qatada's seminars in London, and three went to the tribal areas of Pakistan, while others sought to join the war in Iraq. Bouyeri, like Kelkal before him and some of the Mullah Boys in Leeds (see below), was a social worker, involved in drug prevention in his neighborhood; as such, he was a member of the middle class with a regular salary. The assassination of Theo van Gogh was part of a larger plan that also targeted other public figures and an airport. In form, the case resembles a murder of opinion that occurred against the backdrop of a bitter debate that was then roiling Dutch society.

Holland was long considered the most tolerant country in Europe. Starting in the Renaissance, it welcomed Jews and Protestants persecuted by the Catholic kingdoms. The philosopher René Descartes, who retreated there in 1629, wrote in his notebook: "Three positive things to say about Amsterdam: you can get whatever you want, you are free, you are safe."[5] The liberal tradition of Dutch society is based on a broad acceptance of freedom, as it concerns opinion, morals, and the expression of opposing views. In terms of immigration, the Dutch opted for a policy of welcoming, and a social contract based on effective solidarity through work and a strong multiculturalism. The recognition of religious and identity-based specificities, and the development and teaching of immigrant cultures, were established there earlier than in neighboring countries. The first Muslim populations, mainly from colonies in the Dutch East Indies, settled after the war. Workers from Morocco and Turkey arrived in the 1970s, joined twenty years later by refugees from the Horn of Africa, the Middle East, and to a lesser extent the Balkans.

In the 1990s, the country discovered the presence of its first radical preachers, at the same time as Belgium, Germany, and Scandinavia. An extremely small minority, they attracted attention through their desire to set themselves up as leaders of their respective communities, and through the ambivalent relationship they had with the principles of Dutch multiculturalism. Like communalism in Great Britain, the few Salafists claimed to respect the conditions of the social contract while rejecting the spirit of the underlying societal project. In their view, multiculturalism became a legal lever for establishing parallel cultural counter-societies sheltered from the values of the broader society, which were deemed contrary to conservative Islam.

In an opinion piece entitled "The drama of multiculturalism," published in 2000, an academic close to the Labour Party lamented the general lack of interest in immigration issues and the absence of any real policy in this area.[6] Public debate raged, and after 9/11, it began to tear the Dutch political class apart. Far-right parties, which were particularly xenophobic, made their first real electoral breakthrough, like elsewhere in Europe at the time. Dutch society was ill-equipped to address religious extremism, having built its modern politics around rejecting the latter and keeping the expression of beliefs outside the public sphere.[7] Unlike in France, "communal" belonging was not perceived as harmful, as long as it served the emancipation of the group in question with a view to its adherence to the codes of Dutch society. But the idea of "religious communalism" was perceived as problematic because it was counterintuitive within the Dutch political tradition. Despite objective data showing that the integration of new populations worked in the vast majority of cases, the idea that multiculturalism was failing was widespread.[8]

A sociology professor emerged from the fray: Pim Fortuyn. Colorful and media-savvy, he thrived on controversy, and made the denunciation of Dutch multiculturalism his hobbyhorse. A former Marxist in his fifties and a member of the Dutch Labour Party for 20 years, Fortuyn broke with convention and in many ways anticipated the changes of balance elsewhere in Europe. Liberal in the moral realm, protectionist in the social realm, openly Catholic and openly homosexual, Fortuyn described himself as pragmatic and democratic while accepting that he was a populist, which was difficult to classify at the time. He rejected the far-right label that his opponents applied to him but made numerous sweeping remarks against Islam, describing it as a "backward culture" and an "existential" threat to the Dutch model. These positions strongly polarized public opinion, which had already been jolted by the campaign for the legislative elections in the spring of 2002, in which his party was well placed. Nine days before the election, Pim Fortuyn was shot and killed as he left a radio station. The assassin was an environmental activist and animal rights defender. During his trial, he confessed to wanting to put an end to the stigmatization of Muslims, accusing Fortuyn of turning them into "scapegoats" for electoral purposes. The impact of the assassination was immense: it was the first political murder in the Netherlands since that of Johan de Witt in 1672, a statesman killed in The Hague whose body was then the object of cannibalistic practices on the part of the murderous crowd. Pim Fortuyn's funeral became a national event, while his list won seventeen percent of the vote in the elections.

The upheavals raging in Dutch society did not spare Theo van Gogh. A distant descendant of the post-impressionist painter, heir to a family of anti-Nazi resisters, formed by the activist libertarian spirit of the 1960s, Van Gogh was a public figure. An essayist and director, he had his own television and radio programs, in which he addressed the controversies of the moment in his own politically incorrect tone, alternating vulgar remarks with reasoned positions. True to his reputation as a trouble-maker, he tackled the issue of multiculturalism in a first book, angrily denouncing the hypocrisy, misogyny, and homophobia of certain self-righteous Islamists in the Netherlands who wanted to lock their young followers into a strict identity. He also produced a short film entitled *Submission*, co-directed with Ayaan Hirsi Ali, a Dutch MP who fled an arranged marriage in her native Somalia, and a feminist committed to the emancipation of Muslim women. The film told the story of four such women, who described the physical and sexual abuse they had suffered. They looked directly at the camera, which Islamists interpreted as a sign of defiance, while their naked bodies, lacerated by a whip, displayed verses from the Koran. The filmmakers received death threats as soon as the film was broadcast. Ali was placed under permanent police protection; van Gogh declined this protection on the grounds that he did not wish to live in fear. According to Ali's account of the incident, he said: "If they kill me, don't forget that the rule of law must be protected from extremists."[9]

On November 2, 2004, at 8:30 a.m., van Gogh got on his bike, joining the many others in Amsterdam who cycle to work. At the Oosterpark, on Linnaeusstraat, a man was waiting next to his bicycle. Seeing the director, he pulled out a revolver and opened fire. Van Gogh, having been hit, fell to the ground and then got up. He hobbled across the street, looking for shelter, and in a gesture that Ali would describe as "typically Dutch," shouted to his assailant: "We can talk about this, don't do it!"[10] Catching up to van Gogh, Bouyeri emptied his magazine at point-blank range. Watched by some fifty witnesses, the killer then began to decapitate his victim – which he had practiced at home on sheep – before giving up. One of the witnesses, disgusted, called out to him: "You can't do that!" The criminal turned to him and said: "Oh yes I can, he got what he deserved, and now you know what to expect!"[11]

He then fled, but not before attaching a letter to the polemicist's chest with a knife. In the five-page missive, he vehemently attacks Ayaan Hirsi Ali, accusing her of apostasy. This marked her out as a priority target of the Hague group.

The cruelty of the methods used is reminiscent of those popularized at the same time in Iraq by Zarqawi, who a few months earlier released the first video of Western hostages being executed in orange jumpsuits (to mirror the outfits of the Guantanamo prisoners), which ISIS would make a normal practice ten years later.

Bouyeri showed no remorse during his trial. He refused the advice of a lawyer and stated that he did not recognize the authority or legitimacy of Dutch law. Only divine justice, which he claimed to have rendered by killing Van Gogh, mattered to him. He confided to the police that he had sought martyrdom on that day, as evidenced by a message found in his pocket.[12]

The case was symbolically charged and in many respects paradigmatic. It was the second political murder in two years in a country that had not experienced a single one for three centuries. It occurred against a backdrop of controversy surrounding the identity and model of Dutch society, a debate that has continued ever since, as evidenced by the heated controversy that followed the early release of Pim Fortuyn's killer in 2014. And its effects spread to the whole of Europe. The issues raised by the assassination of Theo van Gogh found a spectacular echo the following year with the publication of caricatures of Mohammed in a Danish newspaper.

The Dispersal of Londonistan

After the Madrid attacks, the noose tightened around Omar Bakri, the last representative of Londonistan. He mobilized support networks in the country's major cities more than ever before and prepared for his succession. In June 2004, he organized one last rally, summoning the European networks of Al-Muhajiroun. Several hundred Islamists gathered in London, including about twenty Scandinavians and Dutch.[13]

On October 8, 2004, Bakri, knowing that he was in the crosshairs of the British authorities, took the initiative and dissolved Al-Muhajiroun. The reason was that some of the militants had shifted to planning violent acts with which Bakri feared he would be legally associated. Rashad Ali, then involved in radical circles in London, noticed that part of the base was escaping his control:

> Omar Bakri explained to his followers that England was a zone where you shouldn't randomly attack people. But Al-Muhajiroun was divided on the issue and eventually broke apart because they couldn't find common ground on it.[14]

Indeed, a few months earlier, members of the organization had killed themselves in a Hamas suicide operation against a restaurant in Israel, while others were arrested while targeting a concert hall in London and a shopping center in Kent. Over the course of the decade, around seventy of the Britons who were convicted of participating in terrorist projects were associated with Al-Muhajiroun (almost 20% of the total), while its networks were responsible for sending several hundred Europeans to Syria.[15]

The self-dissolution of Al-Muhajiroun is indicative of a specific feature that allowed Omar Bakri to maintain his influence in Europe until the 2020s. Unlike his partners in Londonistan, he prepared for his succession and tried to adapt to legislative developments.

In concrete terms, starting in the fall of 2004, Bakri and his accomplices, instead of acting through Al-Muhajiroun, went through a myriad of groups with their own names and legal statuses. This allowed them to continue preaching despite the accumulation of legal proceedings. The groups ostensibly promoted the same objective as Al-Muhajiroun: the establishment of the caliphate in the United Kingdom. They were also anti-democratic in their form, and regularly mounted attacks against Muslim religious authorities, "apostates," Jews, Christians, atheists, homosexuals, and freedoms of all kinds. The most visible were Al-Ghurabaa (2004–2006), The Saved Sect (2005–2006), Ahlus Sunnah wal Jamaah (2005–2009), Islam4UK (2009–2010), Sharia4UK (2010–2012), and Muslims Against Crusades (2010–2011), to which we should add Call to Submission, Islamic Path, London School of Sharia, and Need4Khilafah.[16] These ten or so organizations relied on the same networks. They reproduced popular video and audio content on their websites, featuring the emirs of Londonistan, the American Anwar al-Awlaqi, and their protégés. The heir to Omar Bakri, Anjem Choudary, emerged among these latter, and began to oversee various initiatives. British by birth, a lawyer by training, a long-time protégé of Omar Bakri and founder, alongside the latter, of Al-Muhajiroun, he took up the provocative line and style of his elder. Like him, he was an outstanding coordinator, specializing in spectacular actions conducted at the limits of legality. He played loose with the rules, which he admitted to the press: "Unless the government can prove that we are exactly the same organization, acting at the same time and doing exactly the same thing, it is very difficult for them to crack down."[17]

In the summer of 2005, Omar Bakri flew to Lebanon and was banned from returning to British territory. He settled in Tripoli, declared that he was in favor of committing terrorist acts in Great Britain, and continued to supervise his networks, now led by Choudary, from a distance.

In the mid-2000s, the British capital gradually ceased to be the militant and logistical crossroads of Salafi-jihadism in Europe. But other regional centers emerged, in Leicester, Leeds, Birmingham, Manchester, Luton, and elsewhere in Europe.

As the European version of the Peshawar model, the London preaching machine gave birth to its own theorists, and new modes of action that had repercussions across the continent. Aspiring British jihadists, most of them metaphorical or ideological children of the local ecosystem, were by far the most numerous in the EU, and were now ready to take action.

Leeds and London, July 7, 2005

The only advice I can give you is: total obedience to your emir, whether he is Arab, Chechen, Saudi, or British. Have you heard about that brother who disobeyed? They slit his throat. The lesson I learned from that is: total obedience to your emir, unless he tells you to do something haram [religiously forbidden]. Next, you need a reason to go to Pakistan. So, you're a Brit going there to study because universities are cheaper. You're going to take classes in whatever you want and live a normal life. That's all you're going to do for the first four or five months. We need the intelligence to follow us until they say, "These guys are nothing." When the time comes, we'll launch the operation. Everyone wants to fight, everyone wants to go to the front. We never slow things down, but when we send a brother out, we don't want it to be 50/50, we don't want it to go wrong because everything wasn't 100% ready. We don't want to think that if we had waited another month, it would have gone smoothly, but that you got caught because we rushed into it.

Advice from Omar Khyam to Siddiq Khan, February 21, 2004, in Khyam's car, recorded by the British services.[18]

A few days after this exchange, Omar Khyam and a group of Salafists from Crawley, in the south of England, were arrested. This commando unit, which had frequented the circles of Londonistan, was planning to open fire in the Ministry of Sound concert hall and to poison the hamburgers at a stall at Wembley Stadium.

As for Siddiq Khan, he reappeared a year and a half later, flanked by three accomplices, and killed himself in a suicide attack on the London Underground on July 7, 2005. Aged between eighteen and thirty, the four terrorists were in Britain; they had working-class backgrounds, and two of them had joined the middle class and had a regular salary. Three were of Pakistani origin and grew up in Leeds, while the other was a convert from a Jamaican family in London. All had links with the Islamist environment created by the veterans, and the two leaders, including Siddiq Khan, frequented Al-Muhajiroun circles, and traveled to Afghanistan several times between 2001 and 2005, on the recommendation of friends, as indicated in the above exchange. Once there, they underwent military training and ideological indoctrination under the supervision of a British man in charge of planning external operations for Al-Qaeda.

On their return, these "recruits" become recruiters and activists who were known in their respective neighborhoods. This is a dynamic that took shape after 9/11.

Siddiq Khan, in his late twenties, was a charismatic educator at the Hamara Centre for Healthy Living in Leeds, and was particularly appreciated by young people from the ultra-segregated area of Beeston Hill. Married and expecting his second child, he was known for the religious influence he exerted over a small group in three places of worship in the surrounding area. He also ran a local gang known as the Mullah Boys, which may have been an implicit reference to the Taliban leader, Mullah Omar.

The Mullah Boys were a mix of zealous Salafists and delinquents in search of meaning. They cruised the brick houses of Beeston Hill at night, making it their mission to "preach good and prevent evil." They were known to seize drug addicts they came across and lock them up in the basements of the premises they had at their disposal in order to wean them off drugs by force, for several days if necessary. Their violent methods, sometimes verging on torture, terrified the addicts, and were welcomed by local residents who were tired of drug trafficking and its destructive consequences on the economic and social environment. Siddiq Khan's work was also recognized by the town hall. Thanks to public funding, he founded an Islamic bookshop promoting Salafist literature, and set up at least three sport halls in the neighborhood. One of these, set up in the basement of a mosque on Hardy Street, was nicknamed the "Al-Qaeda gym." As in Toulouse, these places attracted young men and led, by way of physical activity, to raising their awareness of injustice and the persecution of Muslims around the world. As in

Ulm, Khan attracted some followers of the Tablighi Jamaat, one of whom would go on to join the commando unit alongside him.

At dawn on July 7, 2005, Khan and two accomplices traveled from Leeds to Luton. They picked up a fourth individual and equipped themselves with heavy backpacks full of explosives. They abandoned their vehicle and boarded a train bound for King's Cross St. Pancras, where they split up, each taking a different tube line. At 8:50 a.m., they set off their portable bombs. The last accomplice, barely of age, was running late. He wandered out of the underground transport system, hesitantly pushed open the door of a McDonald's restaurant, and tried unsuccessfully to reach the other assailants by phone. Leaving the McDonald's, he walked towards a bus stop and climbed on board the number 30. At Tavistock Square, at 9:47 a.m., he decided to press the detonator, killing himself and 13 people around him. In total, 56 Londoners perished in the attacks, and 700 were injured.

Peter Clarke, then head of the anti-terrorist section at Scotland Yard, describes a nightmare:

> The week before the attacks, my team from the counter-terrorism branch and I spent the weekend considering different crisis scenarios in which we tried to anticipate the worst possible situations. And by a dreadful coincidence, the scenario we chose was multiple attacks on the London Underground.[19]

Unlike the 2015 attacks in France, the investigation did not lead to a special trial, despite the fact that the number of people involved in the bombings was potentially high. No resident of Beeston Hill would reveal any conclusive information to investigators. Siddiq Khan, born in Great Britain, was buried in his parents' native village in Pakistan, where he was celebrated as a "martyr" during his funeral. In July 2006, Al-Qaeda's media channel, Al-Sahab, claimed responsibility for the attacks, broadcasting the video testimony of one of the bombers, recorded a few months earlier in Afghanistan.

Danish Satire, September 30, 2005

The Danish cartoon affair occurred in the aftermath of the London bombings and was the first knock-on effect of what had happened in

Holland in 2004. At first, it appeared to be harmless. Kare Bluitgen, a left-wing author of children's books, wanted to hire someone to illustrate a book about the life of Mohammed for young children. He received a series of rejections from illustrators referring to the assassination of Theo van Gogh, and to a recent incident in which a teacher was roughed up after reciting verses from the Koran as part of one of his lessons.

Flemming Rose, editor of the culture section of the center-right newspaper *Jyllands-Posten,* was aware of discussions about this going on in Copenhagen's intellectual circles. He explained the approach that led to the second stage of the affair:

> At the time I didn't know much about Islam, but afterwards I had an intensive crash course. For me, it started with a completely legitimate journalistic project: I heard about a problem. Some say that artists, writers, filmmakers, and museums engage in self-censorship when it comes to Islam. Others say, "No, not at all, there's no self-censorship." As a journalist, you want to know if it's true or not. We did it in an unusual way, by inviting illustrators to show in actions, not in words, how they approached the challenge of drawing the Prophet Muhammad, based on a fundamental principle of journalism that says, "Don't tell it, show it."[20]

On September 30, 2005, twelve drawings were published under the title: "The Faces of Muhammad" (*Muhammads ansigt*). The drawings fit within a tradition of Danish humor that is quite unlike French or British satire. Some images appeared trivial or self-referential, while others poked fun at the stance of *Jyllands-Posten,* such as the sketch of Lars Refn, whom we met in May 2022, and who explained his approach thus:

> At the time I was working for a weekly technology magazine, I didn't draw cartoons about religion. I said to myself: instead of drawing the Prophet, I'll make a joke. [. . .] I drew a student standing at the blackboard in front of his class, writing in Arabic with chalk: "The editors of Jyllands-Posten are right-wing provocateurs," because that's what I thought. And I said to myself: "Either they won't print my drawing, in which case they'll be censoring me and not respecting freedom of expression during an experiment on freedom of expression, or they'll print it and there will be people who translate the text and have a good laugh!"[21]

Other drawings, such as the one by Kurt Westergaard, adhere to the canons of caricature. The Prophet is represented there with a wick bomb instead of a turban. Here is Lars Refn once more:

> Kurt Westergaard is a cartoonist. A cartoonist, if someone says to him, "You're not allowed to do that," well, he does it. You're not allowed to draw a caricature of [Vladimir] Putin? He'll draw a caricature of Putin. You're not allowed to draw a caricature of the Queen of Denmark? He'll do it.[22]

In the days following the publication of the *Jyllands-Posten* cartoons, reactions were rare. No one thought they would reach anyone beyond subscribers, as Lars Refn noted:

> You have to remember that the Internet wasn't as big back then. We thought we were drawing for the readers of *Jyllands-Posten*, 200,000 people, not the whole world.[23]

On October 17, 2005, the drawings were reproduced in the Egyptian newspaper *Al-Fajr*, the first publication to pick them up. They went unnoticed. In Aarhus and Copenhagen, however, a group formed around three imams, two Muslim Brothers – Abu Laban and Ahmed Akkari – and a Lebanese Salafist, Raed Hlayhel, who runs the Grimohej mosque in Aarhus. The latter had already made headlines by declaring to the press that he had settled in Denmark so that his daughter could receive free healthcare, while stating that he hated Danish culture, refused to learn the language, and prescribed the *burka* for all women.

At the end of October, the three preachers demanded an apology from *Jyllands-Posten* and "reparation" measures, which went unheeded. One of them, Ahmed Akkari, has left the Islamist movement. In an interview conducted in spring 2022, he recalled how they tried to put pressure on the newspaper by mobilizing community and consular networks:

> Our working group [the three imams] had to try other methods, like demonstrating and writing to Muslim ambassadors to rally support for our campaign, in other words show that we were there and that we represented the community. [. . .] We also launched a petition for support and collected around sixteen thousand signatures, sixteen thousand Muslim families who

supported our campaign, which in Denmark is practically the equivalent of a political party.[24]

The initiative was picked up by the Egyptian ambassador. Ahmed Akkari continues:

> It was November and still nothing was happening. And then the Egyptian ambassador contacted our group, which was a turning point in the affair. [. . .] She invited us to come to Egypt to present our cause and obtain the support of the state and institutions, and to meet with Omar Moussa, the president of the Arab League. It was a very appealing offer after two months of silence.[25]

In December, the delegation of radical imams traveled to Egypt and various Middle Eastern countries, where it was received by institutional and Islamist networks. To stir up indignation, grotesque drawings of unknown origin were mixed with those published in the newspaper, one of which shows Mohammed with devil's horns holding little girls by the hand. Ahmed Akkari, who took part in the meetings, denies having compiled the file and describes the course of the discussions:

> A Pakistani and an Egyptian, presidents of two respected religious associations, were also on the trip. These two people were integrated into Danish society and had lived in Denmark for forty years. One was a civil judge and the other a civil servant. They were the ones who presented the affair during the trip to Egypt. They brought with them the famous file that would later cause problems. [. . .] They had hastily put it together the night before their departure, and as is often the case in Islamist circles, they hurried, they improvised a little, not everything had been calculated down to the last detail. In Egypt, one of them presented the facts in a somewhat bizarre way, and maybe everyone got the impression that things were much worse than they actually were. Did he do it knowingly? I don't know. In any case, he was not precise in his wording and that did us a disservice.[26]

The international tour caused the affair's first sparks. On December 2, a Pakistani Islamist group condemned the editorial staff of *Jyllands-Posten* and all the cartoonists to death. In January, the controversy flared up.

Protests broke out in many countries, partly exploited by regimes that were at loggerheads with Europe on many issues. Danish diplomatic missions were stormed – people threw stones at the mission in Tehran and set fire to the one in Damascus. Flemming Rose examined the reasons for the escalation:

> In 2005, under pressure from the Americans, Egypt organized elections and, for the first time in a long time, the Muslim Brotherhood was allowed to participate. The first phase of the crisis was led by the Egyptian ambassador to Denmark, who opened all the doors in the Middle East to the groups of imams. [. . .] The Egyptian regime needed to say to Egyptian voters: "You think the Muslim Brotherhood defends Islam? Well, no, it's us. Look how we defend the faith against the Danish infidels who mock the Prophet." And the same thing happened in the Palestinian territories, where there was an election in January 2006. It wasn't the Islamists of Hamas who exploited the cartoons, but the secularizing Fatah party, which wanted to show that they were true believers.[27]

In this context of religious one-upmanship and political manipulation, Denmark and Norway (where a local Christian magazine reproduced some of the drawings) were accused of waging a "war on Muslims." Following a script that would be repeated fifteen years later against France following the death of Samuel Paty, food companies of these countries were subjected to boycott in the Gulf. Prime Minister Anders Fogh Rasmussen was urged to make a formal apology to Muslims. He refused, stating that the government could not be held responsible for the use of freedom of expression by the press in his country. On January 30, the *Jyllands-Posten* published an apology in Arabic on its website. The campaign only became more intense. It was linked in particular to the global networks of the Muslim Brotherhood, which until then had kept a distance from the demonstrations. Ahmed Akkari, who was present in the affair from the beginning but to that point had been isolated, recounts the definitive shift in his hierarchy:

> Egypt reacted. The imam of Mecca delivered an impassioned sermon against Denmark and the cartoons in front of 1.5 million followers. The Salafists had made their intentions clear and wanted to go to war. That left only the

Brothers. So they took matters into their own hands. Qardhawi [the spiritual leader of the organization] proclaimed a "day of rage" at the beginning of February, and the Brothers rallied so as not to miss out on everything that was happening.[28]

Faced with what was perceived as an attempt at global intimidation and the risk of being censored, several European news outlets decided to reprint the Danish drawings. On February 1, newspapers in Belgium and Germany printed them in full, as did *France Soir*. *Libération* reproduced four the twelve drawings two days later. *Charlie Hebdo* reprinted all the cartoons on February 8 and added a few of its own. The satirical newspaper was taken to court by two organizations, including the French Council of the Muslim Faith, and acquitted a year later.

In the third phase of the crisis, demonstrations broke out all over Europe, some at the initiative of the Salafi-jihadist networks mentioned above. The cartoons were described as an insult to Islam and all Muslims, an act of war, punishable by reprisals. A young Danish man of Iraqi origin who grew up in a Salafist family and later joined the jihadists in Syria described the situation in an interview in the spring of 2022:

> When the cartoons were published in Denmark in 2005, I was fourteen years old and had been in Denmark for two years. I remember that it made me angry, and it was used a lot in the Salafist milieu. You don't forget something like that. It will remain a stain on Denmark. For Salafist groups, as long as Denmark exists, it will never be forgotten. For them, I don't think they'll ever get enough revenge; even if they take revenge every day, they'll think it's not enough.[29]

Unsurprisingly, the strongest tremors were felt in England and Brussels. In London, signs in demonstrations proclaimed: "Mock today, die tomorrow."[30] Militants from Al-Muhajiroun demonstrated in front of the Danish embassy in a climate of extreme tension, chanting: "Europe you will pay, your 9/11 is on the way,"[31] extending the responsibility for the "crime" to the whole of Europe. Slogans implicitly referred to Theo van Gogh's murder: "Butcher those who mock Islam!"[32] Al-Qaeda officially reacted in April 2006. Bin Laden declared that the cartoons were "a crime even worse than the bombing of villages that collapse on our women and children."[33]

The affair's center of gravity then shifted to France. In addition to the official representatives of Islam in France, *Charlie Hebdo*'s acts attracted the attention of a Salafist group active in the north of Paris, later known as the Buttes-Chaumont branch, headed by a certain Peter Cherif. Originally from the Caribbean, he converted to Islam, and was a pioneer who had already fought against the Americans in Fallujah in 2004.

In the spring of 2006, a café-gallery in the twentieth arrondissement, La Mer à boire, continued the discussion by organizing an exhibit on the question of blasphemy entitled "Ni Dieu, ni Dieu" (Neither God, nor God). It showcased old and recent religious caricatures relating to all the faiths debated by regulars at evening lectures. Twenty days after the opening, on an afternoon of strikes against a French employment reform, the establishment was invaded by a dozen boys and girls aged between eight and fourteen. They expressed outrage at the caricatures, accused the waiters of North African origin of being atheists, and tore down drawings and trampled on them. Amused young adults supervised the scene outside, with one of them warning the owner: "This is serious! You are attacking Islam! The Brothers of Belleville are going to burn your house down."[34] The owners, in a gesture of appeasement, covered the drawings visible from the outside with a sheet of paper on which the word "censored" was written. A paving stone was thrown through the window a few days later. On April 4, a debate was organized involving local elected officials, neighborhood anarchists, and regulars, concerning two members of the *Charlie Hebdo* editorial staff, Charb and Wolinski. Two of the young adults who had supervised the children were present. They questioned Charb during the discussions, but without animosity. Nine years later, when the faces of the Kouachi brothers appeared on television screens after the massacre of the newspaper's editorial staff, the waitresses and manager of the establishment realized that one of them was Cherif Kouachi. At the time, the Kouachi brothers, who were from the neighborhood and in their early twenties, attended the seminars of Peter Cherif and Farid Benyettou, imam of the cell known as Buttes-Chaumont, known for its links with the jihad in Iraq.

The cartoon affair revealed dynamics that until then had mainly been observed in England, in particular the large-scale affirmation of Salafist militancy. It also revealed one of the ways jihadism manages to entrap the European democratic debate. The origin of this sequence of events was the murder of Theo van Gogh by an Islamist. And yet, as intimidation increased, the debate shifted from the question of how extremists sought to limit freedom of expression in Europe, to that of whether *Jyllands-Posten* and the cartoonists were partially responsible for triggering the stream of tragedies. Flemming Rose noticed that he received the first waves of criticism from former supporters at the same time as death threats began to come in. He saw this as an early symptom of the self-censorship that takes hold of people's minds:

> The problem with self-censorship is that it's not visible, you can't see it. To notice it, people need to be honest with themselves and transparent about their fear and lack of courage. None of this is particularly heroic, so most people just rationalize their fear by saying, "I really don't see the point in publishing cartoons that might offend people's sensibilities. Why should we do that?" And you hear this from people who would be willing to accept satirical drawings of Jesus, the Catholic Church, politicians, philosophers, or whatever. I think we really need to be on our guard to detect how the mechanisms of self-censorship work. They can destroy, or render impossible, the freedom to exchange or express opinions in a democratic society.[35]

5

The Acceleration of Salafism in Europe

As the cartoon affair became international, civil and sectarian war took hold of Iraq. On February 22, 2006, armed jihadists stormed the Golden Mosque of Samarra, one of the four sacred sites of Shia Islam in the country. They set off their explosives, leading to the collapse of the golden dome, an architectural marvel twenty meters in diameter, one of the most majestic in the Muslim world. They also destroyed the tombs of the tenth and eleventh imams, the equivalent of saints in Shia Islam. In retaliation, more than a hundred Sunni mosques were attacked in the following days. The country's disintegration was set in motion, and the Americans were stuck in a quagmire that they had helped to create.

However, the Americans would score their first victory on June 7, 2006, locating and killing Zarqawi, the leader of Al-Qaeda in Iraq. His body was identified by the scars that had replaced his tattoos. That same year, his successors announced the creation of an "Islamic State of Iraq" and their aim for a return of the "caliphate." For their part, the United States supported the Iraqi army and the Sunni tribes of northern Iraq, in an aim to recapture the provinces occupied by the jihadists, who were retreating as local populations rebelled against their bloody methods. Global jihad entered a new phase of low tide, while in Europe the pioneers continued their emancipation.

Jihadist Cells in Denmark and Sweden

The cartoon affair and the war in Iraq was a rude awakening for the Scandinavian public authorities, which had considered jihad to be a foreign risk. Several attempted attacks against journalists, cartoonists, and the offices of *Jyllands-Posten* were thwarted. Jakob Scharf, then head of the Danish domestic intelligence service, explained the pressure his department faced:

> Starting in 2008, the cartoons became central to Al-Qaeda's propaganda, which explained to a wide audience that terrorist attacks were necessary to protect Muslims from violations by Western countries such as Denmark. That changed everything. Suddenly, Denmark was designated as the number one target in the world.[1]

The first Scandinavian cell was dismantled in western Copenhagen in the fall of 2005, before the cartoon affair, to which it was not linked. This was the so-called Glostrup group, named after a suburban municipality, made up of Danes and Swedes who had links with the jihad in Bosnia. They were led by a Palestinian preacher from the Nørrebro mosque, where the Egyptians of Gamaa Islamiyya had preached in the 1990s. The imam, who was also a Thai boxing instructor at a local club, attended the meeting organized by Omar Bakri in the summer of 2004. In 2005, he was expelled from the Nørrebro place of worship after a report in the leading daily *Politiken* highlighted his jihadist leanings and the content of the hateful sermons he delivered to dozens of young Muslims. Nevertheless, he continued his preaching from his apartment in the Amager district and in a nearby clandestine mosque. The Glostrup group made innovative use of the internet at a time when broadband lines were just appearing in Europe.

A group linked to the jihad in Iraq, known as Vollsmose after a neighborhood in Odense, was dismantled in the summer of 2006 while it was targeting officials of the *Jyllands-Posten*. The arrests continued in the following weeks. In 2008, an American jihadist, David Headley, was arrested while he was planning to "avenge the Prophet" by opening fire indiscriminately in the streets of Copenhagen. Shortly thereafter, the Danish embassy in Pakistan was the target of a bomb attack. In 2010, a jihadist of Somali origin, connected to the aforementioned Salafist circles of Copenhagen and Aalborg, entered the home of one of the cartoonists, Kurt Westergaard, armed with a machete. Westergaard was in the presence of his granddaughter at the time. The cartoonist managed to lock himself and his granddaughter in a secure bathroom designed for this purpose, a "panic room," from which he called the police. In December 2010, a Swedish group was arrested while planning to carry out an attack on the offices of two newspapers, *Jyllands-Posten* and *Politiken*, in the Danish capital. Finally, in 2012, three Norwegians were convicted in Oslo for planning a similar operation. Meanwhile, in France, the offices of *Charlie Hebdo* were the target of a Molotov cocktail attack. Outside of Scandinavia, German pioneers were also establishing the first terrorist cells.

From Ulm to Afghanistan: The Pioneers of Sauerland

In the mid-2000s, Fritz Gelowicz and Attila Selek, the two Ulm pioneers, went on a pilgrimage to Mecca, financed by the largest Turkish Islamist organization, Millî Görüş, which has 29,000 members in Germany. They met another compatriot there who would become the third of the four accomplices. The three friends were unable to reach Iraq from Syria, and instead headed for Central Asia.

When they arrived in Pakistan, they met a fourth man in a jihadist camp in northern Waziristan, Daniel Martin Schneider, who would establish himself as the leader of the cell. Like the British volunteers at the end of the 1990s, they were unable to keep up with the pace set by the military instructors. They fell ill, Fritz with a case of dysentery, and Selek with malaria and hepatitis C. Even Schneider, who had completed his military service in Germany a year earlier, was overwhelmed by the intensity of the program, the difficult living conditions, and the lack of hygiene. The Uzbek leaders supervising the camp concluded that the recruits could not be deployed against the American army in Afghanistan, so they were sent home to carry out attacks. Back in Europe in 2006, Fritz Gelowicz and Attila Selek settled in Frankfurt and then in Ulm, and frequented local Salafist circles. Their group was selfless but also amateurish, a feature of many of the pioneers of the 2000s. They visited each other at their respective homes, and exchanged information on the internet via free WLAN networks, which made them easy to trace. They were trained in bomb-making in Pakistan but forgot the basics. They were located when they tried to touch base with local go-betweens.

On December 31, 2006, they were questioned while idling in front of the American base in Ramstein after having driven more than 150 kilometers from the Al-Ansar mosque in Frankfurt. A few days later, Selek got out of his car and shouted at the police officers tailing him, puncturing one of their tires as they looked on in astonishment and continuing on his way. In February 2007, the emir of the cell, Martin Schneider, was questioned upon his return to Germany from Pakistan. A few weeks later, their objective became clear. Selek got his hands on 26 detonators in Turkey, and Gelowicz bought chemical compounds in pharmacies all over West Germany. The third member, a resident of Ulm, organized seminars in his garden; the agenda included religious lessons, jihadist videos, barbecues, and soccer matches. Seven attendees eventually made their way Afghanistan. One of them would prove to be more pugnacious than his elders, and a year later would become the first German to commit a suicide bombing on German soil. In the summer of 2007, the explosives were ready. The targets were chosen for a day of terror: Frankfurt airport, the mess at Ramstein base, and a nightclub. On September 3, 2007, Gelowicz received an e-mail from the command of a camp located in the Afghan tribal areas. He was ordered to take action within three weeks, before the Bundestag vote on renewing German military presence in Afghanistan, a choice probably dictated by the Spanish precedent. In the early hours of the morning, three of the four were arrested in Ulm. The fourth, Selek, was found a month later in Turkey. The IIZ center in Ulm, which they had founded, was closed after a decade of activity.

The Sauerland cell offers a condensed version of the process of the formation of Europeanized jihadism. The result of the pollination by the veterans, the pioneers formed themselves within the various spaces of Salafism in the Middle East (the institutes of Cairo, Damascus, Mecca) and the lands of jihad abroad (Afghanistan instead of Iraq). When they got to Afghanistan, they were taken in hand by Uzbek combat groups, with whom many Germans of Turkish descent had already trained, for linguistic reasons and to gain access to networks that were built during the jihad in Chechnya in the early 2000s. Their failure to join fighting in the tribal zones led them to consider terrorist actions in Europe. The foreign emirs gave them orders on when to act, but the Europeans retained control over targets, modus operandi, and the precise date of operations.

These developments defined the framework of Western jihadism at the end of the 2000s, which was still under supervision, but beginning to act with greater freedom. Following the example of the Germans, the Toulouse circles went through the same stages, almost at the same time. They studied in Salafist centers abroad, mainly in Cairo and Molenbeek. Once there, several of them started planning to go to foreign fronts. Sabri Essid and Thomas Barnouin, two close friends of the Clains, failed to reach Iraq, and were handed over to the French authorities on February 12, 2007, the same day that the emir of the Sauerland cell, Martin Schneider, was arrested at the airport by the German police. Like their counterparts across the Rhine, Essid and Barnouin were sentenced to several years in prison, while new disciples appeared in their wake. Like the young people from Ulm who went to Afghanistan after meetings in the gardens of the pioneers, the Merah brothers rose through the ranks in Toulouse. Abdelkader visited Jean-Michel Clain in Cairo, while Mohammed embarked on a journey to Algeria and the Middle East that led him to settle in the tribal areas a few years later. There he would face the same tribulations, suffer from the extreme conditions, and develop hepatitis C. He returned to France armed with his gruesome plans, which were supervised from a distance by a Belgian from Molenbeek living in Afghanistan; he carried out his attacks in March 2012.

European Prisons at the Crossroads of the Global and the Local

In the second half of the 2000s, the intelligence services of Baden-Württemberg began to take an interest in a number of imprisoned jihadists, a first in Germany, as Herbert Müller relates:

> My colleagues had to visit various prisons on several occasions because there had been incidents with individuals convicted of terrorism. [. . .] This worried us [. . .], but apart from a few serious cases that were made public, [. . .] we were able to avoid putting dangerous people together. We feared that demagogues would be able to lead other inmates down the same path. As I recall, in Germany and Baden-Württemberg, it remained limited; it was not as problematic as I was told it was in France.[2]

Given what Müller says, the dynamic in Germany seemed to follow those of its French, British, and Belgian neighbors, but with a lag of a few years. For his part, Abu Qatada, the emir of Londonistan who was imprisoned in the south of England at the end of the 2000s, notes:

> You can contemplate great signs of Allah in prison. I have seen how young men come to Islam and how they become students of knowledge. They learn Arabic and Sharia in just a few months and develop an understanding of reality that some Muslims who grew up in the land of Islam continue to ignore.[3]

One sign of the porosity of prison walls was Abu Qatada himself, who was presented as Bin Laden's favorite representative in Europe, and who managed, from prison, to give interviews in Arabic to sympathetic media abroad.[4] He even boasted of having "inspired," from his cell, a spectacular attempted attack on Glasgow airport that narrowly failed on June 30, 2007.[5]

At the same time, in England, France, and the Netherlands, new kinds of prisoner support associations were emerging. In 2006, the organization Cage was founded in Great Britain with the aim of "raising awareness in a unique way about the fate of the prisoners of Guantanamo and other detainees in the context of the war on terror."[6] Its president, Moazzam Begg, was himself imprisoned for two years in the American prison before being released without charge. With Cage, he promoted a specific version of his commitment to freedom. In a document posted online in 2008, he extolled the work of Abdullah Azzam, the theorist of contemporary jihad and inspirer of Al-Qaeda: "In his masterful discourse on jihad during the Soviet occupation, 'The Defense of Muslim Lands,' the charismatic scholar Sheikh Abdullah Azzam revived the famous thirteenth-century fatwa of Ibn Taymiyyah, which states: 'With regard to the aggressive enemy who destroys life and religion, faith demands nothing is more strongly [of the faithful] than to fight against him.'"[7]

Other prominent members of the association justified participation in defensive jihad by referring to Western intellectual principles and international legal concepts. One of them, Asim Qureshi, a "researcher" within Cage, claimed that the jihadist groups in Iraq, Kashmir, Afghanistan, and Palestine were responding to a religious obligation, but also engaging in legitimate defense as recognized by the 1949 Geneva Convention. This claim is mistaken, as the acts in question are indeed "reprisals," which are prohibited by the aforementioned convention.[8] In essence, the site attempted to normalize the idea of jihad among a broad audience, and opened the door to justifying attacks in Europe. For example, at an event organized in the streets of London by Hizb ut-Tahrir in the summer of 2006, the individual cited above stated: "We know that it is incumbent upon all of us to support the jihad of our brothers and sisters in these countries [Iraq, Kashmir, Afghanistan, and Palestine] when they face oppression from the West, Allah Akbar!"[9]

Finally, Cage promoted on its website and in its events, certain of the forerunners of jihad against the West, such as Abu Hamza, the emir of Londonistan, whose testimony was featured on the association's website alongside many other preachers. Similarly, the American Anwar al-Awlaqi, a former star of British Islamist circles who became emir-in-chief of Al-Qaeda in Yemen, was presented as an "inspirational figure."[10] He was the guest of honour in August 2009 at an online conference organized by Cage, canceled at the last minute by the municipal council of the Chelsea and Kensington neighborhoods.[11] Rashad Ali, who at the same time was distancing himself from Islamism and moving toward other intellectual horizons, commented on Cage's appearance in the landscape of English associations:

> Associations like Cage made appearances on British university campuses. They explained to people that they shouldn't cooperate, that the police were trying to prevent Muslims from exercising their freedom of expression, and that it was their duty to free the jihad prisoners. The terrorists were not terrorists, they were prisoners of war who had to be set free. This was Cage's online campaign, these were the words of Anwar al-Awlaqi and other preachers in their interviews.[12]

In 2009, Fabien Clain was imprisoned in the Fleury-Mérogis Prison for his involvement in the Iraqi network in Toulouse. From his cell, he founded an association to help detainees, together with a friend who was in charge of internships in Salafist centers in Cairo, an association to help detainees, in accordance with the French Law of Associations of 1901. Entitled Sanabil ("ear of wheat"), it claimed to aid Muslim detainees and offer them much-needed financial, material, moral, and religious support. Under the guise of these laudable motives, Sanabil actually worked to build a database of jailed jihadists, thus creating a sort of directory of French jihadism. The current director of the French prison administration, then in charge of the overseas prison services, recalled internal discussions on this subject:

> I know that Sanabil was under surveillance and that a certain amount of information had been passed on, that some members were banned from prisons. Some of Sanabil's activities were banned and others were debated. We were keeping an eye on them.[13]

Sanabil would be closed by the French authorities in 2016, after several of its former supporters had taken part in terrorist activities, such as Mehdi Nemmouche, the first "returnee" from Syria to commit an attack in Europe in May 2014, and Amedy Coulibaly, perpetrator of the January 2015 attacks.

In the same vein, Behind Bars, an association for the defense of "Muslim" prisoners, was founded in the Netherlands. The founders were from The Hague, and until the mid-2000s were members of the Salafist As-Sunnah mosque, which was then frequented by certain members of the GICM who were responsible for planning the attack on Theo van Gogh. Following this catastrophe, the Dutch authorities tightened control of the mosque, prompting its chief imam, once an ardent Salafist, to revise his position. Behind Bars was a sort of response to this: the organization was founded by the expelled As-Sunnah zealots, who sought to come to the aid of people who had been imprisoned in Morocco, Pakistan, Somalia, or the Netherlands because of their links with the movement, also reminiscent of the approach of Cage and Sanabil.

Thus, at the beginning of the 2010s, the prison was not simply a site of recruitment, but also an issue around which the movement outside of the prison could be organized. In a period of low tide, seemingly uncoordinated but nonetheless similar initiatives emerged in the various Islamist circles of Western Europe.

6

The End of Jihad in Iraq and the Digital Revolution of Jihadism

After a period of expansion in the mid-2000s, Al-Qaeda networks retreated on various fronts and sank into appalling patterns of violence. Al-Qaeda in the Islamic Maghreb (AQIM, created in 2007) did not succeed in unifying the armed groups in North Africa. The jihad in Iraq was defeated militarily, thanks in particular to the mobilization of local Sunni forces, at the cost of two thousand civilians killed every month. In 2010, the Islamic State in Iraq disappeared and went underground. A domestic dispute revealed the poisonous atmosphere among this organization's leaders: one of its emirs was berated by his wife, who was exhausted by the discomfort of life in a yurt, and despaired of the caliphate's promises of greatness:

> So where is this Islamic State you're talking about? We're living in the middle of the desert![1]

As the second cycle of jihadism was reaching a low point, movements in the West were coming to the end of their reconfigurations, which were characterized, on the one hand, by the growing autonomy of the European networks in Afghanistan, and on the other hand, by the westernization of propaganda, driven in particular by the revival of the cartoons affair in the United States.

The Growing Autonomy of the Europeans in Afghanistan

By 2010, the German volunteers in the tribal areas were numerous enough to found their own brigade (*katiba*), replicating the British

139

model that had been in place since the middle of the decade. In concrete terms, they broke away from the Uzbek training camps and established their base nearby. At the same time, Moez Garsallaoui, a resident of Molenbeek, established a French-speaking unit. He would later welcome Mohammed Merah into the unit, and claim responsibility for the attacks in Toulouse.

European militants took more and more of these so-called fragmented trips to these areas. They reached Afghanistan after transiting through Tunisia, Egypt, or Iran, thus making surveillance more complicated. This was the modus operandi that ISIS would reproduce (rather than invent) a few years later, often using the same individuals and the same networks. This helps to explain the speed with which this organization seemed to emerge from the Syrian sands.

In the summer of 2010, a German arrested by American forces in the Afghan tribal areas revealed a plot hatched at the Al-Tayyeb mosque in Hamburg, the new name of the place of worship where the 9/11 command had gathered.[2] The plan, personally approved by Bin Laden, was one of the most important ever conceived in Europe. Unlike attacks that had been attempted to that point, this one was to have been fully coordinated by a European cell and carried out according to an urban guerrilla plan tried and tested during the Bali attacks in 2002. The terrorists planned to open fire simultaneously on civilians at the foot of the Eiffel Tower, on the square in front of Notre-Dame-de-Paris cathedral, and in front of the Brandenburg Gate, the TV tower at Alexanderplatz, and Berlin Central Station. In October, the American, British, Swedish, and Japanese consulates warned their nationals of possible attacks. In November, the German Interior Minister, Thomas de Maizière, raised the security level to maximum alert. The attack was finally thwarted in late fall.[3] It was the last major attempted attack in Europe in the Bin Laden era. His networks gradually entered a crisis while the security services managed the threat.

The Westernization of Propaganda and the Revival of the Cartoon Affair in New York

The jihad in Iraq and Afghanistan, a by-product of the "war on terror," acted as a magnet that, in the imagination of the pioneers, took the place of the crises in Bosnia, Algeria, and Chechnya of the previous decade. The distant battlefields of these countries became places where European jihadism was welcomed, but these battlefields also initiated dynamics that would take shape in the Old Continent. The interaction of the global and the local would be facilitated by the rise of the digital realm (in particular the creation of social networks such as Facebook in 2004 and YouTube in 2005) and the increasing accessibility of broadband connections.

The German camp in Afghanistan was described on the internet by certain of its members as a site of ideological and military training, but also as being at the cutting edge of new communication technologies. The presence of European engineers and, more broadly, graduates from European universities in the ranks of jihadists contributed to the sophistication of their propaganda.[4] A study published in the early 2010s in England showed that thirty percent of Britons who have participated in Islamist terrorist initiatives have attended universities or institutes of higher education, and that some had doctoral and post-doctoral training.[5] These graduates, who interacted with people in the camps whose background was that of crime and delinquency, highlight the importance of student activism during the 2000s. This was reflected in the growing politicization of propaganda content.

In June 2008, a German convert who had been to Afghanistan and was a former contact of Dr. Youssouf in Ulm took over a Salafist religious center in Bremen, as well as a foundation, the "Family and Culture Club." Supported by around thirty individuals, he organized several meetings with Dutch, Belgian, Swedish, Danish, and Norwegian activists. By the end of the year, two of them were suspected of being the main contributors to the Global Islamic Media Front (GIMF), the media branch of Al-Qaeda, whose leanings were similar to those of Iraqi Jihadism, and which published German content on the internet. Until this point, jihadist propagandists had successfully hijacked the collective imagery and symbolism of Sunni Islam.[6] Now, with the aid of social networks, Salafist concepts were enriched even further by the communication codes of Western youth.

Al-Qaeda videos in classical formal Arabic, for instance, were not always accessible, even to people with a Muslim cultural background. Now, these videos were being replaced by Facebook posts praising the heroes of Islam in the various languages, and in far more accessible ways. The martial iconography of the jihadists was complemented by humorous posts that drew upon the geek culture to reach new audiences. The most viewed videos on YouTube are "lolcats," videos of excited kittens playing the piano or snuggling up to a puppy, and the jihadists began to produce their own versions of these. ISIS even created a Twitter feed entitled "Islamic State of Cat," featuring tender bearded warriors bottle-feeding a kitten found under the rubble of a building in Syria. Where associations in England and France, as discussed above, had previously sought to normalize jihadist ideas, now the aim was to normalize the militants themselves. They were just like everyone else – how could they possibly be considered a danger?

At the same time, in France, Belgium, and the Netherlands, important platforms for discussing and storing jihadist content began to appear, such as Ansar al-Haqq. The internet was becoming a virtual library for globalized Salafi-jihadism.

The main Western contribution to the revolution in Islamist propaganda (aside from social networks) came from the United States. To understand this, it is worth looking at the journey of Jesse Morton, once one of the most prominent faces of the American Islamist movement, who subsequently undertook a long and tumultuous process of repentance. Originally from Pennsylvania, he began living on his own at an early age, after fleeing a dysfunctional home. As a teenager, he developed a passion for the rock band the Grateful Dead, a symbol of the cultural and sexual emancipation of the 1960s. Morton followed them on tour and made a living by selling drugs to the former hippies and neo-hippies who attended their concerts. This ended when, at the age of twenty, he was arrested and convicted for trafficking illegal substances. Imprisoned in Philadelphia alongside a Moroccan veteran of the war in Afghanistan, he converted to Islam. He gradually became open to Salafist ideology, which provided him with explanations for the misfortunes that had landed him in jail. Upon his release from prison after 9/11, he set out on a path of study and Islamist militancy. A curious student, he graduated as valedictorian from Metropolitan College of New York, and in 2006 began a master's degree in international relations at Columbia University.

Around this time he embraced the ideas of Omar Bakri, the emir of Londonistan, and contacted his successor, Anjem Choudary. He organized public demonstrations, during which he flew the black flag and denounced the hypocrisy of the West, which he claimed was at war with Islam. In the heart of Times Square, and also in other cities, he attired himself in the dress of Western Salafists, wrapping his imposing stature in a qamis, topping his shaven head with a kufi, and wrapping his neck in a keffiyeh. With his loud voice and thick brown beard, his piercing eyes concealed behind rectangular glasses, he once introduced himself to CNN viewers by saying: "We must terrorize the infidels,"[7] and sought to provoke people by saying the 9/11 operations were "justified." He spread certain of Osama bin Laden's messages on the internet and expressed his contempt for Muslims who did not share his ideals. He came into contact with the Jamaican preacher of Londonistan, Abdullah al-Faisal, who oversaw the indoctrination of one of the perpetrators of the London attack. Under the combined influence of the various emirs of the British capital, he founded Revolution Muslim, a New York branch of Al-Muhajiroun. He deftly exploited the broad scope of freedom of expression in the United States, guaranteed by the First Amendment to the Constitution, consulting a lawyer to find out how to express ultra-radical views without falling foul of the law. As such, he took pleasure in "legally" subverting democratic values with veiled calls for jihad from the world's oldest democracy. His group remained limited to a dozen Salafists, but the content they produced generated thousands of views and hundreds of comments. Among his recruits were about twenty fellow Americans who had fought in Afghanistan and later for ISIS. Around fifteen of them were also involved in attempted attacks,[8] such as "Jihadi Jane," who aspired to kill one of the Danish cartoonists; another volunteer sought to attack the Pentagon, and yet another was planning an attack on the headquarters of the Lubavitch Jews in South Williamsburg, Brooklyn. The website of Revolution Muslim was used to attract sympathizers, as Jesse Morton explains: "Once you see that they are logging in consistently, you don't really need to take them all the way." The first step was to make it clear that God is the source of all law: "'Then you use that principle to say that all the Muslim rulers, because they don't implement Shariah law in its entirety, they are not Muslim at all, so we can rebel against them. [. . .] What you have to do is frame their personal grievance, making them think that they can contribute to a broader cause. And you do that through the ideology, because believe it or not, Islam can be framed in a way that is incredibly revolutionary."[9]

At the end of the 2000s, the group seemed like nothing less than a shoot from Londonistan that had been planted in American soil. Morton was a prolific recruiter and developed contacts with his compatriot, Anwar al-Awlaqi, who was then head of the Yemeni branch of Al-Qaeda.

They saw their chance to act in April 2010, when the Danish cartoon affair was referred to in the 200th episode of *South Park*, in which the residents of the fictional Colorado town in which the series is set are threatened with legal action by everyone they have mocked since the beginning of the show fourteen years earlier, from Jesus Christ and Krishna to the most iconic celebrities of American pop culture. One of the latter, Tom Cruise, mischievously agrees to drop the charges on one condition: that the residents invite Mohammed into their story. When they hold an assembly to deliberate, one of the characters begins to panic: "If Mohammed appears in an episode of *South Park*, we'll be targeted!" Another muses: "Maybe enough time has passed and we can show Mohammed?" Finally they come up with a ploy: instead of an actual image of the Prophet, we see him hidden beneath a disguise, the envoy of Allah is presented to the local population wearing a bear mascot outfit. The residents of South Park are relieved and thank Mohammed for saving the city.[10]

Jesse Morton's group, capable only of literal readings and lacking in all humour, pounced on the opportunity. The addresses of production companies and artists were published on the internet, and a press release stated that they "will probably end up like Theo van Gogh." Repeats of the episode were postponed, sparking outrage among fans of the show, who noted that sacred figures from other religions were treated much worse in the script. They pointed out that the Prophet had been depicted in the series on two occasions, after the World Trade Center attacks, and in 2006, in the midst of the cartoon controversy, without provoking any reaction. As a response, a resident of Seattle created a Facebook page that evoked Flemming Rose's initiative with the *Jyllands-Posten* five years earlier: "Everybody Draw Mohammed Day." The Pakistani and Indonesian authorities threatened to ban access to the social network in their countries. The page disappeared, sparking bitter protests in the

United States, only to reappear a few days later, which Facebook representatives claimed was due to a "bug."

Jesse Morton and his associates capitalized on the tense atmosphere. They produced the first English-language online jihadist magazine,[11] the first issue of which was devoted to the cartoons. The magazine's raison d'être was to create a transnational movement in the West, promoting an "alternative" worldview based on "principles that reject the Enlightenment and democratic values."[12] The magazine did not last long, but was immediately imitated by Anwar al-Awlaqi, Morton's compatriot, who launched *Inspire*. An exact copy of Morton's initiative, Awlaqi took an editorial line praising globalized jihadism, which would be conceived and written in English, but adopted and disseminated by young people all over the world. The articles discussed recipes for concocting explosives in the kitchen or arguments to use against infidels who criticize terrorist actions. The format was thus the same as the one that ISIS would use to broadcast its messages in dozens of languages over the next decade. Morton summarized his view of the situation, highlighting the contribution of Westerners in modernizing jihadist communication methods: "Contrary to popular belief, jihadist magazines are an American export, not an import to the West."[13]

The American aspect of the cartoon affair thus inspired the mould of media jihad 2.0. The process reveals three key elements that summarize the breadth of the dynamics observed during the 2000s.

The first is the export of the Al-Muhajiroun model and, more broadly, the methods that emerged within the Londonistan ecosystem, to Western Europe and even to the East Coast of the United States, where the potential for the development of jihadism is nonetheless infinitely weaker.

The second aspect is the contribution of these limited digital environments to global jihad. *Inspire*, the natural extension of the many militant forums on the internet, bears the mark of the involvement of Westerners in the international movement. These Western militants were not content to refer to doctrines developed in Peshawar. They appropriated these doctrines and adapted them so as to insert them into the great flow of globalized ideologies that were now spreading across social networks.

Finally, the American developments are interesting for their outcomes. The veiled threats against the creators of *South Park* did not escape the authorities, who responded by taking legal action against all of the individuals involved. Jesse Morton seems to have realized this and fled to Morocco just after the publication of said threats. Most of his companions were arrested. He himself was arrested in Casablanca, handed over to the US authorities, and sentenced to eleven years in prison. The FBI used the tools at its disposal to uproot the parts of the ecosystem that were just forming. The swift and severe reaction, probably dictated by the analysis of the failures of the British, destroyed the preaching machine before it really got going. The hard line taken on jihadism, in part due to the experience of 9/11, was made easier by the minuscule size of the American jihadist circles.

At the same time, perceptions were shifting in Western Europe. The peak of the terrorist threat seemed to have passed, but more people had become receptive to jihadist ideas over the past decade. The hundred or so pioneers in the ranks of terrorist organizations in Afghanistan and Iraq were an indicator of this. The level of support for them during their trials and online activism bore witness to an enthusiasm that had not existed ten years previously. The reconfigurations continued even as the tide was beginning to turn.

III

THE NATIVES – THE 2010s

The final part of the book deals with how European Salafi-jihadist networks were drawn in and then transformed by the war in Syria. Before the rise of ISIS, the European situation gradually became intertwined with the crisis in the Levant (2010–2014). The apex of ISIS's power then resulted in a campaign of attacks (2014–2018). Finally, the group's fall in the Middle East led to reconfigurations that brought new challenges to European territory (2018 to the present).

1

Before ISIS: The Sharia Networks in Europe

The pre-ISIS period was marked by the intensification of intellectual activism and new terrorist ambitions. The dynamic was driven in particular by the Europeanization of the activities of the Al-Muhajiroun group, against a background of upheaval in Syria.

London Calling: The Establishment of Pan-European Sharia Networks (2010)

In 2010, Anjem Choudary, Omar Bakri's successor, was pursuing the objectives of ideological guerrilla warfare instilled in him by his mentor. He stated that he would travel to Wootton Bassett, a village in the east of England, where ceremonies were being held to repatriate the bodies of British soldiers killed in Afghanistan, saying he would hold a funeral counter-march through the streets in which people carried empty coffins symbolizing the "Muslim children massacred" by the British army. The announcement caused an uproar, which was the desired effect. More than 200,000 people joined a Facebook group to express their outrage. Several politicians targeted him, while the far right took offense. Choudary had already been publicly denigrating or desecrating national symbols since 2005. With the help of a few dozen active members and a second circle of several thousand followers, he took advantage of the commotion he caused to present himself as a victim of persecution. When the group he headed, which was modeled on Al-Muhajiroun, was disbanded by the authorities, he cried out against Islamophobia and called for the media, and Muslims as well, to consider the rampant racism in English society.

A few days later, he launched a new organization, the umpteenth copy of Al-Muhajiroun, called Sharia4UK. However, unlike the previous ones, this one had a different dimension, operating at an EU level.

A few months later, a few Danes launched an organization called *Kaldet til Islam* ("Call to Islam"). The founder, Shiraz Tariq, was one of a dozen Scandinavians to have visited Omar Bakri at London rallies. The Palestinian preacher who started the Glostrup cell also moved in his orbit. The head of Danish intelligence at the time, Jakob Scharf, recalls:

Shiraz Tariq was already in contact with Bakri in London in 2004. He organized what he called "religious trips" from Denmark to Great Britain, which influenced the way terrorism developed here in the second half of the 2000s.[1]

Call to Islam became the most visible platform for Salafism in Copenhagen. Its first spokesman, Ryan, of Iraqi origin and then in his early twenties, described its close ties with the former Londonistan networks. From Lebanon, where he now resided, Omar Bakri oversaw the process:

Call to Islam was created in 2010 following a meeting that took place somewhere in Europe, between people who had flown in from Belgium, Denmark, and England. [. . .] The founders had established excellent contacts with Al-Muhajiroun in England. [. . .] Omar Bakri and Anjem Choudary were involved in the creation of Call to Islam. The group asked them for practical advice before taking action, and when they launched a campaign in England, the same was organized here.[2]

Call to Islam emerged at the same time as a constellation of sister structures were established in neighboring countries. A few Norwegians set up *Profetens Ummah* ("Prophets of the Ummah"). In Antwerp, a group led by a Salafist preacher and former drug dealer, Fouad Belkacem, launched Sharia4Belgium. The spectacular actions of the Flemish members of Sharia4Belgium inspired imitators in Amsterdam, Delft, and The Hague, who set up Sharia4Holland. This model was emulated in Germany and Austria by Millatu Ibrahim ("The Community of Abraham") and in France by Forsane al-Izza ("The Riders of Pride"). The latter made their name during a demonstration outside a McDonald's in Limoges to denounce the links between the fast-food chain and the "World Jewish Foundation." Concealing their faces with keffiyehs, the militants denounced "satanic secularism" before throwing stones at the building. At another demonstration, they trampled on the Penal Code and burned the Civil Code as journalists looked on.

Taken individually, each group had its own room for maneuver, but taken together, they formed a flexible, pan-European sharia network under the supervision of their British "parent company." Ryan, the Danish spokesman, explains:

> We knew these groups well, Forsane al-Izza in France, Millatu Ibrahim in Germany, and especially Prophets of the Ummah in Norway, which were closer to us geographically. We had personal ties and visited each other. Their methods were very similar to ours.[3]

The groups demanded the establishment of sharia law in their respective countries and the application of what they viewed as authentic Islam. Ryan continues:

> Establishing sharia law in the West was not a provocative gesture in our eyes. [. . .] For us, it was the truth: this was where we lived, so this was where sharia law had to be established. If I'd lived somewhere else, I'd have wanted to do it there. [. . .] Many of us considered spreading our vision to be a full-time job. [. . .] We were defending the truth, so we had to act.[4]

To achieve this, they used multiple communication strategies, gaining notoriety on social networks, hosting internet forums, and responding to the media interest aroused by their hostility. While their existence testified to the fact that Salafism had reached an undeniable level of activism and visibility in the European public arena, they based their arguments on the persecution of Muslims in the West, who, they argued, lacked basic rights, and were the victims of Islamophobic regimes. They called for the overthrow of the democratic order and the establishment of a "caliphate" which, in their eyes, was a perfect and indeed utopian political model. In Scandinavia, England, and Germany, certain members were invited to appear on television, where they expressed their views in front of unprepared politicians. The spokesman for Call to Islam described the state of mind prevailing in his entourage:

> Any opportunity to provoke the media and political leaders was a good one. As a group, we were very provocative. It was our DNA.[5]

Like Al-Muhajiroun in the late 1990s, those who took part in such public events were frequently portrayed in the press as extremists whose discourse bordered on parody, and whose claims to the truth were ridiculous. To many, their zeal made them seem harmless. But in fact they were very skilled at using their understanding of the workings of European societies to parasitize public debate. The spokesman for Call to Islam continues:

> Our attack on democracy and values really touched a nerve. And we didn't pull any punches! We used language that made them blow their fuse, and we turned the right to freedom of expression against them: here, everyone has the right to freedom of expression, of assembly, of religion, so you can't deprive us of that. [. . .] It took them several years before they were able to set limits, to forbid us from using certain words, like "jihad," "murder," or others that we used to incite people.

Four years before ISIS was proclaimed, groups were openly campaigning in the streets of major democracies for the creation of a caliphate. The demonstrations came at a time when al-Qaeda's jihad was slowing down. Their discourse, like that of Omar Bakri in his day, was rarely subjected to scrutiny, and often provoked little interest. Only far-right activists took them on, seeing in these few dozen activists the sole and typical image of European Islam. By taking the Islamists literally, they conceded their main claim: that of embodying the true face of Islam in the West; the far-right groups thus took the Islamists as their essential counterpoint. As such, the 2010s began with the mutual instrumentalization of religious and political identity groups; these groups, while they were in the minority, shared a grammar of civilizational conflict. They did not yet have a stranglehold on European democratic debate, although Ismaël, then a member of Forsane al-Izza, the French sharia group, already perceived the trend:

Q: *Was the aim at the time [in 2010] carrying out attacks in France?*

A: The context for us was that we were in danger, for me it was: "Muslims are in danger," and it wasn't just because of Sarko [Nicolas Sarkozy, then president of France], it was above all the rise of the fascists, we were the Yin and they were the Yang. We were talking about "Fdesouche" [a far-right web site in France] before anyone else, we were already keeping tabs on them at the time. They [the far-right groups] were arming themselves, they were training, and we told ourselves we shouldn't be naive. That was the starting point. We had to prepare for the worst.[6]

Authoritarianism Runs out of Steam in the Arab World: The First Steps of an Explosion

Thousands of kilometers away, Syria, in the summer of 2010, was experiencing one of its hottest summers on record. For the third time in five years, the agricultural plains of the Jezirah region in the north of the country were transformed into huge infernos. The fires destroyed wheat harvests and bankrupted cooperatives, which accounted for many jobs in the tribal areas. They intensified growing discontent with the country's economic management, and more broadly with nearly five decades of Ba'ath Party dictatorship. The dysfunctional situation led to an exodus from the countryside to the poor, predominantly Sunni outskirts of the main cities in central Syria, where the most important popular mobilizations would later occur.[7] Only time will tell whether the Syrian crisis is yet another war made worse by the ecological crisis and global warming.[8]

At the same time, in Alexandria, Egypt, the fate of a blogger was causing a scandal. Khaled Saïd was abducted by the security services as he left a cybercafé, then tortured for posting innocuous comments online in favor of justice and democracy. His death led to the first protests. A few months later, Mohamed Bouazizi, a young Tunisian street vendor driven to despair, set himself on fire in a public square in Sidi Bouzid, triggering the largest demonstrations of the twenty-first century in the Arab world. The uprisings led to the downfall of two seemingly irremovable heads of state in Tunisia and Egypt, and Bouazizi and Said became icons of the revolution.[9] The winds of protest spread to Syria. At the same time, in May 2011, Bin Laden was traced to a house in Abbottabad, Pakistan, and then liquidated in a raid by American special forces. Shortly afterwards, Anwar al-Awlaqi, the face of American jihadism and leader of al-Qaeda in Yemen, was also eliminated. The organization entered a structural crisis at a time when Arab countries were experiencing an unprecedented wave of democratic and popular change. In many ways, the various iterations of the "Arab Spring" seemed to bury global jihadism and its many representatives.

Rising Waters: Sharia Zones in Denmark and England (2011)

In 2011, the onset of the crisis in the Levant and the decline of al-Qaeda concealed the growing complexity of the European Salafi-jihadist movement.

The focus had not yet shifted to Syria, but the fact that young Europeans were spending more and more time in Salafist institutes abroad, in Cairo and Yemen, in Indonesia and the Maghreb, bore witness to growing trends that had taken shape ten years earlier around the pioneers.

Soulé, a Frenchman who grew up in the Toulouse region and later joined ISIS, described the excitement that reigned in jihadist circles during a prison interview in spring 2016. His parents were from Guinea, and he spoke of his desire to join the Tuaregs in Mali, who, he said, were preparing to apply Sharia law in the north of the country, before moving on to Syria:

> Already, in Mali, in 2011–2012, then with the intervention [of French troops in January 2013], there was an organization a bit like *Dawla* [the Islamic State], and people really wanted to go there! A lot of them were eager to go.[10]

In summer 2011, Anjem Choudary launched a new project in East London. Yellow posters were put up at the entrances to several neighborhoods with the following message: "You are entering a sharia-controlled area. Islamic rules apply." Alcohol, gambling, dancing, dress that was immodest and "contrary to Islam," drugs, and "fornication" were all prohibited, the Islamists proclaimed, at the same time announcing that religious patrols would ensure compliance with these rules. In his usual style, Choudary declared vociferously to the press covering the event: "There are hundreds, if not thousands, of people who are ready to make sure that these laws are applied."[11] This was far from true. No one was present to enforce the group's demands. One of the few disciples on site, a twenty-something convert with fire-colored hair and a red beard without moustache, who had once been sentenced to four years' imprisonment on charges related to terrorism, boasted: "Twenty-five districts have large Muslim populations, including Bradford, Dewsbury, Leicester and Luton [. . .]. We want to turn them all into an Islamic Emirate, where the excesses of Western civilization will no longer be tolerated." Even the event itself was smoke without fire. The stickers were removed by residents and public authorities, and the thousands of leaflets were swept up by maintenance workers. But, as always with the Al-Muhajiroun network, the creation of a spectacle was inherent to their strategy. First, they would seek to capture the public's attention, by announcing an initiative that was likely to bother people and force politicians to react. This, in turn, would bring about a reaction from the far right, which would then play on the hysteria of "great replacement theory." Then, when the press discovers that the plan was an empty shell, citizens who are concerned about the rise of the far right turn their anger on the political system, thereby blinding themselves to the threat of Salafism. The success of Choudary's project therefore lies not in any actual Muslim-controlled zones, but in reinforcing divides around how the question of Muslim influence is to be discussed. Those who try to deal with this subject are then accused of fear-mongering and playing into the hands of the extreme right; those who make these accusations, meanwhile, reinforce a relativist standpoint, buying into the claim, on the part of Islamist movements, that they are organizing themselves in the face of racism. Democratic debate is thereby reduced to the expression of opposing positions, leading to political polarization and the sense that one does not belong to an open and free society. The ideological guerrilla warfare of Choudary's movements has since been widely adopted and indeed become normal; even ISIS has employed certain of their methods, as have other Islamist movements close to Salafism and the Muslim Brotherhood.

Denial and hysteria, the two stumbling blocks of rational thinking, were alive and well at the beginning of the decade of 2010, and prevented people from becoming aware of Islamist activism within democracies. This was in no way limited to the "sharia zones" (which were little more than a communications operation) – the networks in question went well beyond this.

In the days that followed, Call of Islam copied the English initiative and announced that it had established Scandinavia's first "sharia zone." The militants chose the Tingbjerg neighborhood, in the north of Copenhagen, where several of them lived, and where the first Salafists appeared in the 1990s and the first jihadists ten years later. The announcement was always sure to have an impact, because it came in the middle of a legislative campaign. At the very moment citizens were being encouraged to participate in democracy, the Call members were conducting a religious counter-campaign, in which they publicly denigrated democracy, directing people to abstain to express their "disapproval" of godless institutions, and call for support for the local implementation of what they described as the laws of Allah. As in the United Kingdom, this led to a media firestorm, as summarized by Ryan, who was then a spokesman for the movement:

> Call to Islam caused a real shockwave through the country, especially among political leaders. [. . .] Our vision was diametrically opposed to the democratic and secular values promoted by the West, and all the values to which people here in Denmark are very attached.[12]

The Danish "sharia zone" was no more successful than the one in England, and was met with scorn from Muslim circles, which Ryan attributes to the press:

> The media distorted things. Other Muslims contacted us at the time to express their anger with us, but they didn't really know what was going on.

However, Ryan's remarks also mentioned levels of funding (which are unverifiable) for these activities that imply a level of preparation that is far from amateurish:

> For the first project we wanted to carry out in Tingbjerg, we had a budget of 23 million Danish kroner [almost three million euros]. I think we had to give up after a month; we really didn't know what we were doing, and we completely wasted the money.[13]

In addition, and unlike the situation in London, this was only the first step in the project. On this matter, Ryan's arguments are similar to those of the Mullah Boys of Leeds ten years earlier:

> The concept of "sharia zones" in the city of Tingbjerg and in other neighborhoods was not properly covered by the media. It was never about establishing "sharia zones," but fighting insecurity and crime. At the time, crime was very prevalent in Tingbjerg. [. . .] People were fed up and felt powerless. The police couldn't intervene because Tingbjerg is a project that's closed off to the outside world. The criminals knew it better than the police, and they were organized like real professionals. Some families, who had seen that there were many of us [the Salafists of this group] in Tingbjerg, asked us for help. And we accepted. We set up three teams to monitor and patrol: one in the morning, one in the afternoon and one in the evening.[14]

Their approach showed just how respectable many local residents considered them to be. They did not hesitate to intervene with dealers that the police, according to them, were incapable of arresting:

> We hauled in the offenders who were plaguing Tingbjerg at the time to tell to them that from now on there would be zero tolerance. If one of our security guards saw someone smoking a joint, he would take it from them.[15]

What Ryan is describing here is the deployment of religious watchmen. He draws this from a very specific Salafist interpretation of the concept of *hisba*, which is a duty, ordained by Allah, to intervene with fellow believers who transgress God's law, whether consciously or not. Islamic tradition holds that only the governor has the right to coercively "command good and forbid evil" in the public realm. But many European Salafists consider that the practice of *hisba* is the responsibility of every Muslim. It can thus take the form of religious patrols in a neighborhood, as in this example.

Whatever the truth of his narrative, Ryan's arguments are particularly instructive. The deployment of *hisba* by the Call to Islam responded to a local demand: a neighborhood infested with drugs and subject to the law of criminals needed to be pacified. His group, unlike the authorities, had local roots that would enable it to act. Ryan thus downplayed the religious dimension of their actions and emphasized their social necessity. For him, the establishment of divine commandments responds to the first need of any human group: law and order. There is no reason to think that his description is not at least partially true. Tingbjerg is indeed affected by drug trafficking, juvenile delinquency, and unemployment, though not at the levels of difficult neighborhoods in France or Great Britain.[16] But he omits parts of the official statement that his group published under his supervision: "How can we [Muslims] claim to follow the Sunnah [the principles established by the Prophet Muhammad] and defend the best *deen* [religion] when we prefer to live among the infidels, be subject to their laws, imitate them, and not distinguish ourselves from their *kufr* [impiety]? How can we claim to love Allah and His messenger when we are ashamed to call for the application of sharia? How can we be indifferent to the establishment of Allah's order on earth, which is the duty of every Muslim? [. . .] Working towards the establishment of the caliphate is one of the noblest tasks of our time. This can only be achieved if we work collectively, under an emir. It is also our duty to fight the evil that is spreading all around us. Laws made by men are currently in force, but all Muslims have an absolute obligation to work collectively to rid the world of democracy, that great *munkar* [vice]."[17]

The Danes and the British were particularly visible, but the Dutch, Belgian, and German antennae were not to be outdone. Ismaël, a member of the French branch, Forsane al-Izza, confirmed that they sought to ramp up their activities in the summer of 2011:

In fact, there are two versions of Forsane al-Izza. There's the foetus, a sort of first draft, when you don't really know what to do, you don't really know where to go, let's call it activism [. . .] And then when I joined Forsane, we started making videos and everything [. . .] we found a structure. I'm not saying it's all down to me, it's just that the latent force of the thing was revealed. The first period was before summer 2011, the second period was after summer 2011.[18]

At the same time, a civil war was brewing in Syria, even though in the first months of the crisis there was no sign of sectarian clashes. The political opposition was mainly Sunni, but there were also Christians and Alawites, reflecting a country that embodies the religious diversity of the Levant. But Bashar al-Assad's regime decided on a strategy of repression, turning the country into a microcosm of the fault lines of Middle Eastern geopolitics.

The First Attacks in Europe and the Syrian Backdrop (2012)

A year later, the conflict escalated as the war between the regime and the opposition (which jihadists now began to join) became increasingly sectarian. In July 2012, Jabhat al-Nusra, the Syrian branch of Al-Qaeda, established itself in the Aleppo region.[19] Its creation was formalized by a former leader of the Islamic State of Iraq, who had gone underground since the group disappeared at the end of the 2000s. The organic links between the Syrian and Iraqi terrorist components, which existed from the start, are clear.

This, in addition to the easy accessibility of the Syrian theater from southern Turkey, explains the shift in focus in European Islamist circles. Among the first to travel to Syria were the pioneers, the main followers of jihadism at the time. They had the specific feature of having forged links ten years earlier with Middle Eastern organizations, particularly with the Islamic State of Iraq. The departures still took place on a confidential basis in their circles. But since they were the first to take the plunge, they blazed a trail for their followers, who traveled the "highways" of jihad from 2014 onwards. Their level of training, indoctrination, and prior preparation indicates that they had evolved in Europe in "anticipation" of being able to throw themselves into a large-scale jihadist project.

In London, the man who would come to be known as Jihadi John headed for the Levant. In Toulouse, the initiators of the local dynamic continued to develop within the Clain constellation. In Val-de-Marne, Salim Benghalem, a pillar of the movement, a former criminal who was "jihadized" in prison in the mid-2000s and who would one day become an ISIS executioner, also left for the Levant with several accomplices. Boubaker El Hakim, a member of the Buttes-Chaumont network in Paris, left for post-revolutionary Tunisia, where he joined the jihadists of Ansar al-Sharia, who had just been released from prison and were building bridges between Europe and Syria. He set off for the Levant after murdering a newly elected deputy and fervent defender of Tunisian democracy. Omar Omsen, a close associate of Forsane al-Izza residing in Nice, criss-crossed the various neighborhoods where he had contacts. In Toulouse, Lyon, Strasbourg, and the Paris region, he invited these contacts to embark on the path of jihad. He turned out to be one of the first recruiters for the cause, and himself "emigrated" to the "blessed land of Islam" in 2012, as he explained in a video viewed several hundred thousand times on YouTube. Once he arrived in Syria, he founded a brigade and his own camp in the north of the country, where he was still living at the beginning of 2023, a unique situation for a European.

In parallel and sometimes in connection with them, the sharia networks turned to promoting jihad in Syria. The Danes of the Call to Islam joined the battlefields very early on. In 2012, Shiraz Tariq, the founder of this group and an acquaintance of Omar Bakri, went to northern Syria, where he was killed in action. Ryan also went there and emphasized the importance of his group in recruiting volunteers:

Call to Islam was the first group to send members to Syria in 2012, and the Danes were among the first to arrive there. [. . .] There have been 160 departures in total from Denmark, I believe, and Call to Islam is largely responsible for this. [. . .] We knew how to recruit and we had contacts almost everywhere. Among the people who left Aarhus, for example, we were the ones who won many of them over to our cause; they ended up sharing our approach and participating in our activities.[20]

The head of Danish intelligence at the time, Jakob Scharf, confirms:

One of the objectives of groups such as Sharia4UK or the Call of Islam in Denmark was to generate media hype. However, very quickly, the focus of their attention shifted to promoting the conflict in Syria.[21]

Ismaël, from Forsane al-Izza, confirmed that Syria had established itself as the horizon of the European Salafi-jihadist revival, of which they were standard-bearers:

Q: *What was your approach?*
A: The approach was not one of violent militantism, but more the idea that catastrophe was imminent in France, and that's still what I think, by the way,

and I'm not the only one. And obviously Syria was a catalyst for all these young people who thought like that.[22]

The fact that Syria became a hub for these people was not only due to their links with the pioneers, and it was not merely the culmination of their personal journey. Jihad in the Levant also served as an alternative to incarceration for those who were beginning to have legal problems.

In the spring of 2012, in France, Mohammed Merah, a Toulouse native who had returned from the Pakistani tribal areas and was close to the Clain family, committed the first jihadist attacks in the country since 1996, killing seven people, including unarmed soldiers and three children, in front of a Jewish school. The investigation led to the prosecution of the Forsane al-Izza network, whose activities were taking an increasingly bellicose turn. They planned to assassinate a French judge of Jewish faith and made frequent trips to Molenbeek, where they were in contact with Sharia4Belgium leaders and sought to arm themselves.[23] One of the magistrates in charge of the case looked back the affair:

> When we arrested the members of the Forsane al-Izza network in 2012, we worried that we had "caught" them too early, but the investigation of their files revealed that we had arrested them just in time. They were ready to take action.[24]

Several Forsane al-Izza activists, who were the subject of a judicial investigation, fled to Syria without waiting for their trial in France. Ismaël, who was arrested, recounts:

> I also thought about leaving. Especially since, at the beginning of 2012, I could feel the noose tightening.[25]

Similar scenarios were occurring in all the countries concerned. In early May 2012, in Germany, a single event triggered many departures for Syria. For several months, the country had been experiencing a new kind of tension. A group called *Die Wahre Religion* ("The True Religion"), close to the groups we've been dealing with, organized a national campaign to distribute the Koran, imitating a scheme tried out a year earlier in the Netherlands. Young people in full Salafist regalia took to the streets of dozens of municipalities, haranguing shoppers, and demanding the abolition of the German Constitution (Basic Law) and an end to the separation of religion and politics. A far-right group, which had been condemned for its unconstitutional and xenophobic positions, sought to react, and announced demonstrations in front of a Salafist mosque in Solingen and the King Fahd Academy in Bonn, a site of radicalization in the 1990s. The events spiraled out of control when the organizers said they would display the Danish caricatures of the Prophet. A German-speaking jihadist living in Afghanistan published a video in which he called for the immediate execution of anyone associated with this organization,[26] while the most prominent preachers from Salafist circles announced that they would be present on the day of the demonstration "to defend the honor of the Prophet." Two hundred Salafists went to Bonn on the day of the event, the "crème de la crème" of radical Islamism in Germany. Among them were Reda Seyam, a veteran of Bosnia, mentor to the Ulm pioneers, and active in Berlin and Vienna, and Deso Dogg, a rapper who had converted to Salafism and was close to Millatu Ibrahim, the German branch of those promoting sharia. Both ended up joining ISIS and attaining high-ranking positions. There are 250 anarchist militants, close to the "black bloc" movements. The Salafists gathered, prayed in the street, warmed up, chanted "Allahu akbar," and shouted anti-Semitic slogans.

The authorities, who couldn't cancel the event, opted for a form of risk prevention. The few dozen far-right sympathizers were surrounded by police trucks to prevent the caricatures from being seen. One neo-Nazi, seeing a gap, climbed on the shoulders of a comrade and made sure the crowd on the other side of the cordon had a view of the cartoon. This is exactly what the crowd was expecting, and the situation got out of hand. The police were attacked by the Islamists, who saw them as acting in concert with the far right, revealing a hidden desire on the part of the institutions and society to humiliate Muslims. One of them lunged at the police officers with a knife, stabbing three of them, who were evacuated. In the end, 30 police were injured, and 109 Salafists were arrested. A national controversy ensued. Germany witnessed the reality of virulent Salafism and the potential for a return of the far right, just when the spectre of Nazism seemed to have been banished. Several dozen "hardline" Islamists, prosecuted for their participation in the violence that day, fled to Syria to escape their trial.[27]

In Belgium, Sharia4Belgium was gaining in power, and starting to send volunteers, both men and women, to Syria, which its members described as an extension of the "Belgian front." The group disrupted a conference at the University of Antwerp, and sympathizers also joined their comrades from Sharia4Holland to intimidate the Muslim feminist activist Irshad Manji in Amsterdam. A dozen or so others sought to prevent Caroline Fourest from speaking; men with their faces wrapped in keffiyehs and women hidden under *burkas* shouted "stone her!" from the audience. Sharia4Belgium was active both on the internet and on the ground. In Molenbeek, a local offender, Abdelhamid Abaaoud, attended their "religion course." A year later he would leave for Syria, and would eventually become the leader of the commando unit of the November 13 attacks in Paris. One of the teachers at Sharia4Belgium was a Toulousain, friend of the Clain family, suspected of having been the first to consider an attack on the Bataclan at the time when he was active in the Salafist institutes of Cairo.[28] Members of Sharia4Belgium wandered in packs in the city center, as one resident relates: "They came in groups of four, they were young, in their early twenties, and they didn't work. They wore jellabiyas, so they were stood out. The recruiters of women are other women, but they did this more in houses, not on the street."[29] In the summer of 2012, the group was banned, while renowned French and Belgian Salafists organized a "council of Muslim reflections" in Molenbeek. The networks switched their focus to Syria. In addition to almost all the leaders of Sharia4Belgium, no fewer than seventy-nine Belgians out of a total of nearly six hundred who left to fight in the Levant were directly linked to the organization. Fouad Belkacem, the founder of the group in Antwerp, was arrested while trying to join his recruits. In 2015, he was sentenced to twelve years in prison for his role as a recruiter.

Point of No Return (2013)

The year 2013 was marked by the intensification of all the dynamics described above. On the Syrian front, the aims of the various jihadist groups differed. A split occurred between the supporters of Al-Qaeda (Al-Nusra), who favored an Islamist revolution against the regime of Bashar al-Assad, and those of ISIS. The latter sought to resume the

"Islamic State" project in the region and proclaim a caliphate there. The idea was met with opposition from most of the rebel groups and led to extremely violent clashes between the different factions, in which many Western volunteers took part.

Despite this poisonous climate, Europeans continued to flock to the Levant, including most of the future ISIS propagandists. Berlin rapper Deso Dogg, co-founder of the group Millatu Ibrahim, oversaw IS's German-speaking communications. Adams Johansen, former spokesman for a Danish Salafist movement, was also active on the ground. Abu Rumaysah, a British citizen of Pakistani origin, who organized patrols (*hisba*) for Al-Muhajiroun in the streets of London, also flew to the Levant, where he would publish a humorous tourist guide presenting a gilded view of life in the "caliphate." Finally, French Salafists, including the former editor of the YouTube channel "Ana Muslim," are joined the Syrian forces, where they founded the French-language ISIS magazine *Dar al-Islam*, based on the model of *Inspire*.

After the Merah affair in France, the United Kingdom was also hit. On May 22, 2013, a rifleman named Lee Rigby, aged 25, just back from service in Afghanistan, walked to the Woolwich base, in the southeast of the capital. Michael Adebolajo and Michael Adebowale, converts of Nigerian origin in their twenties, were driving in the vicinity of the barracks, waiting for a military target. On seeing Rigby, the driver pressed down on the accelerator and ran into the soldier. The two accomplices got out of the vehicle and mutilated the Briton's lifeless body in front of numerous witnesses. Adebolajo ordered one of the passers-by to record the scene on his cell phone. He brandished a meat cleaver with blood dripping from his hands, gloating that he had "avenged the Muslims killed by the British army" and adding: "An eye for an eye and a tooth for a tooth."[30] The killers were arrested, but the images posted on social networks were soon seen by people around the world.

In July 2013, one of the accused was beaten in the corridors of the high-security prison in Belmarsh where he was being held: pinned against a wall, he lost two teeth. He filed a complaint against five wardens, who were suspended during the investigation, and demanded 25,000 pounds in compensation, sparking popular anger. The charges were finally dropped and the guards reinstated. Four months later, on November 18, 2013, the highly charged trial began at Central Criminal

Court, known as the Old Bailey. The accomplices pleaded not guilty and declared that they did not recognize the legitimacy of the court. Michael Adebolajo introduced himself by his jihadist name of "Mujahid Abu Hamza" and as a "soldier of Allah," a statement similar to that of Salah Abdeslam, the only survivor of the commando unit in the November 2015 attacks in Paris, at the opening of his trial in September 2021. Adebolajo was sentenced to life imprisonment, while his accomplice received a mandatory minimum sentence of 45 years.

As Syria fell deeper into crisis, public debate in the United Kingdom intensified. But just like in the Merah affair, the dominant interpretation portrayed these individuals as "lone wolves," dangerous deviants who were isolated in the British landscape. Like many terrorists before them, however, they were active members of Al-Muhajiroun, and one of them even protested alongside Anjem Choudary in 2007. The public debate dealt with them but not their environment, even though, for the first time in European history, hundreds of nationals were flocking to Syria and planning terrorist operations. A year before the explosion of ISIS, and although this was not yet reflected in the media coverage, jihadism was taking on extraordinary importance in Europe.

Same Combat in Dinslaken and Lunel

The final element of the pre-ISIS jihadist reconfigurations was the appearance of new ecosystems that grew up around patterns of transmission between pioneers and natives. In addition to the movements following the Bonn events and the networks of Millatu Ibrahim, the first departures from Germany were from the industrial belt of the Ruhr, specifically the working-class neighborhood of Lohberg, in Dinslaken, a municipality of six thousand inhabitants. The population of Turkish descent had been severely affected by unemployment since the closure of the mines in 2006, and had been exposed to a great deal of Salafist preaching. The Millatu Ibrahim movement, which was close to Sharia networks, set up a branch (it already had branches in Berlin, Solingen, Hamburg, and Frankfurt). Between 2011 and 2013, Salafist preachers who were well known in Germany brought around twenty young people together at a site provided by the local authorities. They gave them lessons and taught them the group's ideology. Almost all of them ended up in Syria. "We didn't see it coming in 2013, because these young people didn't preach violence," admits a representative of the city's integration council.[31] The pattern is reminiscent of the case of Lunel, France, Verviers, Belgium, and several Scandinavian cities: departures exploded and then quickly dried up after the entire group arrived in the Levant. The cities concerned were often places where Salafi-jihadist ideas were transmitted late. The communication took place directly between pioneers and locals, without the prior establishment of veterans. Thus, the pool of "candidates" for jihad was quickly depleted, because the local preaching machine was recent, not very complex, and only concerned a small group of individuals. The suddenness of the situation was matched by the shock of locals, who were suddenly confronted with an unimaginable reality. This was often followed by resentment toward the "bad press" these municipalities received in the media, which was beginning to take interest in the phenomenon.

2

ISIS, *an Attempt at Jihadist Submersion*

In the summer of 2014, the Syrian conflict was the deadliest in the world. The opposition to Bashar al-Assad was no longer in a position to overthrow him, and the army was incapable of quelling the insurgency. Entire swathes of the country were living in a war economy and falling prey to militias. The country was the battlefield of a three-way confrontation. A civil war was still raging between the regime, supported on the ground by Hezbollah and Shiite battalions, and the insurgents, who were divided but increasingly dominated by Salafist brigades. A diplomatic confrontation pitted the Russians and Iranians, who were close to Damascus, against the United States and the European powers, who pushed for the departure of Bashar al-Assad. In addition, the Kurds were fighting ISIS in the northeast, but saw a window of opportunity to unify their "nation," which straddles Turkey, Syria, Iraq, and Iran, thereby rekindling ancient fault lines.[1] The internal clashes between jihadist groups in the North were superimposed on these multiple layers.

In this chaotic context, ISIS announced, on June 29, 2014, the first day of Ramadan, that it had re-established the "caliphate" of Islam in Mosul, Iraq's second-largest city, ninety years after its abolition in Istanbul.[2] Its leader, Abu Bakr al-Baghdadi, granted himself the status of commander of all Muslims (*amir al-mominin*), and urged believers from all over the world to come and populate the new "State."

ISIS's Warning Shot

The news sent shockwaves through the jihadist galaxy. The organization tried to construct a semblance of administration around a slogan: "Persist and expand" (*baqiya wa tatamadad*). In his first sermon as "caliph" on July 7, 2014, at the Al-Nouri Mosque in Mosul, Abu Bakr al-Baghdadi invited "[religious] scholars, jurists, especially [Islamic] judges, as well as individuals with military, administrative, or logistical expertise, and doctors and engineers in all fields of specialization" to support their project of state construction.[3]

Jihad thus went from being a religious doctrine of liberation to a concrete way of life within a proto-state. This led to a change in status for all those participating in the project and a major upheaval in the political economy of jihadism. The group itself, as all other organizations had done to that point, was welcoming foreign fighters: it condemned to hell those who did not "emigrate" to its territory. In this view, all those who pledged allegiance to the caliphate were brothers and sisters, while all those who did not were accomplices of the impious order – "hypocrites," "apostates," and enemies. The jihadists no longer felt the need to convince "the masses" of the merits of their actions. As the vanguard, they called on believers to respond personally to what they saw as the very embodiment of the Islamic ideal. Did they or did they not wish to live under the caliphate? Were they or were they not "true Muslims"? This polarization of positions (for or against the caliphate), the product of a rational tautology, allowed for the emergence of a divide specific to Muslim eschatology, between "good" and "bad" believers, between the pious and the ungodly. This was all the more pressing given that, according to ISIS's millenarian vision, the "caliphate" was to emerge during the battle at the end of time: the faithful would soon be confronted with the Last Judgment. As a French Salafist named Amine, who was convinced after initially being skeptical, explained the way he saw the dilemma in the following terms:

If you're a Muslim and the caliphate is proclaimed, you have to take a stand. Everyone has to take a stand, that's how it is. At the beginning Al-Baghdadi's arguments about the return of the caliphate didn't convince me; I was especially skeptical of his qualifications. But as time went by, I started to change.[4]

The Echo of the Call to the "Caliphate" in Europe

In Europe, the re-establishment of the "caliphate" was the fulfillment of the ideal that hundreds of extremely ideological militants publicly pursued.

An initial show of support took place in The Hague, the Netherlands, home to the International Criminal Court and a city that symbolizes peace, and also the home city of the murderer of Theo van Gogh, some of those behind the logistics of the Madrid attacks, and the first members of Sharia4Holland. Less than a week after the proclamation of IS, around fifty supporters, led by a local Salafist, carried the group's black banner at a rally in the working-class Schilderswijk neighborhood, presented as a demonstration against Israeli operations in Gaza. No arrests were made, but slogans were shouted: "The dirty Jews in the sewers must be killed," and, in Arabic, "*mawt al-yahoud*" – "death to the Jews." Journalists were attacked and had to take refuge behind police officers. Some of the protestors posted a video on YouTube in which they posed in front of a high-rise building with IS flags around them, with one of them describing The Hague as a "jihad city." Twenty days later, on July 24, a second gathering, identical to the first, was held. The leader of the movement was invited onto live television programs to defend his positions, which he did without going back on any of them.[5] The Dutch government made the public display of the ISIS flag a criminal offense. On the sidelines of the event, several local Salafist imams made ambivalent statements about the IS initiative. One of them, spokesman for a dialogue platform called "Bewust," said: "All Muslims are automatically in favor of re-establishing an Islamic state, but it is still too early to say whether IS is the one we are waiting for. We do not know enough about this organization, and religious scholars are divided on this issue." In the same vein, the spokesman for another group, Moslims in Dialoog, in charge of relations with the Dutch authorities, explained to the press what he believed to be the middle way. Giving unreliable figures, he strangely underestimated the proportion of those opposed to IS. He distinguished three categories: a "small portion" of the Dutch Muslim community who "unconditionally supports IS" and "applauds everything they do." He then mentioned those who were "a little more numerous, who totally condemn IS," before clarifying his position: "As for us, like the vast majority [of Dutch Muslims], we are neither for nor against IS, we have a more nuanced position."[6] The Hague would see nearly thirty departures for IS, mainly from the Schilderswijk neighborhood.

On Saturday, August 9, 2014, on Oxford Circus, London's busiest shopping street, former students of Omar Bakri and Anjem Choudary distributed leaflets calling for the caliphate to be extended to the whole world. Positioned outside the low-cost clothing store Topshop, they accosted shoppers in the manner of the Dutch and Germans before them. The leaflet stated that the "caliphate has been established" and that a "new era has just begun."[7]

It emphasized the responsibility of Muslims to pledge allegiance to the caliph and obey it, and the obligation to emigrate to the heart of war-torn Syria. One passerby, a British Muslim of Iraqi origin and a gynecologist by profession, asked them why they supported ISIS. This led them to harangue her: one of them called her a "whore," while another, a red-bearded convert, said that she "should be killed like those Christians in Iraq." Anjem Choudary, the leader of Sharia4UK, acknowledged that these were indeed his former followers and emphasized to the press that there is "no harm" in wanting to live and raise children under the caliphate. At the end of the month, the security threat in Britain was upgraded from "significant" to "high."

At the same time, the number of departures to Syria and Iraq was increasing dramatically, reflecting the long-ignored geography of European jihadism described in the introduction.

In France, Great Britain, Germany, Belgium, the Netherlands, Denmark, Sweden, and Spain, departures mainly occurred in groups, most often of family members or within extended circles of friends, in environments that had been exposed to the preaching of veterans or pioneers and their entourage. Almost all departures can be explained by these ideological and emotional affiliations in places where consciousness-raising had occurred. They came from a limited number of areas, which were neither the poorest, nor the most marginalized, nor those with the highest proportion of Muslims. The cities and neighborhoods most affected were both the old centers of the phenomenon and their new outskirts.

Given the nature of the ISIS project, departures for the jihad fronts were also thought of as religious emigration (or *hijra*). The ambition to populate a new "empire" under the jihadist flag led to sympathizers coming to the area with their wives and children in a logic of settlement, migration in the strict sense, which intrinsically resembled colonial logic. In this sense, it was very different from the logic that drove the supporters of freedom to go and fight for the Republican cause against Franco's fascism during the Spanish Civil War of the 1930s.[8] Indeed, the extremely localized dimension of the departures hewed to most examples of international migration, which is explained better by social capital, such as family or local contacts, than poverty levels.[9] The American researcher and authority on the subject, Myron Weiner, notes: "If there is a single 'law' in migration, it is that a migration flow, once begun, induces its own flow. Migrants enable their friends and relatives back home to migrate by providing them with information about how to migrate, resources to facilitate movement, and assistance in finding jobs and housing."[10] Robert Leiken makes a similar point: "migration research almost always exhibits a flow from a *particular* point of origin to a *particular* destination as if these two points were somehow metaphysically linked."[11] From Toulouse to Raqqa, from Copenhagen to Aleppo, or from London to Mosul, new kinds of pairings were emerging between Europe and the Levant, updating the geography of contemporary jihad.

The "caliphate" project opened doors to people left aside by Al-Qaeda's selective recruitment: children, the elderly, recent converts, opportunists, and the unstable, but also women. ISIS took care of "sorting" the volunteers once they arrived in Syria, where they were closely supervised by the jihadist administration. The totalitarian structure in place allowed the group to assign individuals to various tasks that served its military and colonial interests. The most brutal were assigned to conducting interrogations, watching over detainees, or opening new fronts. Experienced thieves, familiar with police procedures, participated in external operations requiring false papers, transportation, and the purchase of assault rifles. "Intellectuals," ideologues fascinated by doctrine, musicians, or aspiring journalists, such as the German rapper Deso Dogg or the Clain brothers, were made responsible for propaganda and ideological dissemination through all possible channels. In addition to these groups, there were throngs of religious fanatics, criminals in search of spiritual or personal redemption, long-standing Salafists, and newcomers for whom joining jihadism was their first form of commitment. The common ground between all these groups was the same as the one that had existed thirty years earlier: adherence to a set of common values defined by Salafi-jihadist dogma, which was still used as a moral code and presented as a creed (*aqida*). Other recurring features should be mentioned. Firstly, the fact that, apart from some criminals, most of the supporters of ISIS were Islamist militants before becoming jihadists. They were generally sensitized to this by movements close to the Muslim Brotherhood, Hizb ut-Tahrir, the Tabligh, or Salafism (and sometimes all four). Where this was not the case, and they had joined ISIS with no previous experience of militancy, members of their entourage had been involved in these movements and exposed them to their teachings. Half of the Europeans concerned also shared a criminal past and a spell in prison. Linked by the internet, they would in turn generate new departures in their circle of acquaintances, giving rise to the beginnings of a "massification" of the phenomenon in highly exposed environments.

The 6,000 Europeans who went to Syria indicate the scale of the phenomenon. However, this figure is low when compared to the number of potential sympathizers in Europe (see chapter 3). ISIS's zeal, their indiscriminate attacks, and the apocalyptic tenor of their discourse discouraged even some of those who were the most motivated to join them.

Women, the Blind Spot of Jihadism

While September 11, 2001 marks the birth of European jihadism, because it led to the appearance of the pioneers, the creation of the "caliphate" marks its maturity and the point at which it became aware of itself. In this respect, its ability to incorporate women was undoubtedly its most fundamental upheaval, the one most likely to lead lasting reconfigurations. Female activists were the key element in creating a truly European jihadism, which is a feature of the age of the natives.

Women had no involvement in jihadism before IS. Bin Laden sometimes praised them for their support.[12] But they had been a point of contention since the movement's inception. Leading ideologues, such as the Jordanian Al-Maqdissi, systematically condemned the arrival of women in a territory at war.

The militantism of women, less spectacular and less visible than that of men, received little public attention until the end of the 2010s;[13] this was also due to their limited involvement in major terrorist projects until then. A few emblematic figures emerged from the shadow of their spouses, such as the Belgian-Swiss woman Malika El Aroud, a "pioneer" of the 1990s. Another Belgian, Muriel Degauque, is also important for having been the first Westerner, and the only one to date, to complete a suicide attack, in Iraq in 2006, as we mentioned above. Many others, less famous, have been leaders behind the scenes, such as Filiz Gelowicz, wife of the Ulm terrorist, supported by dozens of people during her trial in 2009, and the subject of glowing coverage on the German-speaking Salafist forum Ahlus-Sunna. Female involvement, focused on indoctrination between "sisters" and the consolidation of internal ties within the movement, gives pride of place to the "invisible" methods typical of jihadism at low tide. It therefore went largely unnoticed until the rise of ISIS.

By establishing itself as a "state," the IS opened its doors to women, who represented about seventeen percent of the contingent originating from Western Europe – just over 1,000 individuals (including 385 French women). In total, they made up thirteen percent of the estimated 41,000 foreigners in the country, or just over 5,000 people.[14]

But these numbers, however large they may have been, were insufficient to guarantee a spouse for each combatant, not to mention to satisfy their desire for polygamy, which led the IS to "outsource" women from populations designated as inferior, notably the Yazidis. These followers of an ancient syncretic belief system were accused of "polytheism." During the summer of 2014, thousands of Yazidi men were massacred, and 7,000 women were taken captive and reduced to sexual slavery.[15] Girls and their mothers were sold for a few hundred dollars (more for virgins) in human markets run by the organization in Mosul. A video filmed by IS members showed several of them jeering as they discussed the trade in minors: "Where is my little Yazidi?" asked one of them. "If she is fifteen, I have to inspect her, check her teeth," adds another.[16] According to the understanding of universal Islamic morality provided by the ISIS sheikhs, these cloistered women had a duty to be submissive to their masters, just as the latter were submissive to Allah. According to the cycle of order and submission: "Slaves will give birth to their masters."[17] The ISIS dogma with regard to sexuality can be summed up as puritanism in the service of male impulses. Beyond religious justifications, this arrangement maintained internal order. It was an integral part of workings that were entirely oriented towards war and the exercise of total power over each individual, which requires spaces for the release of primal urges. The treatment meted out to homosexuals, thrown from the tops of buildings and stoned once on the ground, was another sinister manifestation of this.

From a sociological standpoint, women are representative of the transformations that are characteristic of the natives. Western women tend to be younger, less trained, and less educated than their male counterparts. The proportion of converts is also higher. They are often more deeply integrated into the jihadist worlds they join. Johannes Saal notes, for example, that two thirds of those belonging to the movements in the German-speaking countries were already married to jihadists; this was true of only 12.5 percent of men.[18] The women were also divisible into categories, just as the men were. In addition to the propagandists and logistics experts, some women, craving structure, saw in the ultra-standardized and ultra-conservative ISIS straitjacket a religious redemption, a "purification" similar to that of criminals or traffickers who saw the practice of jihad as an outlet capable of washing away a life spent in sin.

Their place under ISIS rule depended on their marital status. A woman who wanted to be a jihadist had to have married a jihadist. This, and the fact that single women were kept in closed spaces (*maaqar*) until they accepted a suitor, explains the speed with which some chose their fiancés. The strict separation of sexes under IS encouraged women to exercise strong social control over each other, as is clear in the remarks of Aïssam, a French jihadist, who recalls his wife being chastised by other women for her hasty marriage to him:

> It's not easy. My wife was insulted by the other women because she left the *ma'aqar* too quickly! They criticized her for not having been patient enough.[19]

The entrance of women into the movement shows that the cause was not limited to fighting or attacks. Though they were in principle forbidden from participating in armed struggle, they played various roles: spouses, mothers, educators, and propagandists in charge of bringing in other followers. On a symbolic level, their arrival gave substance to the jihadist project, bestowed upon it a family dimension, and implied a level of diversity within IS. Their arrival suggested that the volunteers were settling in and planning to populate the "caliphate," and thus played into the idea that ISIS was founding a new world in its image. The establishment of a "state" meant jihadism was a way of life and a societal project, and the families within it were the repositories of the "culture" it sought to transmit, the education and values it aimed to instil in its offspring. The primary duty of mothers was thus to raise and educate their children according to the principles of Salafi-jihadism – in other words, to indoctrinate them and pass jihadism on to them as a sort of inheritance.

Female involvement thus led to a deepening of the jihadist phenomenon, all the while that it reshaped the latter. Where jihadism was once structured in closed microcosms, semi-professionalized male terrorist cells, it was now, under IS, taking shape in family cells, following more complex modalities that were at once horizontal and vertical. On a very small scale, this paved the way for the creation of jihadist lineages, and thus for processes of tribalization of the European movement outside periods of high tide.

Approximately 1,500 minors from Western Europe – a quarter of the total population – grew up in this setting. Although the figure is difficult to verify, at least 730 babies were born to foreign parents under the "caliphate," and almost none of them possessed a birth certificate.[20] From a very young age, they were taught the glorification of jihad and martyrdom; they received their first military training before puberty. Infant mortality rates were among the highest in the world, and living conditions, in an existence punctuated by war and lack of healthcare, were deplorable. Among the testimonies to have emerged from this period, many referred to women giving birth alone, contracting illnesses in the absence of medical assistance, and seeing their infants die. ISIS defined children under the age of nine within its ranks as "innocents," who, should they die, would be accorded an immediate place in paradise. This served as a sort of "overcompensation," in that the dead child was granted the ultimate reward by Allah, that of eternal paradise. Starting from the age of ten, children became eligible for the physical and military preparation program, with a view to training the battalions of tomorrow.

Apart from these responsibilities, women were strictly regulated by the ultra-conservative orthodoxy in force under ISIS, and kept in an even stricter totalitarian stranglehold than their male companions. Within this interpretation of Islam, women had the status of perpetual minors, and could never do without the supervision, in the literal and figurative sense, of a *mahram* (a male contact, often a close relative). They were invisible under their full veils, and everything was done to prevent them from escaping their reproductive role, on which the internal balance of ISIS depended. When the men were not fighting, women had to stay by their sides. When they went to the front, their wives were taken care of by their peers. When all the brigades were deployed at the same time, the women were grouped together in the *maaqar*, where they were not allowed to have contact with the opposite sex. A French jihadist in Raqqa said the following about this in an internet conversation:[21]

These methods of partitioning social life were presented as a guarantee of women's "purity" and a means of preventing adultery (which was punishable by stoning).

In practice, however, the very high male attrition rate under ISIS often led to women remarrying a number of times, following successive waves of "martyrs." Many Western women became widows several times, each time remarrying and thus bearing children with several different fathers. High death rates and the close supervision of women paradoxically led to the emergence of a kind of involuntary female sexual vagrancy within the ultra-rigid framework of jihadism.

Because female jihadists were not sufficiently understood in their specificity, their importance tended to be underestimated, and this was reflected in the treatment they received. Until 2016, European countries did not systematically condemn female "returnees." Yasmina, a French convert whom I met in a prison in the Paris region, shared her observations:

> Women don't run many risks when they return from Syria. [. . .] Of the 50 to 80 women who have returned, only about ten are in prison. I also know girls from my neighborhood who have left and have not been questioned [by the French authorities]. So basically jihad is attractive and cheap for women . . .[22]

This is an example of women being overlooked. The few female volunteers who made the news were those who participated in attempted attacks, like the four French women involved in the so-called gas cylinder case aimed at blowing up Notre-Dame-de-Paris.

The Attacks

As with the Islamists in Peshawar in the 1980s, Europeans saw moving to the "caliphate" as an opportunity to break from the "godless" order in which they grew up. As such, they applied the precepts of the American Anwar al-Awlaqi, whom some jihadists I have met, such as Ryan in Denmark, consider to be the "Bin Laden of European jihadism." In 2005, al-Awlaqi explained that emigration to Islamic countries and participation in jihad in the West should be considered on the same level: "Some will say, 'I was born in the West, so where do I go?' Well, if you are aware of the fact that the West is not just any land of impiety, that it fights Islam in the media and on the battlefields, then your obligation is either to retaliate with the sword, or to go to a Muslim country (if possible) and wage jihad there."[23] He added that those who remained in the West had a moral obligation to fight wherever they happened to be, because they were in the position of infiltrators "behind enemy lines." Jihad, he argued, should become "as British as five o'clock tea":[24] "They live in the lion's den and form the first line of defence in the battle of ideas."[25]

Pledging allegiance to ISIS meant engaging in "disavowal": namely, the ontological denial of the West and the values associated with democratic societies. Ismaël, the French supporter of Forsane al-Izza, explained this as follows:

Leaving for Syria meant choosing a side. Those who left chose to deny their Western identity, and the idea of returning to commit attacks in France was the high point for them, it was perfect.[26]

In Salafi-jihadist logic, leaving to join IS, making the *hijra*, became the first act of jihad. Likewise, those who didn't leave were justified in killing any "infidel," anywhere in the world, for the glory of jihad.

The campaign of attacks in Europe was the peak of the third cycle of Western jihadism, the most serious thus far. Between 2013 and 2018, the western part of the continent was hit by dozens of attacks. France, Germany, Great Britain, and Belgium, which accounted for three quarters of departures from the entire EU for Syria, were the hardest hit.

The unique feature of this period lay in the fact that ISIS's terror administration centralized the preparation of attacks, which were divided into three types. First, the *orchestrated* attacks in which ISIS sent those it had trained in the Levant back to Europe. Secondly, attacks in which it tried to *remotely control* supporters on the ground, pushing them towards targets to strike at home. Finally, those in which it sought to *inspire* the action of strangers who grasped the general meaning of the struggle, to act within enemy societies with all the means at their disposal.[27] The first category required sophisticated logistics, lengthy preparation, contacts in both Syria and Europe, and abundant funding. This category includes the November 2015 attacks in France and those of March 2016 in Brussels. It disappeared with the destruction of IS infrastructure from 2017 onwards. Remote-controlled operations accounted for the majority of terrorist acts claimed by ISIS in Europe. They required coordination among those ready to take action and target symbols – examples include the assassination of Father Jacques Hamel during a mass at Saint-Étienne-du-Rouvray on July 26, 2016, or the series of murders in Germany in 2017. Inspired operations were often carried out by unstable individuals who were quickly radicalized. Such operations were unpredictable, and while they were low-cost, they were no less dramatic than the others: examples include the events of July 14, 2016 in Nice, or December 21 in Berlin. This third form of attacks survived ISIS's organizational decline, and became a new low-tide, terrorist "norm," characteristic of the early 2020s.

The Terror Cell and the Networks of the Aleppo Hospital

It is impossible to understand the campaign of attacks in Europe without looking at a specific cell that took shape in a branch of the Aleppo hospital in 2013. At that point, Al-Nusra and ISIS were plagued by fratricidal clashes; ISIS was about to begin its conquest of Raqqa, where it would proclaim the caliphate a year later.

The path taken by the head of this cell itself summarizes many of the developments in European jihadism since the 1990s. Oussama Atar was a Belgian in his thirties, born in Brussels into a working-class family, with grandparents who came from Morocco. His journey was shaped primarily by the artisans of the preaching machine that took shape in his neighborhood. He grew up in Laeken, a neighboring municipality of Molenbeek, where some GIA veterans were beginning to be active. In his late teens, he frequented the circles of the Syrian sheikh Bassam Ayachi, who founded the neighborhood's first Salafist institute, and who had enormous influence in the local jihadist milieu. In the summer of 2001, they set off together for Aleppo in a camper van, a trip from which the young Atar returned with clearly defined ideas. In 2004, after spending several months learning Arabic in Damascus with Belgian and French pioneers, he crossed the Iraqi border. There, he took up arms against the US Army, and most likely took part in the battle of Fallujah alongside Al-Qaeda troops led by Zarqawi. Wounded as a result of mishandling a grenade, he was arrested by American forces in 2005 and imprisoned in Abu Ghraib. The prison complex, with an inscription at the entrance stating that "America is the friend of all Iraqis," is known to have been the site of CIA torture programs. Atar was then transferred to Camp Bucca, a huge detention center that at the time housed several men who would go on to form the highest level of ISIS leadership. While there, he developed close relationships with the future "caliph" Abu Bakr al-Baghdadi, and the future ISIS spokesman Al-Adnani. He perfected his Arabic dialect and acquired comprehensive knowledge of jihad. Anne Speckhard, professor of psychiatry at Georgetown University, who was tasked with implementing a "deradicalization" program that ended in the summer of 2007, describes a scene she would see daily: "On the surveillance cameras, we could see these extremists teaching other inmates how to make explosive devices by drawing in the sand. At night, they organized sharia courts and broke the arms of those accused of being informants."[28] Starting in 2006, Atar's family, supported by six leading members of the Brussels bar and a few Belgian diplomats, began taking steps to bring him back to his country. In 2010, the campaign received public support from local politicians and human rights associations,[29] who claimed that Atar was being held illegally in Iraq and was in poor health (he was said to be in need of treatment for kidney cancer), and that his return would not represent a security threat. He was repatriated in 2012, and all these assumptions were proven false. The Belgian State Security Service also looked favorably upon his return, confident that he could be used as an informant in radical circles;[30] this was reminiscent of failures in France (Mohammed Merah) and Germany (Martin Schneider, head of the Sauerland cell). The people involved in the "Save Oussama!" campaign, whether from civil society or the world of politics, seemed to have been struck with amnesia, hardly remembering their various roles in the course of events. Atar was placed under judicial supervision, the terms of which he soon broke; he visited his cousins in prison and encouraged them on the path of jihadism they had already begun to take. Among his circle of friends in Laeken and Molenbeek, the number of departures for Syria was increasing. He himself set out for the Levant at the end of 2013, where he was welcomed as a "legend" by Western jihadists.[31] His former comrades from the Iraqi prisons now led the most dangerous terrorist organization in the world, and catapulted him to the head of the external operations cell that would terrorize Europe for several years.

Atar became one of the most highly ranked Europeans in ISIS. He surrounded himself with zealous individuals who distinguished themselves by their cruelty while guarding some twenty Western hostages in the Aleppo hospital. Among their executioners were four hooded torturers with British accents, known to their captives by the nicknames John, Paul, George and Ringo, the "Beatles of jihad." Like Jihadi John, who was linked to an aborted attack in London in 2005 and had tried to join Shabab in Somalia four years later, their journeys often spoke volumes. In the basement of the hospital, they organized bare-knuckle fights between prisoners exhausted by poor nutrition, sparing the winner from being tortured. Several Belgians treated French-speaking hostages with the same sadism, such as Abdelhamid Abaaoud from Molenbeek, recruited by the Sharia4Belgium networks, and Najim Laachraoui; both men were involved in the Paris attacks a few months later.

The 2014 Campaign

In February 2014, a jihadist from Cannes who had recently returned from Syria was arrested by the French authorities as he was about to carry out an attack in Nice. Like many pioneers, he had traveled to the Levant in 2012 from the Salafist institutes in Cairo. The project was orchestrated from Syria in coordination with Jihadi John and approved by Osama Atar.

On May 24, Mehdi Nemmouche, a resident of Roubaix who made a name for himself as the executioner of French people at the Aleppo hospital, arrived in Molenbeek. To avoid possible surveillance, he took care to transit through Asia. His profile was one of the models valued by IS: he was a former criminal who turned to Salafism, much like Merah, to whom he would dedicate his massacres. In the middle of the afternoon, he entered the Jewish Museum of Belgium and murdered four people. He was arrested six days later at the Saint-Charles train station in Marseille, with the murder weapons in his suitcase. The first "returnee" of ISIS to carry out an attack on European soil, he was sentenced to life imprisonment. His case served as an alert for the authorities, but not so much that they were able to foresee the coming wave of attacks.

In the Levant, meanwhile, a campaign to execute the first Western hostages was taking shape. The "caliphate" had just been proclaimed, and IS had declared war on the United States and several Western countries via a series of macabre videos published on social networks and promoted in the group's media.

The detainees were shown kneeling in orange jumpsuits, recalling Zarqawi's reference to the clothing from Guantanamo ten years earlier. The torturers, members of the external operations cell, looked at the camera and addressed heads of state and government leaders. The aim was to push the Western powers to launch a ground intervention that would lead to a new military quagmire in the Middle East. ISIS leaders hoped to rally all the jihadist factions, and pushed an apocalyptic narrative when they took to the microphone. On August 19, 2014, James Foley, a photographer held by the organization, was the first to be murdered by the "Beatles of jihad." The video of his beheading was posted on social networks, and Jihadi John called out to Barack Obama on camera: America, he said, should prepare for "a bloodbath." The journalist's execution actually turned out to be the first dip in ISIS's fortunes, because no matter how strongly the international powers responded, they were not going to risk a ground operation. Barack Obama returned to the Iraqi issue, which he had neglected since 2011, and formed an international coalition to defeat ISIS. Applying the lessons of the victory in Iraq during the previous decade, the plan was to provide material support to regional allies, mainly Arab-Kurdish forces, and to guarantee them extensive air cover. On September 10, shortly after the "Beatles" executed another American reporter, Steven Sotloff, eighty-five nations joined the coalition and bombed the terrorist group's positions. Brahim, a French jihadist, discusses what he sees as a major mistake by IS:

> What killed IS was that they rushed things. When they slaughtered the American journalists, I was in prison in Fleury-Mérogis. I saw it on TV and I said, "They're dead!" [. . .]. The people of *Dawla* [ISIS], by attacking everyone, destroyed themselves.[32]

Three days after the first attacks, the spokesman of the "caliphate," Al-Adnani, called for attacks on the coalition countries, first and foremost the United States. France was also mentioned five times.[33] The declaration confirmed the turn towards terrorism that the group had taken since its early days, and the formation of the external operations unit in 2013. It was yet another validation of ISIS's ambition to plan deadly operations at the heart of European democracies.

This chronological reminder is essential because it contradicts the propaganda of ISIS, which, in accordance with jihadist custom, systematically presented its misdeeds as "reprisals" for actions attributed to those they designated as enemies. Thus, the attacks of 1995 in Paris, of 9/11, of 2004 in Madrid, and of 2005 in London, not to mention the massacres in Toulouse and Montauban in 2012, or the killing of the British soldier in 2013, were systematically portrayed as legitimate and proportionate responses. The victims, whether they were three-year-old children or Parisians sitting on a terrace, were inserted into a game of equivalence that suited the Salafist logic of allegiance: they were all morally and politically guilty simply by "belonging" to godless societies that they did not "disavow." The IS propaganda effort thus sought to invert relationships between events so as to claim that their acts belonged to an Islamic form of "legitimate defense." This was reminiscent of the logic of the London-based "intellectuals" close to Anwar al-Awlaqi, who attempted to show that jihadist attacks were compatible with the Geneva Convention.

Once again, this rhetoric targeted public, democratic debate, seeking to relativize jihadist horrors and create political polarization. The strategy itself was not surprising. What was surprising was that similar arguments appeared in the European media and intellectual spheres. The idea that the attacks were planned "in reaction" to the bombing of ISIS positions was put forward, for example, by some defense lawyers during the first weeks of the trial for the attacks of November 13 in Paris, in which we testified.

An editorial that appeared a few years later in ISIS's English-language propaganda magazine offers a key to interpreting this: "We hate you, first and foremost because you are infidels [. . .], because you live in liberal and secularized societies that permit what Allah has forbidden. [. . .] As for the atheist fringe, we hate you and wage war on you because you do not believe in the existence of our Lord. [. . .] What is important to understand is that, even if some claim that your foreign policy is the cause of our hatred, it is in fact secondary [. . .]. The truth is that even if you stop bombing us [. . .], we will continue to hate you, because the main cause of this hatred will not go away until you embrace Islam."[34]

The year 2014 ended as it had begun, with jihadists stepping up their torture, and their tirades against Europe. In mid-September, the executioners lectured the British Prime Minister, David Cameron, while they murdered an English humanitarian, David Haines; three weeks later, they killed Alan Henning, a taxi driver from Manchester who had come to volunteer to help the Syrian people. On November 17, 2014, Jihadi John, in association with Maxime Hauchard, a convert from Normandy, murdered the American journalist Peter Kassig and twenty-two Syrian prisoners, calling them "apostates." The presence of the Frenchman was intended to respond to a statement by Marine Le Pen, who claimed that "French jihadists do not come from the Norman countryside," it was a sign, in other words, of their desire to insert themselves into national political debates and directly confront the far right.

January–February 2015: The Bloody Return of the Cartoons

A few weeks later, the first attacks in Paris took place. The sequence of events is now well known. On January 7, 2015, the Kouachi brothers, who moved in the Salafist circles of the Buttes-Chaumont neighborhood in Paris and in the entourage of a Frenchman who had taken part in the jihad in Iraq, entered the newsroom of the satirical weekly *Charlie Hebdo*. They shot twelve people and left eleven wounded. The following day, Amedy Coulibaly, a former criminal who was radicalized in prison and was a friend of the Kouachi brothers, shot a policewoman in Montrouge; on January 9, he opened fire in a Hyper Cacher supermarket. He was killed in the ensuing assault by special forces, shortly after the Kouachi brothers, and left a video pledging allegiance to ISIS. His wife went to Syria, where she was honored with the status of "martyr's widow."

The *Charlie Hebdo* massacre gave concrete form to a scenario that dozens of activists in Scandinavia and elsewhere had considered for the offices of *Jyllands-Posten* and the cartoonists who had participated in the newspaper's initiative. Flemming Rose, the journalist behind the initiative, who has since been under continuous police protection, looked back on that tragic day:

> I think it was the worst work day of my life. I was sitting in an editorial meeting when I received a text message telling me there had been gunshots at Charlie Hebdo. [. . .] I knew several of them, I had worked with Wolinski . . . It was truly horrific . . . but I have to say I wasn't that surprised. I think no one who followed what happened at Charlie Hebdo between 2006 and 2015 was surprised by what happened that day. [. . .] The fact that two men could walk into their offices and open fire with Kalashnikovs changed the entire security landscape in Europe. I know from my own experience with police protection that the way the services operate in the face of the jihadist threat changed that day in Europe.[35]

As Flemming Rose suggests, the attacks triggered the first serious reckoning with jihadism just as the latter was reaching its third peak. On

January 11, the largest demonstrations since the liberation of Paris took place, with some 50 heads of state from all over the world marching at the front of a procession of more than 1.5 million citizens in the capital; four million people in total took part throughout France. In the space of a few weeks, the authorities tried to make up for their many delays. Departures for Syria were systematically impeded, police cooperation within the EU was strengthened, and programs to combat radicalization were created or revised. Close attention was paid to the propagandists on the continent and in prisons. In the UK, Anjem Choudary was prosecuted for having publicly called for people to join ISIS, and sentenced to five years in prison. He would be released three years later, in 2018. His mentor, Omar Bakri, the emir of Londonistan now based in Lebanon, boasted at the same time of having sent "hundreds of Europeans to fight in Syria," including his own children, who would die fighting for IS.

Return to Copenhagen: The Endless Spiral of "Revenge"

A month later, Copenhagen was the scene of a series of attacks whose targets mirrored those in Paris: cartoonists and intellectuals, a Jewish community center, and police officers on duty. On February 14, 2015, a debate was organized at the Krudttønden cultural center, entitled "Art, Blasphemy and Freedom of Expression," with the stated aim of considering the assassination of the *Charlie Hebdo* editorial staff in the city where the cartoons affair began. The discussion was opened by the French ambassador to Denmark, François Zimeray, and took place in the presence of Swedish cartoonist Lars Vilks and Femen activist Inna Shevchenko. Just as the latter was about to speak, a gunman entered the room and pointed a gun at the speakers in front of an audience of about thirty participants. He killed a film director who tried to intervene and injured three police officers during his escape. The following night, he reappeared in front of the capital's main synagogue. A security guard prevented him from entering the synagogue, where seventy young people were celebrating a bat mitzvah, and paid with his life. The assailant was shot at by the police but again escaped. Late that night, in the north of the capital, he attempted to break into the home of a well-known person who was under police protection – it seems that he planned the break-in in advance. Spotted by the guards, he opened fire, but was fatally hit. He was quickly identified as Omar el-Hussein, a 22-year-old Dane of Palestinian origin. A talented Thai boxer, he became involved in petty crime in the poor neighborhood of Nørrebro, where he grew up. He attended the local Al-Farouq mosque, where the Egyptians of the Gamaa Islamiyya preached when he was a child, and an imam close to Omar Bakri when he was a teenager. It was in the entourage of this imam, who was himself a Thai boxing teacher and Palestinian, that the Glostrup jihadist cell and Call to Islam emerged. In January 2014, Omar el-Hussein had been imprisoned for a knife attack on a commuter train. During his one-year stay at the Vestre penitentiary, he was reported to the intelligence services for his activism in favor of the "caliphate." His cellmate came to the attention of the authorities after publishing messages of support for IS from a concealed phone. Their names appeared on a list of 39 convicts described as ISIS supporters, another indicator of the growing radicalization in the normally very calm Danish prisons. According to several international media outlets, Omar el-Hussein was in contact with Saïd Mansour during his imprisonment.[36] Mansour, discussed above, was the Moroccan ideologue who welcomed the veterans with open arms in the 1990s, gave his public support to the blind sheikh after the 1993 World Trade Center attacks, and was the propagandist of choice for the Spaniards responsible for the 2004 Madrid attacks. Omar el-Hussein was released on January 30, 2015, and captured attention before his release by announcing his intention to join the jihadists in Syria. Fifteen days after his release, he posted an oath of allegiance to ISIS on his Facebook account under the nom de guerre of Abu Ramadan al-Muhajir ("he who has made the *hijra*"). Instead of going to the Levant, he made his way to the cultural center, where the French ambassador was about to give the opening remarks, and opened fire in the name of ISIS. Bo Yde Sørensen, the prison union president, looked back on El-Hussein's prison journey in an interview conducted in May 2022:

> Reality caught up with us. In 2015, the political class and the prison administration realized that we had not focused on the real issues, that we had turned a deaf ear to the reports sent by the guards. In this particular case, the guards had warned that he was dangerous. The police had been alerted about things to watch for when he got out of prison. This information was ignored.[37]

Like the perpetrators of the January attacks in France, the Dane was the product of the presence and indoctrination of veterans and then pioneers in specific local contexts. His development in prison was also typical. The union president continued:

> We have been aware of this problem for many years, ever since the first Islamists arrived in prison. For several years, we did not fully grasp the extent of the problem in Denmark. The Danish prison administration paid little attention to it, despite warnings, until 2015.[38]

Two days after the tragedies in Copenhagen, at a time when France was in the grip of a debate to find out "Who is Charlie?",[39] Denmark was confronted with its own controversy. People flocked to the place where Omar el-Hussein died with his weapons in his hands, to lay wreaths of flowers as a sign of remembrance and appeasement. Several said that these civic gestures were a reminder that Omar el-Hussein, despite the horrific acts he had committed, was "a compatriot in every sense of the word," a person who "probably suffered" and "also deserved to be forgiven by the national community."[40] A dozen men who presented themselves as the terrorist's "brothers," their faces hidden under keffiyehs, failed to appreciate these expressions of compassion. They appeared at the scene and tore up the bouquets on the grounds that it is forbidden in Islam to adorn the graves of martyrs with flowers. They chanted "Allahu Akbar" in el-Hussein's honour and placed leaflets on the ground expressing indignation at what they perceived as the different treatment of the "victims," which, they claimed, revealed the "Islamophobia" of the Danes. The leaflet claimed, by way of evidence, that the body of the synagogue security guard, a Jew, was covered with a shroud, while that of the killer remained on the pavement for several hours before being honorably concealed. In their logic, the heroic victim who prevented a massacre should be viewed in the same way as the person responsible for it. As they left the scene, they tagged a wall, in Danish and Arabic: "May Allah be merciful, may your soul rest in peace, Captain." This term is an honorary title used in local gangs, a reflection of the fact that El-Hussein had been both a criminal and a Salafist, common among the people I'm referring to as the natives. His funeral, on Friday, February 20, in a mosque in Brøndby, was attended by nearly 3,000 people, double the usual turnout. The April 2015 edition of *Dabiq*, the ISIS magazine, contained a hagiography of the young man.

Verviers, Prelude to November 13

At the same time, as if by clockwork, Belgium experienced an extremely serious terrorist incident. If the Copenhagen murders were a "ripple effect" of the *Charlie Hebdo* attacks, what happened in Belgium was a prelude to the November 13 attacks.

On January 15, special units carried out an assault on a former bakery in Verviers, Wallonia. The surprised terrorists, several of whom had just returned from the Levant and were heavily armed, immediately responded. The exchange of fire resulted in several deaths among the criminals. Thirteen people were arrested, including nine from Molenbeek. Not by chance had the terrorists chosen Verviers to finalize preparations for an attack. The city is located in a "border area," like many of the other municipalities we have looked at, and is close to both Germany and the Netherlands. An "insignificant town," in the words of Victor Hugo, who did not spend much time there during his wanderings along the Rhine in 1842,[41] Verviers was at the heart of the European wool industry from the Middle Ages until the de-industrialization of the 1970s. Since then, it has been a modestly sized Walloon city with a fragile economy. Certain figures from the Brussels jihadist movement lived there in the 2000s, and a handful of individuals from the city joined ISIS. Members of the November 13 commando had connections and obtained weapons there. A Belgian investigator in charge of the case stated: "There isn't a family in Verviers that doesn't have a cousin in Molenbeek or Antwerp."[42]

The Verviers team, commissioned by Oussama Atar, was to work towards goals similar to those of the November 13 terrorists in the Netherlands and France.[43] It was led by Abdelhamid Abaaoud, who was present that evening but escaped the police. He returned to Syria and reappeared in Europe eleven months later as the head of the Paris commando unit. Alain Grignard, the Belgian police officer, summarized his distress:

With the Verviers case, we realized that there might be another cell, but we were unable to make use of this information. They had gone underground, only coming out to carry out the attacks on November 13. [. . .] When the Paris attacks happened, it was a shock.

From Raqqa to Paris via Brussels: November 13

Between the end of 2014 and summer 2015, all the November 13 teams travelled to Molenbeek via Hungary, Austria, and Germany (with a stop in Ulm). As with the departures to Syria, the terrorists traveled in groups, leaving approximately ten days between convoys.

The operations were directed from Syria by Oussama Atar, following a plan reminiscent of the GIA attacks in Paris twenty years earlier: a logistics group hidden in Brussels supported a commando unit that targeted the heart of Paris. Like the German or British Al-Qaeda representatives ten years earlier, the cell on the ground had a certain degree of autonomy in the execution of the plan. Unlike them, they were much better trained.

The Belgian part of the operations was supervised by two of Atar's cousins, former thieves who were radicalized in prison, and Najim Laachraoui, a close friend who was a faction leader in the sordid basements of the Aleppo hospital in 2013. They finalized the preparations, established the plans, and made the explosives, following recipes learned in Syria. The attacks were carried out in the French capital by nine people, led by Abdelhamid Abaaoud. He was not the "mastermind," but the most reliable lieutenant to guide the unit on the ground.

The backbone of the unit was made up of the relatives, childhood friends, and brothers in arms of Oussama Atar; they had all passed through a rigorous selection process. Most of them lived in the municipalities along the Brussels canal, particularly Molenbeek and Laeken, and some had known each other since childhood.

T Minus Four Days

On November 9, 2015, the Brussels team made the final choice of targets and decided on the date: the assault would be launched on November 13, 2015. Among the targets considered were the Arc de Triomphe, military barracks, an airport, and far-right groups. There are certain very precise mentions of a school in Belgium with explicit comments: "You jump over it," "dozens of nurseries."[44] The team ended up deciding on a sports venue, a cultural event, and areas with a lot of nightlife.

T Minus Two Days

On November 11, the unit went into "operational" mode. The members turned off their phones, and a few made cryptic farewells to their loved ones. Salah Abdeslam, who until then had been in charge of ferrying the would-be attackers from Eastern Europe, shared a kebab with his girlfriend for what he knew would be their last dinner together before the assault. Instead of enjoying his food, he burst into tears for no apparent reason, to the astonishment of his girlfriend, who suspected nothing. He then settled debts that he had refused to pay until then, reflecting a tenet of Salafist doctrine according to which one must pay one's debts before dying so as not to take them into the afterlife.

T Minus One Day

On November 12, the group crossed into France and spent the night at the northern and southern extremities of the capital. The Brussels team abandoned a planned attack the following day against Schiphol Airport in Amsterdam. Three thousand kilometers away, Jihadi John, one of the "ISIS Beatles," was located in a vehicle in Raqqa. The executioner of American and Syrian journalists, who intended to provoke a bloodbath in the United States, was immediately killed by a drone strike. He had likely been in contact with the members of the Paris unit when a few months earlier they had carried out reconnaissance at Old Trafford stadium in Manchester, and in gaming halls in Birmingham.

November 13

The members of the unit split into three groups. Shortly after 9 p.m., they hit the area around the Stade de France, which they had not managed to infiltrate, and the café terraces of the tenth and eleventh arrondissements; they also entered the Bataclan theatre during an Eagles of Death Metal concert. They committed a massacre unprecedented in the history of contemporary France, firing thousands of rounds from assault rifles and detonating their explosive vests in crowded parts of the capital. They killed 131 people and left hundreds more "injured or deeply shocked," in the words of the presiding judge at the opening of the trial. The attacks were the most spectacular in the West since 9/11. They were conducted in an "urban guerrilla" style, a jihadist fantasy that until now had been carried out only in Mumbai and Bali, but had fueled many thwarted attempts in Europe, such as the 2010 plot against Berlin and Paris.

T Plus One

Late that night, Salah Abdeslam, who had not been able to activate his defective explosive belt, asked two childhood friends to come smuggle him back to Brussels. Driving back in the early morning hours, their vehicle was stopped at a roadblock. The assailants had not yet been identified, and Salah Abdeslam waited nervously for his identity check to be completed. A Belgian journalist who was recording the reactions of motorists to the attacks asked him for his opinion on the atrocities to which he had just contributed. His response: "This is the third check. Frankly we found it a bit excessive, huh? But we understood a little bit . . . the reason why, in fact, afterwards, we knew the reason why."[45] After pocketing his identity card, Salah Abdeslam disappeared in Belgium.

A few hours later, the Clain brothers, the Toulouse jihad pioneers, claimed responsibility for the attacks on behalf of ISIS. The statement, written in advance, mentioned a detonation in the eighteenth arrondissement that did not take place, but where Salah Abdeslam's phone had been in the evening. A state of emergency was declared in France. The mandate of the international coalition was extended to Syria, and fighter jets began to pound ISIS positions.

T Plus Four

On November 17, the head of operations on the ground, Abaaoud, was located in a hideout in Saint-Denis. He died alongside two accomplices in the ensuing assault, just as he was planning new acts of violence in the La Défense neighborhood.

The resolution to all this took place in Brussels five months later, and shed light on the ambitions of the external operations cell.

From Paris to Brussels, the Resolution: March 22

On March 19, 2016, Salah Abdeslam, the only survivor from the Paris unit, was arrested in Brussels, 400 meters from his home, after a routine police visit to a derelict building. He was wounded in the arrest while his accomplices opened fire or fled.

Recordings found in the hideout of Najim Laachraoui, who was directing the group from Brussels, help us to understand what happened next. In the first audio message, sent when Salah Abdeslam's hiding place had not yet been discovered, Laachraoui communicated with Oussama Atar, who was overseeing the situation from Raqqa. He analyzed what he saw as having gone wrong on the evening of November 13. He expressed regret at the lack of a backup plan for Abaaoud, which prevented him from "striking a second time." It seems he was the only one who was meant to return alive. Laachraoui then insisted on not attacking Belgium, which serves as their support base, in order to "do England, like we talked about."[46]

He sent a second voicemail to Atar shortly after the arrest of Salah Abdeslam, in which he made harsh remarks about the latter, who "once again" missed the opportunity to die a martyr even though he was "equipped to." He worried that he'd see his name in the media, and expected to be arrested soon. He lamented not being able to carry out "all the projects" he had planned, including striking the Euro 2016 soccer tournament in France. He ended his farewell with a special greeting to two of the four "Beatles," and a declaration of brotherly love for Atar, whom he would welcome, he said, to the *firdaws* ("paradise"). The next day, together with other members of the Brussels cell, he took his own life in the suicide attacks on Zaventem airport, while Atar's cousins did the same in the capital's metro, killing 48 people.

After March 2016, ISIS, deprived of operators in Belgium, lost much of its room for maneuver in Europe. The measures taken by the public authorities continued to dry up the organization's supply of men by systematically hindering departures. The intensification of air strikes weakened the group's advance in Syria and Iraq, and the organization was now losing ground. Turkish intervention helped to suffocate the terrorists. IS tried to give itself some breathing room by stepping up actions against European societies, in the hope of triggering episodes of civil war, a logic very similar to that of the GIA twenty years earlier. Unable to reproduce orchestrated attacks, the jihadists fell back on whatever remote-controlled attacks were available.

2016–2018: The Resourcefulness of the "Caliphate" System

The summer of 2016 saw an increase in the number of deadly incidents against a backdrop of political polarization within European democracies. The jihadists tried to influence events by adapting their terrorist language to the specifics of the debates in each target country. In doing so, they sought to trigger outbursts of anger in the form of clashes between ethnic and religious groups, employing the logic Al-Qaeda had used in Iraq. We will now look at certain attacks that occurred in this period, which will allow us to trace the evolution of ISIS in its phase of strength.

The period was marked by a political explosion: on June 23, 2016, to everyone's surprise, the United Kingdom voted for Brexit. For the first time in the history of the EU, a member state decided to leave.

In France, the networks mobilized from Raqqa by the Franco-Algerian Rachid Kassim targeted two police officers in Magnanville on June 13, a priest during mass in Saint-Étienne-du-Rouvray on July 26, and Notre-Dame de Paris on September 4. In Nice, a man drove a nineteen-ton truck up the Promenade des Anglais during the July 14 celebrations, killing 86 (including dozens of children), injuring 458, and traumatizing thousands more.

Four days later, a tragic week began in Germany. The continent's leading economic power broke with the cautiousness of its neighbors and opened its doors to 850,000 asylum seekers. The decision, as Chancellor Angela Merkel, supported by Sweden and Norway, explained, was a duty in the face of the greatest humanitarian catastrophe since the Second World War. However, since it was not coordinated with other EU nations, it led to an unstoppable human procession through the Eastern countries, and gave new life to far-right movements, who were convinced that this was a decisive stage in the "great replacement." Aware of these political fault lines, ISIS networks in Germany tried to recruit individuals from among the exiles, in order to fracture public opinion, weaken the government, and encourage the spread of xenophobic discourse.

On Monday, July 18, in Würzburg, Bavaria, the *Land* that had taken in the largest number of refugees over the previous year, a 17-year-old Afghan asylum seeker, who had been staying with a host family for two weeks, attacked passengers on a regional train with an axe and a knife. He left the train after the alarm was pulled and walked back along the railway line. He was shot by special forces as he ran towards the police in a violent rage. ISIS claimed responsibility for the attack on Twitter, and a flag of the organization was found in the perpetrator's room. The following Sunday, July 24, 2016, in Reutlingen, a small city not far from Ulm, a Syrian man murdered a pregnant woman with a machete, and injured several people in front of a kebab restaurant. He was arrested by the police after a driver incapacitated him by hitting him with his BMW. On the same day, 200 kilometers to the north, in Ansbach, another Syrian blew himself up at the entrance to a pop music festival, injuring 15, after first pledging allegiance to the "caliphate." The attacks shook the political debate in Germany, where the Pegida movement, which openly described itself as "anti-Islam" and claimed to be the only force capable of defending German and European values, swung into action online and in the media.

On December 19, 2016, in Berlin, a Tunisian drove a truck into a Christmas market, much like the attack on the Promenade des Anglais in Nice, killing 12 people and injuring around 50. The attacker fled to Italy, where he was killed by the carabinieri after opening fire at a roadblock. At the same time, two Syrian members of IS, who were living in Germany and Sweden, were arrested by Danish police. They were planning to undertake a series of indiscriminate knife attacks in the streets of Copenhagen before detonating their vests.

On December 31, Istanbul, already targeted in a very serious attack in the summer, fell prey to more ISIS carnage. Foreign jihadists entered an open-air nightclub and killed 39, in a "reprisal" against the Turkish armed intervention, which now prevented foreign volunteers from reaching Syria.

Great Britain was targeted in the spring of 2017. On March 22, a year after the Brussels attacks, a British convert drove into pedestrians in front of the Houses of Parliament at 120 kilometers per hour. He killed four of them and injured around 50. He then drove his vehicle into the security barrier at Westminster Palace, got out, and stabbed an unarmed policeman, before being shot by a security guard. The 52-year-old assailant was a repeat offender who had turned to Salafism in prison in 2005. He had been on MI5's radar since 2010 for his proximity to a Luton group that was planning an attack on a military base, and had frequented Sharia4UK circles between 2012 and 2016. Before the attack, he sent a text message stating that he was outraged by British policy in the Middle East and wanted to "take revenge for Islam." ISIS published a short statement on Twitter glorifying the "soldier of Allah who answered the call of the caliphate," a clear sign that they had inspired him. On May 22, 2017, in Manchester, a 22-year-old British man of Libyan descent blew himself up inside Manchester Arena, one of the largest concert venues in Europe, during an Ariana Grande concert attended by thousands of teenagers. He killed 22 spectators and injured 116 others; the youngest victim had just celebrated his eighth birthday. Finally, on June 3, 2017, three jihadists drove their rented van into the pedestrian area of London Bridge, killing two. They then got out of the van armed with knives and explosive vests (but without the Molotov cocktails they had in the trunk) and went off to stab passers-by. After eighteen minutes of horror, the police intervened and neutralized the three criminals, who were responsible for eight deaths and 45 injuries.

Eleven days later, during the France-England friendly soccer match at the Stade de France, the Republican Guard performed an Oasis song, *Don't Look Back in Anger*, which became a rallying cry in refusal of division in Manchester after the terrible events. The whole stadium joined in to sing this anthem of 1990s Cool Britannia. Five days later, on June 19, 2017, Darren Osborne, a 47-year-old Briton with links to the far-right English Defence League, imitated the ISIS model, mowing down a crowd of worshippers outside Finsbury Park mosque, where Abu Hamza had preached twenty years earlier – the same time Oasis released their hit song. He killed one man and injured ten believers. Andrew Parker, head of MI5, declared that the security threat had considerably increased, and that 2017 was the most intense year of his 34-year career.[47]

Similar attacks took place in Sweden (a truck rammed into people on April 7, 2017 in Stockholm) and elsewhere in Europe. On August 16, a house in Alcanar, Catalonia, exploded. Two trainee bombers were killed. One of them, a 44-year-old Moroccan and Salafist imam of the Ripoll mosque, had just returned from Belgium. He had been served an expulsion order in Spain in 2014 for drug trafficking, but the order was suspended after his lawyer appealed on human-rights grounds.

Like the attacks that had been brought forward in Brussels, the unintentional detonation prompted the rest of the commando unit to take action. The next day, a follower of the same mosque drove his van at high speed down the busy alleys of Las Ramblas in Barcelona, killing thirteen people and injuring 130 more. He fled on foot through the Boqueria market, fatally stabbing another person in order to steal his vehicle. Nine hours later, five other members of the cell went to Cambrils, where they killed a woman and injured six other people before being shot dead by the police. One of the assailants, who had arrived in Spain in 2005, was a futsal player in a local team. In 2015, he was asked a question on the social network Kiwi: "What would be the first thing you would do if you were master of the world?" His answer was unequivocal: "I would kill all the infidels and only spare the Muslims who follow their religion."[48]

These attacks, though they were rushed, reawaken memories of the bloody events of 2004, but also sealed the decline of this cycle of deadly acts, due to the collapse of IS in the Levant.

3

After ISIS: The Jihadist Decline and Islamist Reconfigurations in Europe

The end of the 2010s was marked by a reversal of the tide. ISIS's influence was crumbling, under pressure from all sides. By the end of 2017, Arab-Kurdish forces had regained control of Mosul in Iraq and Raqqa in Syria, and were pushing back jihadist positions.

The "ISIS moment" indirectly enabled the Syrian regime to remain in power, as the Western powers were unable to exert the same pressure on it at a time when, in the east of the country, they had to concentrate their forces on defeating ISIS.[1] Bashar al-Assad was made a vassal by his Russian and Iranian allies, who deployed troops and militia groups on the ground to ensure his survival and recapture most of the lost territory. As a final symbol of Assad's loss of sovereignty, the Pyrrhic victory was proclaimed not by him but by the master of the Kremlin, Vladimir Putin, in the summer of 2018. After eight years of conflict, 400,000 victims, and the departure of six million of his people, the Syrian dictator now reigned over a field of ruins. Millennia-old cities such as Aleppo were largely destroyed, while ancient sites such as Palmyra were the scene of heinous massacres and reduced to ashes. The crisis gave rise to "the largest refugee population for a single conflict in a generation," according to the United Nations High Commissioner for Refugees (UNHCR), Antonio Guterres.

The Fall of the "Caliphate"

The defeat of ISIS can also be explained by an internal collapse. Purges intensified as the organization declined. As with the GIA in Algeria twenty years earlier, the group's brutality, the increase in its attacks abroad, and the violence inherent to its project led to its implosion. Like many totalitarian movements throughout history, IS members devoured each other in a blind ideological advance. Their failure to fulfill the Koranic prophecy was interpreted by part of the leadership as the result of insufficient doctrinal purity within the command. Starting in the summer of 2016, 38 members of the group accused of providing information to the enemy were executed, while the "reshuffle" of the ideological committee gave rise to a settling of scores against a backdrop of widespread suspicion. Men and women suspected of desertion disappeared.

The weakening of the group affected the positions of some of its most faithful servants, like the best placed pioneers, who remained loyal to the "caliphate" despite their imminent defeat. Sabri Essid, from Toulouse, mentor of Mohammed Merah and a close associate of the Clains for twenty years, was presented as a "martyr" killed in a coalition bombing, though in fact he was silently liquidated by IS. Rachid Kassim, responsible for the campaign of remote-controlled attacks in France in the summer of 2016, hid from the coalition by living among women and children. He was shot in February 2017 as he slipped out of his hideout. Other Europeans, while still viewed in high regard in jihadist circles, were caught up in the dead end of defeat. German rapper and propagandist Deso Dogg was killed in a targeted strike. His compatriot Reda Seyam, who went to Bosnia in the 1990s and played a central role in structuring the movement in Germany, met the same fate, though he was head of jihadist education in the province of Mosul. Similarly, the Belgian Oussama Atar, head of external operations and mastermind of the attacks in France and Belgium, was flushed out and eliminated. His death symbolically closed the cycle of terror: he was the last of the seven leaders who planned the November 2015 attacks to still be alive in the Levant. By March 2019, ISIS's minions were reduced to a patch of Baghouz in Syria. Until the very last moments, the religious police (*hisba*) patrolled the enclave of a few square kilometers, which was the last elementary particle of the "caliphate." Among the diehards were the Clain brothers, Toulouse pioneers and voices of IS's media war. They were located on the basis of information provided by children present in the camp. A missile struck the position on March

23, sealing their fate. The Arab-Kurdish forces set out to conquer the stronghold and abolish IS law. In a final video, Abu Bakr al-Baghdadi, the puppet "caliph" of a stateless state, payed nominal tribute to the Europeans mentioned here. On the run for three years, he was tracked down in a hamlet near the Turkish-Syrian border, where he took refuge in a cellar, killing himself and his three children during the ensuing raid by American special forces. The "caliphate" had disappeared, along with all its symbols.

Ephemeral Caliphate, Permanent Utopia

The structural causes that favored the emergence of a jihadist sanctuary in the Middle East twice in the last twenty years are still present. The war in Syria has contributed to the worsening of an axis of crisis, which now extends from North Lebanon to Iraq via northern Syria and southern Turkey. The territorial strip, approximately 1,000 kilometers long, is home to 600,000 displaced persons, and all the ills that have afflicted the region since the invasion of Iraq in 2003.[2] Among the Sunni-majority population, a feeling of dispossession predominated, from the standpoints of politics, identity, and religion.[3] In addition to the presence of jihadist groups attempting to regroup, there is a concentration of armed forces from international and regional powers: Russia, Iran, Syria, Turkey, the United States, and Europe, as well as the Kurds. The result is a security situation that is liable to ignite. In addition to the absence of a long-term political settlement, the region is dealing with an economic decline caused by eight years of conflict in Syria, twice that in Iraq, and the collapse of Lebanon. The shift of a single variable has immediate effects on the entire equation. In October 2019, the announcement of a withdrawal of American forces from Syria by Donald Trump was interpreted by the Turkish army as a green light to launch an offensive against the Kurds, whose forces oversaw ninety percent of the European jihadists detained there. Pressure from the Pentagon led the American president to change his mind, but the situation is clearly precarious.

The 6,000 Europeans who went to the Levant can now be divided into three groups. The first consists of those who either died on the spot or are missing. The second includes those who have been imprisoned in

Kurdish or Iraqi prisons. The third group are those who have returned to their countries of origin (half of these are minors).[4] The last two categories reflect problems specific to the post-ISIS era. The issue of people – including hundreds of women and children – imprisoned in Syria remains unresolved, and constitutes a legal, political, humanitarian, and security gray area. The management of imprisoned returnees opens onto the question of jihadism in prisons, and also what will become of these people at the end of their sentences.

Growing Up in the Al-Hol Camp

The detention camps in northeastern Syria provided a glimpse of the last remnants of the caliphate in which the abandoned generation of ISIS grew up. The majority of ISIS fighters captured by Kurdish soldiers were held in three prisons in Qamishli, Dashiqah and Hasakah. Women and children lived in supervised camps in Ain Issa, Al-Roj, and above all the largest camp, Al-Hol, which was home to 65,000 people from more than 60 countries.

The camps, which resembled gigantic shantytowns, were overseen by Kurdish soldiers, who lost 11,000 brothers and sisters in arms in the fight against ISIS. The living conditions were indecent, as one would expect in an area devastated by civil war and terrorism; the Kurds had few resources and limited appetite for comforting the families of foreign jihadists. Several reports from NGOs and United Nations agencies expressed alarm at the health situation, but also the environment in which so many young children were growing up – there were 7,300 children in Al-Hol alone.

The gathering of tens of thousands of IS sympathizers in this camp led to the reproduction of an order similar to the one that was in force under Daesh – only worse. Women's actions focus on social control, using methods typical of jihadist circles, based on three pillars: educating the young, deploying *hisba* (morality police), and maintaining security pressure on camp supervisors, similar to the behavior of returnees when they form cells in European prisons.

Minors were taught the canons of ideology – to worship martyrdom and avenge their fathers captured or killed for the cause. As an American diplomat in charge of this case said at the end of September 2022:

> It's not just the living conditions that are deplorable, it's everything else too. Children learn to count using pictures of rockets and Kalashnikovs, they learn to read from books glorifying jihad against the infidels.[5]

The authorities supervising the camp feared that prolonged stays in these environments would create "the next generation of militants."[6] The proliferation of *hisba*, groups of women who set themselves up as moral leaders of the camp, ensured a hold over the population. The patrols did not hesitate to threaten aid workers with death and put pressure on fellow inmates who appeared to be distancing themselves from IS. "The *hisba* represent the greatest challenge for the camp's administration and security forces," note the authors of a report on the situation.[7] In the first half of 2022, incidents involving 200 women and their children were recorded, and at least 24 members of the camp management were murdered, including a humanitarian worker. The American diplomat in charge of the case mentioned several escape attempts:

> ISIS operatives within the camp have dug tunnels under Al-Hol that are regularly discovered.

There were also links with ISIS cells abroad. At the end of January 2022, the men's prison in Hasakah was the target of the largest offensive since the fall of the "caliphate." The attack was coordinated with the support of inmates orchestrating a mutiny.[8] The insurgency was quelled after a week of fighting, with nearly 300 jihadists dead and around 100 Kurdish soldiers. The standoff continued, and the new leader of ISIS, Abu Ibrahim al-Hachimi, was killed a few days later in a drone strike, as were several of his deputies in the weeks that followed.

Most of the men and women in the camps wished to be repatriated. They made their requests publicly through lawyers, who are often media-savvy and sharp-tongued. The European authorities agreed on the legal and moral responsibility to repatriate minors, who made up the majority of French nationals, but were slow to implement their decisions. The question of the return of the elderly was subject to greater circum-spection, and its treatment differed from one country to another. The political cost of these decisions was high: 89 percent of French people, for example, declared themselves "concerned" by the prospect of repatriations in 2019.[9] Sticking points included the question of what would become of these individuals in European penal institutions. The vast majority of prisoners were die-hard supporters of the cause who, as ISIS passed from one debacle to the next, allowed the doors of any possible return to slam shut.

For women, the hesitation concerns in particular the possibility of legal proceedings. In criminal terms, their time as militants in Syria and Iraq is difficult to document. The absence of serious offenses, such as participation in acts of violence, suggested medium sentences, if not short sentences or no sentence at all. There was a clear risk that they would recruit people in prisons, and the small size of female detention centers threatened to make them disproportionately influential. The director of the French prison administration spoke of how he became aware of this issue in 2016:

> We didn't fully appreciate the risk posed by female jihadists. The prevailing view was that the women were in the grip of the men, that they were lost souls who had found solace [in jihadism], that they were more victims than anything else. One of the first decisions I made when I arrived in the Île-de-France region was to organize a general search of the maternal ward [where the pregnant prisoners were placed] of the Fleury-Mérogis Prison, because they were starting, five or six of them, to bring this ward under their control, to forbid the South American [inmates] from celebrating Christmas, and so on.[10]

Security, political, and judicial issues were intrinsically linked, as evidenced by the heated debates surrounding the revocation of nationality for certain ISIS members in Great Britain and Scandinavia. But the "let them rot" strategy, which consisted of letting European nationals stew in the security Bermuda triangle where Turkey, Syria, and Iraq come together, was not at all effective. The US State Department advocated for the repatriation of Europeans so as not to see them fall into the hands of ISIS or the Syrian regime, but the backdrop for this was American legislation favoring extremely long prison terms (often life sentences) and solitary confinement for Americans who had joined IS.

The issue is extremely complex. Potential solutions could be explored at EU level, based on a legal structure that has yet to be devised by jurists, perhaps somewhere between the model of the "major trials" of jihadists in France and those of the Nazis in Nuremberg after the war.

The Prisons

Almost all the men who returned to Europe were tried and in most cases convicted, with varying degrees of severity depending on the legal framework. Scandinavia and the Netherlands stood out for the leniency of their legal response, while France and Great Britain tended to increase sentences after 2015. Olaf, a Danish jihadist we met in Copenhagen in the spring of 2022, did not face imprisonment despite having spent two years with ISIS, due to a lack of material evidence. The same was true of one of his compatriots, who spent four months in the Levant, even though there is little doubt about what he did:

> Q: *When you were there, were you engaged in jihad?*
> A: I can't answer directly for legal reasons. So I'll just say that when you go to a conflict zone, you adapt to the circumstances. [. . .] I was in a war zone where chaos reigned, and I joined a group that shared the same vision as mine in Denmark. So obviously, I didn't go to Syria to hand out flowers and chocolate [*smile*].[11]

In the post-Daesh period, prisons returned to their role as the most important space for the movement, as they were in previous phases of weakness. Now, however, the numbers are much higher: around 1,500 people directly linked to these networks are currently behind bars, which is a first in the history of the EU. In Denmark, Bo Yde Sørensen, the president of the main union of security guards, believes that the problem lies in the threshold effects reached after the Syrian crisis.

I have dealt with the development of jihadism in French prisons in a previous work,[12] one of the conclusions of which was that European jihadism does not simply run its course in prison. Naturally, every individual journey is unique; incarceration weighs on morale, even for the most determined, and some give up or gradually withdraw from militancy. Since most sentences are between a few months and 15 years, most of those who returned from Syria will be those released from prison in the 2020s. But since jihadism also refers to a belief and, even more so, a utopian project, it does not simply evaporate from the minds of individuals as a result of imprisonment.

Prisons are complex places in which seasoned militants seek to extend dynamics in which they were already involved. The incarceration of volunteers returning from the Levant resulted in the importation of certain habits developed under ISIS, including threats to staff and the safety of buildings, but also of attempts, by intellectual fringes, to lay the foundations for European jihadism. Ismaël, convicted for his involvement in the Forsane al-Izza group, referred to the movement's "self-determination" as a collective priority. By this he means the need to free themselves from the control of Middle Eastern groups that in his view hinder the expansion of the cause:

> We suffer from a lack of self-determination. I am Western, I am French, people think we are not political, but that is not true. We are very, very political. So, we're not all highly educated, sometimes we don't get all the references, but we always talk about geopolitics and politics among ourselves, we talk about it all the time when we're out and about. It's not as rigid as in communist and soviet circles, but it's politicized. I could have fought the Kurds, but I respect them because they have complete self-determination. They've been getting a good beating for twenty years, but they're not giving up. They educate the young and they fight. The question of self-determination is central for us.[13]

Salafi-jihadist ideology, here likened to the Kurdish ethno-nationalist independence project, is presented as an instrument of intellectual, physical, and moral emancipation, compatible with living in the West. The dissemination of this discourse to ordinary prisoners suggests that it is being popularized within French society. Another activist, Brahim, expressed its ambition:

> Things are going well for us here [in prison]. And as for the West, it's going to turn society upside down when we get out. Because in detention people harden. And they don't harden towards violence, they harden ideologically. They harden when they're in contact with people who are even more hardened than them, I see it among the [ordinary prisoners].[14]

A current is emerging within the prison movement that promotes a synthesis between the political pragmatism of Al-Qaeda and the religious intransigence of ISIS. The popularity of Zarqawi, the first emir of the Islamic State of Iraq, killed in June 2006, who was the instigator of the "caliphate" project, is a recurring theme. Ismaël goes so far as to hold him up as a "role model" for young people from poor suburbs:

> Zarqawi is us! The young kids from the suburbs, here . . . We're all Zarqawi! He messed up a lot, he did a lot of harm, and I'm talking from a universal moral point of view. He's in jail, he's reading, he's learning from his worldly mistakes, just like us. And the real connection is that neither him nor us are afraid to really go for it. On the contrary, Zarqawi, he slit people's throats on video, he's the only influential emir who got his hands dirty. I devoured his videos. Osama bin Laden never did it, no one did it before him. [. . .] Zarqawi is the peasant who became a knight. The lowlife thief with black teeth who found his king and became a knight. That's us.[15]

As these words suggest, the militant environments reconstituted in prison become acclimatization chambers for Middle Eastern jihadism, which the natives are now seeking to adapt to the European context. The physical destruction of the "caliphate" does not mean the disappearance of the ideology that gave it its strength, or that of the utopian project – to build an Islamic state and impose sharia law – which was able to galvanize supporters all over the world. Thus, for Amine, a Franco-Algerian imprisoned for trying to join IS:

> I've come to terms with it. I'm going to return to my country of origin. But the ideal Islamic State is a dream, that's for sure.
> Q: *You're disappointed in Dawla [ISIS] as an organization, but not in the caliphate project?*
> A: Well, it's like I just told you: no one can say that an Islamic state is not a good thing.[16]

While the organization may have been defeated and discredited, this is not the case for its general project. In the eyes of its supporters, ISIS is a promising vehicle that has broken down on the road to the caliphate ideal. This is undoubtedly the most commonly shared observation among the jihadists we met in detention.

There is much to indicate that this is also true of France's European neighbors. Olaf, the Dane who spent two years with IS before returning to Denmark, where he lives freely, says he is in favor of a jihadist synthesis, one that he hopes will be more "pragmatic":

> Salafi-jihadism is plural. A political party can encompass several tendencies, and the same goes for Salafi-jihadism. I would say that it contains several currents, but two main ones can be distinguished. The first consists of seeing things in an extremely binary way, where everything is black or white. It is a narrow, limited Salafi-jihadism, that of IS. And in my opinion, it's not the right one: we've seen the harm it has done to Islam. The good Salafi-jihadism, for me, the one I advocate, is the one that opens your eyes, the one that is pragmatic, the one that allows you to embrace several points of view.[17]

The Materialization of the Security Threat in European Prisons

The French prison situation applies in part to Great Britain, Belgium, and Germany, where the conditions of detention and the sociology of penal institutions are comparable (prison overcrowding, lack of resources). The Netherlands and the Scandinavian countries, on the other hand, have quite different prison cultures, based on alternatives to incarceration and prison facilities that are in better condition, less crowded, and better equipped in terms of human and material resources. However, they still exhibit several similar trends.

From a security standpoint, the various countries have been hit by attacks within prison establishments. The situation took on extraordinary proportions in France in the summer of 2016,[18] when control of the Fleury-Mérogis Prison, the largest in Europe, was temporarily in the balance. Guards have been violently assaulted by offenders on several occasions, and even killed in 2019.[19] The authorities, while they have not solved everything, have made several plans to strengthen the system and better manage the jihadists, who are spread throughout French prisons. The director of the prison administration, Laurent Ridel, looked back on this extremely busy period:

We have made progress. In 2016–2017, due to the massive concentration of Islamist prisoners in the Paris region, some prisons could have been overrun. This did not happen. Currently, we must remain extremely humble, because there are elements of good and bad luck in the management of a very complicated prison population, but the situation is healthier than in 2016–2017, when there was still overcrowding. This is the effect of dispersion, and for once we did it in a very pragmatic way, without a preconceived model and with input from the professionals.[20]

In 2016, in the calm Danish prisons, 274 violent incidents and threats against prison staff were recorded, an increase of a third compared to previous years.[21] For the first time, a minor imprisoned for acts of terrorism, who had links to the movement in Syria, stabbed a supervisor with a piece of broken glass. This act took place at a time when the prison system, known for the weight it gives to rehabilitation, seemed to be one of the best equipped to manage this type of prisoner. Scandinavian imams speak of the quality of detention conditions, which are notoriously lacking in Western European establishments. Individual cells are the strictly applied norm, individuals reported for radicalization are separated (at least in principle), and the guards have significant resources at their disposal to carry out their duties, which results in calmer relations with the inmates.

Similarly, in the United Kingdom, in February 2020, a jihadist attempted to stab three security guards in Winchester. In Holland, in February 2021, a jihadist convicted of a knife attack on a tram in Utrecht failed in his assassination attempt on a member of staff at Rotterdam Prison, considered one of the calmest in Europe.

Penal Institutions Under Pressure

Peter Clarke, the former head of the counter-terrorism unit at Scotland Yard, who was appointed inspector of prisons for England and Wales, is less optimistic than the French officials. In an interview conducted in spring 2022 in London, he described the "jihad-generating" environment of the prisons he inspected:

The closed environment of a prison encourages the development of subcultures and individuals who seek to establish their power through crime or ideology, or a combination of them, which we have observed. I think there's a lot of potential for things to go wrong, and I'm not talking about prison security, but the security of public spaces. [. . .] We've had three attacks in the last two years [2020–2022], carried out by people who were released after being convicted for terrorist offenses.[22]

Similarly, a Danish supervisor summed up his feelings during an interview in Copenhagen in the spring of 2022:

I've been a supervisor since 1995, and for many years now we have noticed that highly Islamized prisoners gain the upper hand over other prisoners and try to spread their ideology, a growing phenomenon in prisons. We find messages advocating an extremely violent form of Islamism hidden on all kinds of media, such as game consoles.[23]

Administrations face identical challenges and constraints regardless of the state of their prisons. They can disperse the detainees linked to terrorist organizations within their establishment, but then they run the risk of disseminating jihadist ideas to new audiences. Or they bring them together, but then they expose themselves to creating virulently militant microcosms, new synergies preventing any possibility of repentance and, in the long run, reintegration. At the beginning of the 2020s, Western countries confronted with this phenomenon tended to set up mechanisms combining both techniques, based on the case-by-case evaluation of profiles. Bo Yde Sørensen detailed the subtle balance behind such measures:

With the Islamists, we take great care to ensure that they can never come into contact with each other. We're trying the dispersal method. The more Islamists we take in, the more complicated it is to apply. We try to disperse them, so that they are left alone with their ideas. We don't isolate them socially – they are in contact with ordinary prisoners. This does not protect against the risk of them trying to recruit, but they are not in a position of strength, which would be the case if there were two, three, four Islamists together. [. . .] Their low numbers in Danish prisons still makes it possible to manage the problem, I'm convinced of it, but the prison system is under pressure.[24]

Collusion between certain criminal and jihadist circles, leading to the "jihadization of crime" and the "criminalization of jihadism," is a fear raised by observers of the prison environment in the post-ISIS period. The Danish union leader said this:

> I must say that we have not yet solved the problem of collusion between Islamists and criminal gangs. [. . .] Islamism is a problem in itself that is difficult to manage and that poisons prison life, whether the individual comes from Nørrebro [a neighborhood in Copenhagen that is heavily affected by jihadist dynamics], from the Saïd Mansour network, or has just returned from Syria. As soon as they bring Islamism inside the prison walls, they become difficult to manage.[25]

The Islamists' discourse has no effect on the prisoners as a whole, and many Muslims remain impervious to it. However, the Salafists assert their influence through the production of a coherent collective, organizing themselves into community-based networks that are perfectly suited to the prison system. By contrast, Muslims who resist "communitarian" confinement formulate their religious commitment individually. They do not seek to form denominational groups, as Islam does not constitute the sole foundation of their identity. They therefore protect themselves from the bullying of the communitarianists, whom they rarely oppose head-on, and this avoidance ensures that they do not become the targets of the surrounding Salafist activism. As such, this fragmented majority, split into myriad individual positions, abandons religion to the preying of the active minority. By "withdrawing" from it, the non-Salafist inmates allow the communitarianists, *mutatis mutandis*, to more easily redefine the contours and meaning of Islam within the prison, and to do so at different levels. And by asserting themselves as noisy collectives, Islamists have a greater *de facto* influence on internal order.

In the UK, a report published in spring 2022, reported by the BBC and to which we gained access, describes the intimidation methods to which staff members in some prisons are subjected by radicalized inmates. Supervisors are prevented from entering the establishment's mosque, and fear being labeled "Islamophobic" in interactions with those convicted of terrorism, who put pressure on other inmates and use Salafist precepts as instruments to control the social order.[26] Peter

Clarke speaks of a professional culture, particularly at the level of the administrative hierarchy, that seeks to avoid controversy and in some cases prefers to ignore disturbing realities even if it prevents them from assessing the situation properly:

> Emirs were able to emerge and gain influence in certain wings, to the point of offering a kind of control over the social order of the prison . . . I think this was a fundamental mistake whose consequences are still being felt today. [. . .] Up to now, I would say that prisons have dealt with the problem posed by extremists by providing questionable responses. [. . .] I have discovered a culture of resistance within the prison system that consists of saying, "Our job is just to ensure the security of prisons; the rest is society's problem." [. . .] There are just over 200 people incarcerated in connection with jihadist terrorism in England. How many of them pose a threat to their fellow inmates or to society upon their release?[27]

Attacks carried out by individuals who have just completed their sentences, such as in Copenhagen in 2015 or more recently in Vienna in the fall of 2022 (four dead and 23 injured) are a reminder that the challenge of managing ex-prisoners is not only the responsibility of the prison service. There will be several hundred such people in Europe in the 2020s, a first in the history of the continent. The question of whether they will "reintegrate" into European societies or the Salafist circles from which they come and in which they have flourished is a major challenge.

The Neighborhoods

There are several signs that predication has not disappeared in the areas from which there were many departures for Syria. To take just a few examples, in July 2018, an imam at the Al-Farouq mosque in the Nørrebro neighborhood of Copenhagen, known as a place where jihadism developed in the country, was once again the focus of media attention. He was prosecuted after a video of one of his sermons was posted in which he calls for the murder of Jews, with the black and white banner of the Prophet often used by jihadists as a backdrop. Refusing to respond to the press, he stated on his Facebook page that the authorities were seeking to criminalize Islam and divine principles, and that he was a victim of Islamophobia. In Dinslaken, the first German city to be affected by departures for Syria, the former networks of the pioneers were dismantled, but the Lohberg neighborhood once again fell prey to Salafist preaching. The imam, who asked the militants of Millatu Ibrahim to bring him people who were "broken" and "fragile," still preaches in the same place of worship and now welcomes some of the 600 Syrian refugees who have settled in the region. "It's starting all over again!" a local government representative told a regional media outlet in 2016. The situation is reminiscent of Trappes or certain neighborhoods in England, such as in Birmingham, which have been demonized to a certain degree. Councillors in these areas tend to repeat relativist positions that are more or less marked by denial. For example, an educator in Dinslaken who observed the departure for the Levant of several of the young people he supervised refused to comment on the presence of jihadist ideology.

Wherever figures are available, they seem to show that in the early 2020s, Salafism occupied a more important place than ten years earlier. In Germany, where the domestic intelligence service regularly publishes figures on the subject, militant circles tripled in size between 2011 and 2018, rising from 3,800 followers to 11,300.[28] These figures remain tiny in proportion to the Muslim population, barely 0.3 percent of the total, but are to be linked to the risk posed by the mobilization of a few hundred jihadists over the past decade. In France, the figures communicated by the Ministry of the Interior to the press in 2018 refer to a Salafist community of 30 to 50,000 people, including 10 to 12,000 who are particularly "virulent," six to ten times the levels estimated in 2004.[29] It is difficult to make comparisons between countries because different methodologies are used and estimates may be made in different ways. However, in England, the trends seem comparable, as they do in Scandinavia. Swedish security services, for example, pointed out that the Salafi-jihadist milieu has grown in size and influence, increasing from 200 to 2,000 individuals between 2010 and the fall of ISIS in 2017.[30]

For all these reasons, a detour through Molenbeek, in Brussels, allows us to identify certain dynamics in the areas strongly affected by departures to Syria since the fall of this organization.

The Two Molenbeeks

The first observation to be made is that there are several Molenbeeks, just as there are various Trappes, Lunels, Birminghams, Bethnal Greens, Dinslakens, Nørebros, Malmøs, etc. It is therefore impossible to reduce these cities or neighborhoods to dynamics that, while they are certainly worrying, have emerged in restricted human environments. It is necessary, however, to deal directly and precisely with the development of the sectors in question.

In 2017, a study entitled "What Does Molenbeek Think," published by the European Institute of Peace, on the political and religious opinions of the inhabitants of the center of Molenbeek provides several useful quantitative elements.[31]

When cross-referenced with our field survey conducted at the same time in this municipality,[32] it sheds light on the development of the local situation since the 1990s, and the current perception of issues relating to Islamism in a locality that is sadly emblematic of European jihadism.

The first observation highlights a strong identity-based divide between residents, not from a socio-economic point of view, but on the basis of their subjective ideas. A clear distinction appears between those who present themselves and are described as "Belgian Belgians" and the others, referred to and defining themselves as "Moroccans" or "Muslims" (more than 80% of the population of central Molenbeek). These elements draw the symbolic contours of a space of "Moroccan" identity in the historic center and maritime district of Molenbeek, which imagines itself, and is perceived, as being separate from the rest of Belgian society on the basis of its belonging to Islam.

The second observation reveals that the religious norm is widespread in these neighborhoods among the majority population and is generally well respected. After nine months of investigation, the report concludes, in line with our observations: "The majority of members of the North African community live according to sociocultural norms associated with Islam. It is clear that Muslims in Molenbeek consider Islam and its values to be central in religious, civic, and cultural terms alike."[33] The researchers emphasize the identity dimension that religion plays in this, which exists in a tense relation with "Belgian society as a whole, which is generally based on a well-established secularized view of the display of religion in the public sphere."[34] For residents of Molenbeek originating from North Africa, religion is fundamental: 92 percent of them declare that it is "important" or "very important," compared to only 24 percent of "Belgian Belgians."

As we have noted, Salafism and the external signs that it circulates provide several of the predominant religious and social codes in the historic center. The low degree of gender mixing and the display of feminine and masculine religious symbols, for young and old, testify to the force of a unique Islamic order and not to the prevalence of traditional Moroccan Islam. In the center, the vast majority of women, whether of Moroccan origin or converts, are veiled, and often very strictly. This is even truer of young women, who are more strictly veiled (*jilbab* or *niqab*) than older women, a sign of the recent generational dimension that Islamic revivalism is taking on. Those who do not wear a veil are subject to social or family pressure within the community. Others express a visceral attachment to it: "When the employer's requirements conflict with the young woman's religious convictions, the latter prevail."[35]

Children in these neighborhoods grow up in a clearly established Islamic environment, marked by the Salafi-jihadist norm that began to emerge in the 1990s. The large number of mosques and Koranic schools (which replace the traditional Belgian school curriculum or "supplement" it with Saturday classes) meets a constantly growing local demand. The municipal area officially has 24 mosques, 16 of which are grouped together within the city's advisory council. The religious centers are often of very good quality and of a much better standard than Muslim places of worship in France. During a visit to three of the largest mosques in the city, we noted that each had its own school (several hundred places each, often considered insufficient) and recreational spaces. They oversaw particularly dynamic associations that operated on the fringes of the religious, social, and political spheres (support and catch-up classes, library, meeting room, cultural events, etc.). This, as most of the interviewees agreed, indicates that the Muslim faith is well funded in one of the poorest municipalities in Belgium. In addition to Koranic education for children, there is a significant number of seminars for adolescents and college students, educational outings, and socio-religious activities that are usually the responsibility of socio-cultural associations. These three "cathedral" mosques are among the most influential in the municipality, which has forged excellent relations with them. However, they only represent a portion of the faithful. The authorities acknowledge the existence of many other "unrecognized" places of worship, most of which are discreet prayer rooms on the ground floor of residential buildings,[36] like the one frequented by the members of the November 13, 2015 commando unit, a stone's throw from the town square. The six square kilometers that make up the center of Molenbeek would thus seem have no fewer than 45 places of worship for 50,000 residents, the highest proportion in Belgium. Despite the efforts of the various mayors in this area, the number of prayer rooms officially recognized in the Brussels-Capital Region remains very low – fourteen on the eve of the attacks of November 13, 2015 – which can be explained in part by reservations expressed by the State Security Service, concerned that some of these places are hotbeds of radicalism.[37]

The way in which time, which is punctuated by Muslim religious festivals, is experienced in the municipality is also significant. During Ramadan, when collective religious fervor is at its height, the tendencies described above are exacerbated. Fasting is observed everywhere in public spaces. While naturally this obligation does not apply to non-Muslims (a minority in the central districts), social control is so effective that no one breaks it. Smokers hide, and those passing through the town square spontaneously put away their water bottles out of respect for those fasting, or to avoid giving the impression of provoking the faithful. Another observation from the aforementioned report: "Although there is no desire to impose the rule [. . .], transgressing the norm for a non-Muslim would be frowned upon. Many non-Muslims thus feel uncomfortable smoking on the street in Molenbeek during the month of Ramadan."[38] Residents of Moroccan origin who do not obey the increasingly numerous "prohibitions" are particularly ostracized and pay dearly on a social level.

Molenbeek is thus not "held" by jihadists, as some commentators claim. Nor is it deserted by the public authorities, who are investing in the municipality. It has undeniably been the object, for the past 30 years, of a religious activism that operates in all aspects of life and has strong political and social effects. It is in the light of these elements that the relationship to the attacks by ISIS, in which residents played a leading role, should be considered.

One aspect that highlights both the gap between Molenbeek and the rest of society, and the influence of identity-based ideas on residents, appears in the responses regarding how returnees, and those responsible for the Paris and Brussels attacks, should be dealt with.

The prevalence of conspiracy theories, which are "legion in the cafés of Molenbeek, where men talk about politics and world affairs," is also expressed in the sense of mistrust of the "system," which refers to both politicians and the media. Members of identity-based communities thus construe their environment according to a logic of a besieged citadel. This can be seen in the outright rejection of all that is foreign to the community, with the intrusion of "Western culture" being perceived as harmful and opposed to the values of Islam.

The dissociation between the reality of jihadism in Molenbeek and the perception that its inhabitants have of it is considerable. For the people of Molenbeek, "terrorism" is the least of the difficulties they face, even though some have been victims of it, as this resident explains: "My cousin's wife was killed in the Brussels metro attack on March 22 [2016]," lamenting the general lack of support.

While, as we have seen, most of the residents of the center knew people who went to Syria (the members of the November 13 commando unit, Mohamed Abrini, Salah Abdeslam, and Abdelhamid Abaaoud, were "neighbors," former "classmates," young people "known" to all our respondents), jihadism is nevertheless considered to be exogenous to the municipality. For almost two-thirds of the respondents of Moroccan origin, religious extremism in Molenbeek is an illusion of sorts: sixteen percent consider it "totally non-existent" and 47 percent "weak."[39] As for "the reasons why radicalization may have taken place in Molenbeek," the majority point to socioeconomic issues, and ten percent say that it "did not take place," almost as many as those who blame the Belgian public authorities (13%).

As for security issues, only three percent of respondents in Molenbeek consider "violence linked to religious extremism" to be a priority, far behind those (17%) who believe that "there is no security problem." Jihadist departures or attacks in Belgium and France are treated with the same detachment. They are seen as the actions of individuals and depicted from a psychopathological perspective. Jihadists are "mad," "vulnerable," or idle people who "do not know religion" and are "manipulated" by others. The internet is viewed as one of the main reasons for their radicalism. At the same time, respondents who identify as Muslim emphasize the responsibility of Belgian politicians. They view Western injustice as a factor in the success of local jihadism: "Western foreign policy is mentioned as one of the structural factors that help make the recruiters' discourse audible. Many young Muslims believe that 'the West unjustly attacks the Muslim world' and speak of 'real hatred.'" A feeling of solidarity with the community of believers is another reason: "Many Muslims in Molenbeek express compassion for the fate of Muslims around the world. They often feel concerned about the fate of the ummah and, through it, of other Muslims in countries such as Syria or Palestine."

On the other hand, the people of Molenbeek do not see jihadism as being the product of local networks, and even less the result of local dynamics. The majority opinion among Muslim respondents is that religion is used as a pretext to recruit the "ignorant," who are made vulnerable by their lack of religious knowledge. The solution would thus be to intensify the spread of Islam at the local level. For almost a quarter of residents (24%, the largest single share), strengthening "religious education" would be the most effective way of preventing "radicalization." This observation is all the more surprising given that there is already an abundance of educational offerings in the municipality.

Regarding the "fate to be reserved for jihadists returning from Syria," three-quarters of the responses are in favor of reintegrating ISIS and Al-Nusra jihadists. Almost half of the respondents said they were in favor of care from social services, and no punishment: "Assistance [to Belgian jihadists returning from Syria or Iraq] with a view to their reintegration" is thus favored by 43 percent of Molenbeek residents.[40] "Strict supervision" of these individuals is suggested by a third of those surveyed. The "imprisonment" of jihadists is in last place (less than a quarter of those polled).

Finally, the coverage of the Paris and Brussels attacks and the role Molenbeek may have played in their preparation is perceived as an injustice inflicted by journalists, reflecting a latent Islamophobia and a desire for sensationalism in the media. The latter are maligned for allegedly stigmatizing the inhabitants of an entire municipality and, by way of them, an entire religion: 73 percent of respondents "strongly disagree" and twelve percent "disagree" with the media's coverage of the city.[41] Those who expressed their agreement with the media coverage of Molenbeek are mainly of European origin.

The responses of the majority of Molenbeek residents, who on the one hand blame the Belgian state, and on the other consider that the management of jihadists returning from the front should be their priority, do not reflect a schizophrenic disorder. They are consistent with the identity-based perceptions that the Salafi-jihadist preaching machine has been able to disseminate in the center. Extremism is thought to be "absent" in Molenbeek because it has become part of the everyday reality in which a large part of the inhabitants live. The denial of jihadism makes it possible for people to close ranks within the "community," to strengthen bonds of solidarity, and to strongly reject "Belgian society," accused by some of being responsible for the production of these "monsters" that they nonetheless tend to perceive as "weak," "vulnerable," or even "non-existent."

The lack of denunciation and indignation in the municipal center following the attacks is thus partly explained by the bonds of proximity that often unite neighbors. A few days before the arrest of Salah Abdeslam, the Molenbeek police chief said (correctly) he was sure that the most wanted man in Europe was hiding in his sector. He deplored the fact that local informants did not provide all the information they had, recalling, for instance, the case of Beeston Hill, in Leeds, after the London attacks in 2005.[42] At the same time, he indicated that, of the entire population for which he was responsible (nearly 100,000 residents), at most 1,000 people were responsible for all the problems the others inherited.

The case of Molenbeek is in no way exceptional. The municipality in the center of Brussels, with its rich and diverse history, possesses a number of factors that have allowed it to become the staging ground for multiple terrorist operations and to contain a particularly dense Islamist environment. In this respect, it is more an ideal type than something unique. The specific characteristics of the elements mentioned are also relevant to the situation in other neighborhoods.

Cities that have been affected by numerous departures for Syria and the resulting negative publicity (Lunel, Trappes, Birmingham, Dinslaken, The Hague, Aarhus, Malmø, etc.) tend to close in on themselves. Residents and local government representatives opt for denial and resentment towards the media or "outsiders." For instance, the deputy mayor of Dinslaken, Eyüp Yildiz (Social Democratic Party), argued in 2015 that the Lohberg neighborhood had never been so isolated,[43] though it is difficult today to gather on-site testimonies, as we have observed. In Birmingham, where a scandal (which continues to be the object of polemics) broke out over the supposed influence of Muslim Brotherhood-inspired ideas among public-school teachers, the situation is quite similar. In Trappes, sadly considered the "capital of French jihadism," the statements of a teacher denouncing the influence of Islamist ideas in schools sparked a debate that only served to further polarize positions.

In light of all this, we can consider another aspect that is characteristic of the post-ISIS period in Europe: the difficulty of collectively assessing what led to the flourishing of European jihadism. If we reject both denial and hysteria, does this mean that the only response left to us is one of silence? The need for precise and measures analyses that neither neglect facts nor express ill will toward local situations that are sometimes fragile has never been so pressing.

The Murder of Samuel Paty and French-Bashing: Symbols of the Post-ISIS Period?

The sequence of events in the fall of 2020, which culminated in the murder of Samuel Paty, a history teacher at a secondary school in Yvelines, is fundamental in many respects. Its scale and consequences may be harbingers of reconfigurations in European societies in the post-ISIS era.

September 2020 saw the beginning of the trial for the attacks of January 7–9, 2015, in which the journalists of *Charlie Hebdo*, along with their guests and bodyguards, were massacred. The atmosphere was especially tense. The day before, the satirical newspaper republished all the original Danish cartoons on its front page, as well as their own cartoons from 2006, under the heading: "All this for this." Al-Qaeda immediately spoke up, promising reprisals. The court that would host the trial was also targeted. Threats against the judiciary should not be underestimated: they have been a constant since the 1990s.

Salafi-jihadists consider the expression of a justice that has its source in democratic principles to be illegitimate, believing that the origin of all legality lies in the divine commandments of sharia. According to their logic, the assassins of January 2015 literally applied a divine sentence against those who were guilty of the worst of crimes, namely "insulting" the prophet of Islam. They were perceived as champions of the cause, and the very idea that they should be condemned by men, according to rules external to Islam and decreed by "infidels," was an additional injustice and an unacceptable breach in their eyes.

The public debate provoked by the trial concerned the same old issues that have been troubling European democracies since the Rushdie affair: freedom of expression, the right to blaspheme, the consideration of religious convictions, and political censorship. At the end of September, two smokers having an argument in front of the former premises of *Charlie Hebdo* were attacked by a young man armed with a machete, a Pakistani refugee convinced that he was carrying out divine justice. His criminal act against what he believed to be employees of the weekly magazine was praised on TikTok by a Pakistani imam from western Paris who is a home teacher.[44]

On October 2, 2020, in Les Mureaux, Emmanuel Macron announced a plan to fight against separatism and defend republican principles. The plan aimed, among other things, to provide the state apparatus with legal and administrative instruments capable of circumventing the pitfalls that have allowed radical Islamist movements to organize within the framework of the law, particularly through non-profit associations. The president's objective was to be able to act directly upon the "breeding ground" on which the dynamics of radicalization appear – the very dynamics that can lead to terrorist acts. Laurent Nuñez, the national coordinator of intelligence and counter-terrorism and an advisor to Macron, who worked on the development of the plan, summarized what it meant in an interview in the winter of 2022:

> For 20 years, the fight against terrorism has focused on the risk of violent acts. The entire system is geared towards identifying individuals or structures that are likely to lead to such acts. The President is now asking us to work on a second plan, in order to have a mechanism to fight against radicalization. The instruments of the public authorities have so far been totally insufficient in

this respect. We worked in ad hoc ways [. . .] without any systematic action. The action that will be taken will now target ecosystems, associations that argue that religious law takes precedence over the law of the Republic, that a certain number of the Republic's laws must be rejected.[45]

A few days later, Samuel Paty, a teacher at the Collège du Bois-d'Aulne in Conflans-Sainte-Honorine, tried to address current issues with his students as part of a civics class. He showed a few cartoons in class, after having taken numerous linguistic and pedagogical precautions. In particular, he invited students who did not wish to be exposed to them to close their eyes or look away. One student, who was absent that day but claimed to have been kicked out of class, was told about the lesson. She declared that the teacher deliberately sought to shock the Muslim secondary school students, including herself, and judged that she was the victim of an act of Islamophobia. Her father exploited the situation and gave a false version of the events in a video he posted on YouTube. He accused the instructor of underhanded intentions that he had clearly never had, and expressed indignation at certain drawings that the teacher had in fact never shown.

The parent thereby unknowingly reproduced the events of the original cartoon affair in 2005, when imams on tour in Egypt had invented drawings to demonize the newspaper. The controversy escalated in radical circles and around the person of Samuel Paty, who received little support from a school board that seemed not to grasp the seriousness of the situation. The teacher was slandered in a new video, this time posted online by a radical preacher well known in militant circles, at the request of the girl's father; the preacher specialized in the subtle intimidation of schools, presenting himself as a "mediator" to the establishments where incidents related to the application of the principles of secularism broke out. His participation in the campaign against the history and geography teacher evoked, in every possible respect, the second phase of the Danish cartoon affair, during which popular anger in the Muslim world, fostered in part by unscrupulous regimes, had ended up whetting the appetites of Al-Qaeda. In Conflans-Sainte-Honorine, in 2020, the false complaints of a parent and a peddler of Islamist anger, boosted by the algorithms of Facebook and Google, were enough to attract the attention of an 18-year-old man, who was from a Chechen family who had fled Putin's war, had been living in France for twelve years, and attended school in the Eure. He had already been displaying clear signs of adherence to the basic principles of jihadism (which had been normalized by ISIS) for some time, as evidenced by his computer searches, the positions he took in online debates, and the few testimonies concerning his religious ideas.[46] On Friday, October 16, 2020, a school holiday, he was dropped off in front of the Bois-d'Aulne school, where he waited for Paty – he paid some students a few hundred euros to identify him. As the teacher was making his way home, the young Chechen attacked him in the street. Following the advice of some jihadists in Syria with whom he had spoken, he beheaded the teacher. He was then killed by the police.

These acts were the latest in a long and tragic chain of events. The fatwa against British writer Salman Rushdie in 1989 forms the tack; the assassination of filmmaker Theo van Gogh in the Netherlands was the first link; and the many sequels to the Danish cartoon affair, from the *Charlie Hebdo* cartoons to the *South Park* episode in the United States, the attacks in Paris and Copenhagen in 2015, and the string of local polemics in Stockholm, Oslo, and elsewhere, were the successive links in the chain. The case of Samuel Paty is quite different, as he was in no way an interested party in any of these cases. He was a teacher, killed for trying to untangle the ins and outs of a societal debate, in the exercise of his duties and in application of the school curriculum. His assassination is an abridged version – a particularly dramatic one – of the formal developments of jihadism in the post-ISIS era.

The first of these developments was the crystallization that took place around the cartoons, whereby the terrorists sought, through bloodshed, to trace the limits of freedom of expression in Europe. The collusion, in this regard, between the various protagonists of this tragedy, from the father to the jihadist by way of an Islamist close to Salafist and Brotherhood positions, each drawing on a chivalrous ideal of defending an aggrieved religion, reveals certain continuums that remain to be explored today.

Second, the barbaric act in Conflans-Sainte-Honorine is reminiscent of the methods used in Raqqa when jihadist organizations ebbed back to the Levant. In addition to the reimportation of murderous methods, the killing of a teacher at a time that was supposedly one of "low tide" gives an indication of the depth of the Salafi-jihadist influence within

European societies. Even in periods of decline, their precepts, which are devastating for democracies, are now liable to be applied.

Third, the murder is a sign of the pressure now being exerted on representatives of the education sector, and in particular on teachers, who are especially neglected by the state despite being essential vectors for the transmission of the democratic principles that are so ardently contested by Islamist militants. In this sense, the death of Samuel Paty symbolically places education at the center of debates during the period of low tide that defines the early 2020s in Europe.

Fourth, the attack shows the distorting effects produced by modern communication tools, which on the one hand mix the real with the virtual, and on the other hand blend sacred beliefs with fantasy. The assassin of Samuel Paty acted after his exchanging private messages with individuals present in northern Syria. His online activity demonstrates an exposure to the moral considerations circulating in the radical circles active on the platforms known as the Islamosphere.

Just as millions of others are pushed toward their "centers of interest" by the logic of algorithmic isolation, he developed in the viral space of the Salafist digital counter-society. His daily news feed was marked by stories about violent incidents presented as an expression of "systemic" savagery, repeated "Islamophobic" acts, and "institutionalized" mistreatment of Muslims in Europe. The cumulative effect of such stories gives rise to a vision of the world that appears coherent, in which Islam is threatened with disappearance in France, and in which injustice, Islamophobia, and racism form the pillars on which democratic society is built. The lies against Samuel Paty triggered his act, but they were just one more distorted reflection produced by the ideological, communicational, and political environment in which he virtually socialized, and through which he filtered his perception of reality. In this sense, the killer's journey represents a tragic conjuncture for Western societies in the age of digital Salafism: the conjuncture of algorithmic isolation and doctrinal injunction.

Fifth and last, the affair reveals the growing polarization around the interpretation of jihadism and its causes. This was not immediately apparent in France, where the various political forces manifested a unity that had never been seen before, but it erupted in February following the divisive controversy over "Islamo-leftism in universities."

Outside of France, there was a general lack of understanding of the Paty affair, which was first evidenced in the United States. In the aftermath of the tragedy, some of the coverage by the American liberal press, long a standard-bearer for freedom of expression, was puzzling. In the articles that appeared in the *New York Times* and *Washington Post* (whose motto since 2017 has been "Democracy Dies in Darkness"), the word "jihadism" simply did not appear. In the former, the term "Islamist" was used only twice, once in a quotation attributed to President Macron, and a second time at the conclusion of the article, in the remark that "some did not hesitate to point directly to Islamism."[47] Even more surprisingly, the article in the *Washington Post*, which has since been deleted, employed an Associated Press dispatch that gave pride of place to remarks made by the Chechen dictator Ramzan Kadyrov, known for his cruelty. The long quotes from the autocrat, who physically annihilates any form of opposition in his country, seemed to offer advice: "When France has a proper state institution of inter-ethic and inter-faith relations, then the country will have a healthy society."[48] In the same vein, a host of opinion articles sought to present the murder of the teacher not as a terrorist act with its own logic, but as an unfortunate situation resulting from the intolerance of the French secular model, applying the framework of American racial issues to European jihadism.[49]

As for the pro-Trump press, it denounced not an "Islamist" but an "Islamic" attack, positing barbaric acts as fundamental to a religion practiced by more than 1.5 billion people worldwide. It saw the attack as proof that Donald Trump, who was then campaigning for re-election, was right to impose his "Muslim Ban" (a ban on Muslims entering the United States).[50]

The understanding of the attack on both sides of the political spectrum tended, if for opposite reasons, to concede to the jihadists their main claim: that of being the legitimate representatives of Islam, viewed by the left as having been "offended," and by the right as intrinsically "violent" and "backward." Both missed the political reality of the jihadist phenomenon, reducing religion and its adherents to caricatures, in every sense of the word. The coverage of the Conflans-Sainte-Honorine attack by the major American newspapers reveals a shared misunderstanding of jihadism, Islam, and the situation within EU democracies; the blindness of these newspapers is potentially a threat to the entire public debate in the West.

The French institutional model has at the same time been targeted by others, following the announcement, by the authorities, that they would disband two associations. These were BarakaCity, which was led by a major figure of French Salafism, and the Collective against Islamophobia in France (CCIF). These groups and their supporters, in a context marked by the *Charlie Hebdo* trial, the murder of Samuel Paty, and the announcement of a plan to combat "separatism," accused the French government of waging a "war on Islam." France was also caught in a diplomatic storm which was led by state but also non-state actors, who were linked in particular to the Turkish and Pakistani authorities and certain Gulf countries. All of this again harked back to the final phase of the Danish affair: political admonitions, real and virtual demonstrations, boycotts (on this occasion, a boycott of dairy products in the Gulf). The entire sequence of events ended with new tragedies: on October 30, 2020, a Tunisian illegal immigrant who had arrived in France two days earlier murdered three parishioners inside the Notre-Dame basilica in Nice; on November 2, an Austrian man returning from Syria, where he had just been released from prison, committed a series of attacks in Vienna, a city whose dynamics are an extension of sorts of those observed in Germany over the past twenty years.

The context at the start of 2020, when Samuel Paty was murdered, was no longer the same as in January 2015, when delegations from all over the world had marched in Paris to defend freedom of expression. France now had to deal with external pressure from international partners who seemed determined to misunderstand it. Certain of the accusations that were bandied about echoed attacks that had been leveled at France in the large body of Islamist literature since the 1970s. The country was thereby depicted as the "mastermind of Godlessness" (*Ras al-Kafirin*), a title many Western countries have been saddled with over the past thirty years, starting with England in the 1990s. The true target of this term lies in the founding values of European democracies and the EU.

The Return of the Taliban and the Death of the Al-Qaeda Leader

On May 1, 2021, the United States began the final stage of its military withdrawal from Afghanistan. The decision made by Donald Trump was implemented by Joe Biden. Almost eighty percent of Americans, who were keen to turn the page on "endless wars," agreed with the withdrawal. The terrorist threat within the country, meanwhile, now seemed like a thing of the past.

The announcement triggered an all-out offensive by the Taliban against the positions of Afghan government forces. Deprived of air cover from the US Air Force, the eyes and ears of the CIA, and the supervision of officers on the ground, the Afghan army disintegrated. The desertion of officers, who could see the writing on the wall, led to demoralization at the front and the collapse of defense lines. The relentless advance of the Islamists forced Western troops to accelerate the evacuation of their nationals and protected persons. Even before this process was complete, the Taliban entered Kabul without a shot being fired on August 15, 2021, and returned to power after the president, Ashraf Ghani, fled into exile. The institutional and administrative foundations that had emerged in the capital were swept away by the establishment of a new "Islamic emirate." Hard-won women's rights were abolished and schooling is gradually being banned for girls, while the strictest form of Sharia law is redefining the legal framework.

The speed with which Kabul fell testified to how poorly the Americans had evaluated the weak phase of the Taliban networks. The Taliban had been defeated in three weeks in 2001, but devised a strategy of slow reconquest by consolidating their foundations within the country's social and ethnic anthropology. Through a game of tribal alliances, preaching, and warlike intimidation, the insurgents established the conditions for a territorial hold that was more suited to the political and religious sociology of Afghanistan than the "state-building" methods of Washington's strategists, which did not put an end to either insecurity or corruption.

In contrast to ISIS's ultraviolent and provocative escapades, the Taliban cloaked their military progress and the re-establishment of an extremely strict order in cautious and pragmatic language. Playing with codes of communication and the spirit of the times, the government announced with great fanfare on social networks that it sought to be "inclusive," while warlords guaranteed to apply divine punishments "gradually."[51] The same radical clans came to power as at the end of the last century; sons sometimes replaced their fathers in official posts. The success of the Taliban encouraged other radical groups: ISIS renewed its attacks, particularly against schools and women, in the hope of recuperating the ground they had lost; meanwhile, a United Nations report published six months after the evacuation of Kabul noted that Al-Qaeda was again operating freely.[52]

In the summer of 2022, despite the promise made many times by the new masters of Afghanistan not to serve as a staging ground for terrorism, a spy drone spotted Ayman al-Zawahiri, the head of Al-Qaeda, theoretician of global jihad, and an indispensable figure in the movement since the time of Peshawar. He was located in a popular district of Kabul, where the Taliban intelligentsia had appropriated the residences of former high-ranking officials. He was living in a lavish residence that had been allocated to an assistant to the all-powerful Minister of the Interior Haqqani, which left little doubt as to the support he enjoyed within the regime. The situation was reminiscent of that of his predecessor as head of Al-Qaeda, Osama bin Laden, who was tracked down in Abbottabad, Pakistan, in an area that is home to the country's military elite and whose French equivalent would be Saint-Cyr. Unlike Bin Laden, Zawahiri did not live entirely behind barricades. He followed a routine, occasionally taking advantage of the open-air terrace at his disposal, which was concealed from prying eyes solely by bamboo windbreaks. At dawn on July 31, 2022, as he was stretching his legs on the balcony, the laser guidance system of an R9X "Ninja Bomb" Hellfire missile locked onto him. The rocket, which is just over five feet long and weighs over 100 pounds, rushed towards its target at the speed of sound. The nickname "Ninja Bomb" refers to one of its features: a fraction of a second before impact, it deploys six sabres across its entire width, katanas three feet in length that render its target helpless. Such was the lethal precision of the device that sealed the fate of the Al-Qaeda leader, the official use of which marked a new stage in the development of automated warfare.

The elimination of Zawahiri closed a chapter that had been opened on the morning of September 11. International jihadism is undoubtedly going through a phase of weakness and of intense and profound reconfiguration. The same is true of the political foundations of European democracies.

4

The Return of Hot Wars and the World after October 7

On February 24, 2022, Russia invaded Ukraine. The European Union was suddenly faced with the manifestation of the Kremlin's anti-democratic and imperialist ambitions. The stakes in this situation are very different from those described in the preceding pages, but it does recall some of the pitfalls we've already looked at, in that the threats repeatedly put forward by both jihadist activists and Kremlin supporters have been underestimated or even denied. All too often, commentators and politicians have taken refuge in a relativization of the ideological dimension behind their actions. In both cases, the threat to European models is only taken seriously when the threat of war sweeps through public opinion. Extremely serious events have to take place, such as Russian tanks breaking through the border to annex Ukraine or jihadists seeking to decimate the patios of Paris cafes with their Kalashnikovs, before we see the beginnings of an ephemeral collective awakening. This lack of understanding prevents European states from awakening to the threat of autocracies and Islamists, and, more broadly, to the authoritarian and totalitarian drifts that they contain within themselves.

Yet the Russian invasion of Ukraine also proved that the EU can mobilize quickly in an emergency. At the end of February 2022, starting with the first Russian bombardments, decisions inconceivable the day before were voted on unanimously by EU members: a program of massive and coordinated sanctions against Moscow, European rearmament, and a reassessment of gas supply agreements. European democracies are not condemned to inaction, and are able to act when threats become reality.

But it has taken them a long time to realize this, and their ability to achieve political union around these key issues is anything but assured. A sign of the persistence of these weaknesses is that, at the time of writing, the outcome of the Ukrainian conflict depends less on European aid than on American military involvement, which Donald Trump intends to halt if he wins the 2024 presidential election. Indeed, for the Kremlin, the shortest route to Ukraine's defeat lies in the potential victory of the Trump-Vance ticket. Forging the terms of debate, influencing candidates' opinions and citizens' perceptions, and therefore the outcome of elections, is an effective way of weakening democracies, as Islamists and dictators have clearly understood.[1] The problem is that, in democracies, elections are the most important legitimating factor for governments. If they are called into question, and if doubts persist about their authenticity – whether on the basis of information that is substantiated, as in the manipulation campaign in favor of Brexit in 2016, or unfounded, as with the claims of Trump's supporters 2020 – the fundamental pillar of Western democratic societies is weakened. This is why, in the age of global information warfare, public debates in Western democracies have become a battleground on which the West's declared enemies seek to involve themselves.

The October 7 Explosion

The fate of the American election, and of the conflict in Ukraine, hinges on another global crisis that was brutally reignited on October 7, 2023.

At sunrise, commandos from Hamas and affiliated groups set off from Gaza towards Israel. They pierced the land border at its weakest points, rounded the maritime border in inflatable boats, and invaded the southern territories. A dozen motor-powered hang gliders attacked a rave that was taking place nearby, leading to atrocities. Houses in the surrounding villages and kibbutzim were targeted. IDF officers, surprised in their own homes as they woke up by well-informed individuals who were armed to the teeth, had no time to sound the alarm, and were slaughtered along with their families. Nearly 1,200 Israelis were killed in the assault, while 252 others were kidnapped, abused, and held hostage in the underground labyrinths of Gaza.

The attack had all the ingredients of a powerful explosion: the element of surprise, barbaric acts against civilians, instantaneous broadcasting of the massacres, and, for the entire duration of the raid, a reversal of the balance of power with the Israelis.

On a symbolic level, the assault took place fifty years after the Yom Kippur War and the day after the Jewish religious celebration of Sukkot. The acts of violence, described as the most heinous since the Shoah, were compared to the anti-Semitic pogroms of Eastern Europe.[2] In their scale and gravity, the October 7 attacks were a major upheaval in international geopolitics, comparable to those of September 11, 2001. More than twenty years after the attack on the Twin Towers, they serve as a reminder of the leading role still played by Islamist organizations in the Middle East.

The event reveals how much prospects for resolving the Palestinian question have receded, and how much people have forgotten about a reality that has continued to worsen since the failure of the Oslo Accords in the 1990s. In terms of security, the extent of the shortcomings is a cause for concern, despite the considerable resources devoted by Israel to monitoring Gaza. More generally, what did Israel expect would result from a dreaded blockade imposed on an overpopulated enclave, controlled with an iron fist by Hamas, whose raison d'être, as stated in its charter, is the physical annihilation of the Jewish state? What can we expect from the colonization of the West Bank and East Jerusalem by ultra-Orthodox Hasidic Jews, in violation of previous guarantees? The problem is by no means limited to these issues, which of course do not justify the atrocities of October 7. But their persistence reflects an ever-increasing lack of interest, on the part of Israeli society and also regional and international powers, in resolving the Palestinian question. As a sign of the times, fewer and fewer Israelis speak fluent Arabic, which a majority were still able to do at the turn of the millennium. The horror of the October 7 raid is a reminder that Israel cannot remove itself from its regional context by the simple fact of not thinking about this context. A symbol of this is the festival that Hamas targeted: young Israelis danced in the open air, oblivious to what was brewing a few kilometers away in the tunnels on the other side of a wall wrongly considered impenetrable.

The Images and Narrative of the Global Information War

There is no need to detail the October 7 atrocities here, as they have been the subject of extensive media coverage. But there is much to be said about the extreme nature of the violence of the attacks.

We should first note that Hamas deliberately broadcast images of the most heinous acts, celebrating them in real time for the whole world to see. This echoes a visual grammar and a propaganda method popularized during the previous decade by ISIS. From the start of the attack, social media platforms were saturated with videos being shot by the units, from the beginning of the raid (destruction of control towers and crossing of the border), the acts themselves (massacres of civilians, hostages paraded in Gaza), and their "justification." There was no delay in the claiming of the attacks by this or that group: the executioners proudly put themselves on display. They certified that they were indeed committing these acts, resulting in viewers being stunned to witness the literally surreal scenes. This modus operandi was surprising because, although Hamas emerged as a radicalized outgrowth of the Muslim Brotherhood, whose use of terrorist methods is well known, it does not belong to the international jihadist movement. Its members have been repeatedly condemned by ISIS, which did not hesitate to excommunicate them as part of their competition for hegemony in Islamist circles. The methods of Hamas and its accomplices on October 7 therefore reveal the extent of their "ISISification," which is a paradigm shift within the organization. It is probably explained by the transformation and ideological hardening of the movement under the influence of Yahya Sinwar, who spent most of his adult life in Israeli jails and was the subject of a prisoner exchange shortly before the attacks. What is Hamas after October 7 in doctrinal terms? The answer to this fundamental question, which is often left aside, would provide many elements to better understand the dynamics at work in the Middle East since the fall of 2024.

The second thing to note is that exposure in the very degraded space of social media has become an effective way to call attention to issues. Terrorists can instantly capture the attention of the global masses. Disseminating gory images and immediately inserting them into a broader narrative, into a "great cause," is a method well known to social network propagandists.[3] Providing the first explanations for seemingly unspeaking events, and defining the framework for their reception, is a way of pervading people's minds.

In order to pre-emptively discredit the Israeli response, the Hamas brigades had only to imitate a *modus operandi* perfected by ISIS: broadcasting their atrocities online and justifying them in the name of a higher moral imperative. Different audiences referred to the attacks as "Hamas's revenge," or "the defense of the people of Gaza," "the Palestinians," or even "Muslims." Such justifications were accompanied by the demonization or dehumanization of the "enemy," which could mean settlers, Zionists, or Jews and their "accomplices." All of this was combined in various ways to mitigate or trivialize the violence of the acts and make them understandable – acceptable, if not justifiable – to very diverse groups, sometimes even to those who are pacifists and oppose the use of violence. This was particularly surprising among certain student activists, who were quick point out linguistic "micro-aggressions" in universities but remained silent in the face of the extreme violence of October 7 on the grounds that the atrocities were committed in the name of a just cause. Israel's response, which was completely disproportionate, and its justifications for destroying Gaza, which overwhelmingly affected civilians, were constructed according to similar patterns (only the motives had been reversed), giving pride of place to the narratives of the religious extremists in the government majority.

Thus, in addition to the traditional confrontations on land, at sea, in the air, and in cyberspace, October 7 revealed the new importance of using information as a weapon. Hamas, an organization infinitely less powerful than Israel, gave worldwide visibility to barbaric acts of humiliation, while paradoxically producing a discourse favorable to its cause.

Gaza has become the epicenter of an information war in which control of the narrative is king. It didn't matter that the raid condemned the Gazans to a response of unprecedented magnitude and exposed all the other peoples of the region, starting with the Lebanese, to a regional war with incalculable consequences. For Hamas sympathizers, it represented an "act of resistance," whose jubilant violence could be explained by the asymmetry of the conflict: the technological and military weakness of the Palestinians against Tsahal, the harshness of the blockade suffered by the people of Gaza, and the colonization of the West Bank by Israel.

Social networks operate topologically: the circulation of content is not hampered by physical boundaries but by ideological and cultural barriers. People who are right beside each other can thus exist in completely different informational and ideological spaces. They are rallied not on the basis of geographical or genealogical affiliation, as in the physical world, but on adherence to an idea and a grand narrative that allows people to filter the news and, above all, interpret it. The dissemination of interpretive frameworks that give meaning to current events through a pre-established worldview thus becomes key to international influence. An attack on southern Israel can therefore profoundly disrupt public debates in Western societies if it receives enough attention to capture and unite different collective imaginaries. By an effect of metonymy, attacks perpetrated by the most radical brigades of an Islamist movement partly rejected by the population, which exposed civilians in Gaza to even more suffering, could be perceived as a liberating act, even a victory for the Palestinian cause. This type of narrative, which took hold in the days immediately following the attack, would have a huge effect on how the conflict was made sense of, particularly in American and European public debates. In an unexpected way, the Hamas attack contributed to widening divisions in areas very far from the conflict.

On the Peaks of Despair: The Relentless Violence of the War in Gaza

On the evening of October 7, the framework of dissuasion that reigned between Israel and Iran was broken. The Israeli command feared new offensives on all fronts: in the South (Gaza), in the North (Lebanon and Syria), in the East (West Bank and Iran) and in the South-East (Yemen). The spectre of a regional war, one potentially involving nuclear weapons, loomed. Hamas belongs to the "axis of resistance" that Iran had been building for forty years to stand up to Israel. Iran sees this axis as an arc of power that extends from Tehran to Beirut via Baghdad and Damascus, based on three non-state organizations: the Lebanese Hezbollah, the Houthis in Yemen, and the Palestinian Hamas.

The emotion in Israel and internationally gave Prime Minister Benjamin Netanyahu, who had been plagued by legal proceedings and broadly denounced, an incredible amount of leeway.

On October 21, the Israeli army entered the overpopulated Palestinian enclave with the aim of destroying Hamas. The IDF set about mounting a relentless response in Gaza, guided by the aspirations of hawks who disregarded the fundamental tenets of international humanitarian law, at the risk of fueling global outrage against Israel and unbridled anti-Semitism. Israel set up a war machine designed to strike Hamas wherever and whatever the cost. It also seemed to be pursuing the objective of making Gaza "unlivable," displacing the mostly young civilian population and striking at areas whose safety humanitarian organizations had sought to guarantee.[4] Ignoring international pressure, including from Europe and the United States, Israel pursued a policy of total destruction, despite the strategic limitations, with potentially disastrous long-term effects of this policy. Massive bombing and ground operations reduced Gaza to ruins in the first weeks of the war. By the summer of 2024, there were nearly 40,000 deaths (most of them civilians and a large proportion of them children), hundreds of thousands of displaced, injured, and traumatized people, devastated cities, and the return of diseases from another century, such as polio. At the diplomatic level, the process of normalizing relations with Israel, led since 2020 by Saudi Arabia, Morocco, and the United Arab Emirates, has been suspended, much to the chagrin of these countries, which have invested significant political capital in these efforts.

At the same time, Israel launched a campaign of targeted assassinations against the strongmen of the "axis of resistance" deemed responsible for October 7. On December 23, 2023 and January 20, 2024, two Iranian generals were assassinated in Damascus, Syria. Meanwhile, important players in Hamas, including the organization's second in command, were killed in the southern suburbs of Beirut, Lebanon. On April 1, General Mohammad Reza Zahedi, commander of the Al-Quds forces in the Middle East, was also killed in a strike against the Iranian consulate in Damascus.[5] His death, and the destruction of the consulate, threatened to set the whole region ablaze. Tehran responded during the night of April 13 to 14, launching three hundred drones and long-range devices towards Israeli territory, with participation from Iran's auxiliary forces, the Yemeni Houthis and the Lebanese Hezbollah. Almost all of the missiles were intercepted by Israel, thanks to the intervention of American forces deployed in the region and the help of the Gulf States and Jordan. Iran had warned regional governments of the imminence and unprecedented scale of its response, probably to avoid an uncontrollable escalation that would cost it dearly.

On July 30, 2024, the assassination in Beirut of a senior Hezbollah military official, Fouad Chokr, followed by the elimination in Tehran of Hamas political leader Ismaël Haniyeh, reshuffled the deck. Haniyeh, a major figure in the "axis of resistance," was neutralized in an apartment secured by the Revolutionary Guards upon his return from the inauguration ceremony of the new Iranian president . . . The humiliation for Tehran, struck at the heart of its security apparatus and losing someone it was protecting, was enormous. On August 25, in response, Hezbollah launched an initial series of 340 strikes against Israel, almost all of which were thwarted by the Iron Dome. Tension reached a new high as Iran prepared yet another retaliation, liable to trigger an open regional war, in which it would probably be the main loser.

A Climate of Intellectual Insurrection: The Post-October 7 World

The 7 October assault and the war in Gaza mobilized European Islamist circles in ways rarely seen previously. From the first hours following Hamas's operation, the news generated spontaneous expressions of joy in different zones within the militant geography discussed in this book. In Malmö, Sweden, a procession of cars paraded on the evening of October 7 to celebrate.[6] Similar events were reported in Brussels. Hamas itself sought to exploit this phenomenon: Ismaël Haniyeh, for instance, called for terrorist acts against Jewish targets around the world, starting on Friday, October 13, 2023.

On that day, in Arras, a former student in one of the city's schools, of Ingush origin and raised in an ultra-radicalized environment, attacked several teachers, killing well-established teacher of literature, Dominique Bernard, and injuring several others. The attack took place almost three years to the day after the murder of Samuel Paty. The young man's statements to judges indicated just how ideologically laden his act was. He admitted to having wanted to attack a "history teacher" and, more broadly, the school institution that had sought to make him "a democrat" (which should be understood to mean a citizen, or someone who adheres to democratic principles).[7] According to the young man's jihadist logic of loyalty and disavowal, citizenship was in every way opposed to the jihadist doctrine of Islam that he, along with several members of his family (including his father and older brother), had embraced. The jihadism of the natives, of which this individual is a clear representative, targets the school as an institution. Far from an isolated terrorist attack, the act points to a worrying trend for France and its neighboring countries.

The following day in Brussels, an IS sympathizer killed several Swedes, who were in town for a soccer match, with a Kalashnikov. A few days later, on October 20, ISIS, which had remained silent regarding these acts that it had not incited, issued a call to attack Jewish targets all over the world, particularly in Europe, without mentioning Hamas. Against the backdrop of a terrible war in Gaza, Islamist communities online were seething with direct calls to "choose a side," flinging accusations, at all those who challenged their version of the events, of "Zionism," complicity in the colonization of Palestine, and even the deaths of Palestinian children. Islamists aimed to channel pro-Palestinian sympathy into tacit support for their own narratives. The daily news from Gaza, which produced images of unprecedented suffering, facilitated the dissemination of extremely politicized messages making the "West" an accomplice to the genocide of innocent children. These narratives, also encouraged by Iran and Russia for obvious reasons, aimed to establish the idea that the world is divided into a good camp and an evil camp, with European and American democracies being the embodiment of the latter.

In London, demonstrations in support of Gaza brought together no fewer than 100,000 people from October 18 to 20. They were infiltrated by a small number of people from Islamist groups who held a collective prayer in front of 10 Downing Street, the Prime Minister's residence. Among those present was Hizb ut-Tahrir, which, under the leadership of Omar Bakri, was one of the first vehicles for the jihadization of European Salafist circles. The same movement was becoming prominent in Germany. The renewed activity of "Londonistan," though it has not been commented upon much in England, is a cause for concern. While European jihadism is still at low tide, the war in Gaza is weighing heavily on Europe, from the standpoints of both politics and security.

In addition to the debates that divided the European left over how to think about the October 7 Hamas massacres, there were demonstrations and blockades of American and European university campuses in the spring of 2024. During these protests, student organizations aligned with far-left identity concerns tended to view the situation in the Middle East through the lens of colonialism, if not the American racial question or struggles against patriarchy and for the recognition of gender identities. The fact that these causes are all antagonistic to the model promoted by Islamist movements was not perceived as a fundamental contradiction, and Hamas was rarely mentioned. The polemic that arose from this unnuanced framework, which ignored historical, cultural, and political contexts, further polarized public debates that were already fraught. The far right also entered the fray, using October 7 as a pretext to demonize Islam and immigrants, and viewing the defense of Israel as an easy way to make up for a centuries-old legacy of violent and murderous anti-Semitism. Important elections – the European elections of June 9, 2024, the French and British legislative elections a few weeks later, and the US presidential campaign – took place in this deteriorated political climate. The French elections almost led to institutional paralysis following the dissolution of the National Assembly by President Macron. In England, the new Labour government immediately faced an unexpected crisis, caused by riots orchestrated by the far right after false information, widely relayed by Russia on social networks, circulated about the identity of the murderer of three girls, fans of Taylor Swift, on July 29, 2024 in the north of England. Antifascist counter-demonstrations were organized peacefully in London, but caused unease in some areas in the north and west of the country after groups with an Islamist bent infiltrated them and engaged in physical confrontations with far-right activists, sometimes using the situation in Gaza as a pretext. It is difficult to know whether the situation, in which different groups intermingled and confronted one another, is symptomatic of the climate of intellectual insurrection produced by the information war and nourished by the various dynamics of the post-October 7 world. But it is impossible to exclude this possibility, which should lead us to address the insurrectionary fire smouldering on the main social networks.

The ISKP: Prelude to a Return to Jihadism?

The sequence of events that began with October 7 and the war in Gaza has created extremely unfavorable background noise for the West, facilitating Islamist propaganda of all kinds.

The IS, which was initially discreet, is seeking to capitalize on these dynamics, by pursuing reconfigurations in three geographical areas.

In the Sahel, jihadist factions have taken advantage of the many pro-Russian coups and the departure of French forces to expand their activities. The renewed dynamism of the various groups in this immense and instable area could spill over into West Africa and other areas, and should be monitored closely.

In Central Asia, the return of the Taliban to Kabul in the summer of 2021 led to a strong resurgence of ISIS in the region, under the new name of the ISKP (Islamic State-Khorasan Province). The movement welcomed many jihadists who were involved in Syria and Iraq, and who had escaped via Turkey. ISKP has rebuilt its logistical and operational capabilities and launched several large-scale attack projects, indicating that waters are rising significantly for this branch. As a sign of their new capacities, ISKP carried out the most deadly jihadist attack in Iran's history on January 3, 2024. During a tribute ceremony for Qassem Soleimani, the former legend of the Al-Quds forces who was killed in Iraq, two terrorists set off their explosives, killing 91 people. On January 28, two assailants attacked a church in Istanbul and killed a worshipper during mass before being arrested by the police. On March 22, four members of ISKP entered Crocus City Hall, a concert hall in the suburbs of Moscow, murdered 144 people and injured 86 others, a toll higher than in the attack on the Bataclan in 2015. The Ukraine War undoubtedly diverted Russia's attention from the jihadist threat. They are also clearly cooperating less with the United States, whose embassy in Moscow had warned them of the risk of attacks on concert halls a few days earlier.

Iran, Turkey, Russia: in the space of three months, ISKP has struck at the countries involved in the defeat of ISIS in Syria. These countries signed the 2018 Astana agreements, which sought to bring a resolution to the Syrian conflict. While the countries diverged on the essential objectives they were pursuing in the country, they agreed on one point: to neutralize the mediation attempt by Europe and the United States. Since then, the "Astanaization" of international relations – that is, the strategy of containment with regard to Western influence in crisis resolution – has spread to other areas (the Mediterranean region, sub-Saharan Africa, and the Middle East).

All of this is a reminder of the opportunism of the jihadists, who strike where they have the capacity to do so, but also realize that they are indeed geopolitical actors in their own right, who know how to take advantage of the benefits that their enemies unwittingly offer them.

The rise of ISKP did not leave Europe unscathed: a few small-scale attacks took place there, and several were foiled. A policeman was killed in Mannheim, Germany, in May 2024. A young man was arrested in Saint-Étienne in June 2024 while plotting an attack during an Olympic Games event. In August 2024, Taylor Swift's Austrian tour was canceled after the authorities uncovered a deadly plot, preventing a huge tragedy. In late August 2024, an IS member stabbed festival-goers in Solingen, Germany, killing three people. The crime, committed by a 26-year-old Syrian, took place during the city's 650th anniversary celebrations and was quickly claimed by IS as revenge for the Palestinians of Gaza. Reactions reflected German struggles to address jihadism in a substantive way, with politicians arguing over dubious proposals that were reminiscent of the mechanisms of anger and forgetting that I have dealt with over the course of this book. The first such proposal aimed to ban bladed weapons in public spaces, as if jihadism could be addressed by reflecting on the size of a blade. The second sought the deportation of emigrants of Syrian and Afghan origin, as if, in 2024, the subject could be considered as something extraneous to the country in question. On the same day, a man armed with a handgun and draped in a Palestinian flag attempted to set fire to a synagogue in the seaside town of La Grande-Motte, in France's Hérault department. These two incidents are evidence of attempts to exploit the conflict in Gaza in order to conceal and legitimize criminal, terrorist, or anti-Semitic acts in Europe. These attacks, combined with the paralysis of public debates that struggle, in France, Germany, and elsewhere, to address the fundamental issues, reveal an extremely problematic trend for Western Europe: the jihadist nature of any terrorist act risks being concealed or even justified through the simple invocation of "Gaza" by its perpetrators. In this context, anti-Semitic acts have increased in severity and number, doubling in 2023 in France, and tripling in the first half of 2024.[8]

The most recent terrorist incidents in Europe reveal another clear trend: the involvement of networks from the Caucasus (Chechens, Ingush, etc.), often linked to IS networks in Syria, some of which have shifted to Central Asia and benefited from the reawakening of ISKP. The individuals concerned are increasingly young and even, for two thirds of those arrested between October 2023 and June 2024, minors. This should be seen as symbolic, as we have emphasized, of the coming of age of jihadists who are "native" or have received jihadism as an "inheritance" in their upbringing, or through their socialization on social networks, a phenomenon now referred to as "TikTok jihad."[9]

We must not overlook one final area in the ongoing jihadist reconfigurations: northern Syria and Iraq, where nearly 10,000 IS militants operate clandestinely, and which is evolving in the background of the conflict in Gaza.

The structural causes that have favored the emergence of a jihadist sanctuary twice in the last twenty years are still present. They have even worsened for millions of displaced persons. This area is still criss-crossed by all the fault lines running through the Middle East and has not recovered from the repeated wars that have taken place there, particularly since the US invasion of Iraq in 2003. Far from politically stabilizing, the region has been militarily locked down by the accumulation of armed forces: Syrian, Iranian, Russian, Turkish, Kurdish and Western, to which we must add the numerous Shiite and pro-Russian (Wagner) militias, the jihadist groups that work underground (ISIS) or administer territories (Hayat Tahrir al-Sham).

The most widespread feeling among the Sunni Muslims who represent the majority of the population there is one of dispossession, whether from the standpoint of politics, religion, or identity; in this, the feeling is not unlike the one that dominates in Gaza and the Palestinian territories, although the causes are different and the comparison is limited. Sympathies for Islamist projects run deep. Indeed, the nation-state model is being called into question throughout the region, in favor of a Russo-Iranian and, to a lesser extent, Turkish neo-imperialism – all of these countries have benefited from the retreat of Western powers, a historic change in the Middle East since 1945. The governments in

Lebanon and Iraq depend on external sponsors to resolve the structural crises that are overwhelming them. The regime of Bashar al-Assad in Syria has not fallen, but it is effectively functioning as a Russian–Iranian protectorate.

In the absence of forces capable of bringing about a new regional equilibrium, the equation remains unstable: a change in one variable tends to immediately affect the overall picture. The announcement of the withdrawal of American troops from northern Syria in the fall of 2020 was immediately followed by a Turkish offensive against Kurdish positions.[10] The development of war in Gaza and the conflict between Iran and Israel would take a completely different turn if it ignited this arc of crisis. In the event of an Israeli invasion of Lebanon or a maneuver of similar magnitude in the region, the risk would be that the various forces that prevented the return of ISIS in the Syrian-Iraqi north would pull out of the area in favor of new front lines. This type of scenario, which is far from certain, would create the pull factors that ISIS still lacks in order to become a meaningful force once again.

October 7, its immediate consequences (the war in Gaza), and its political and security repercussions in Europe also reflect the brutal reconfigurations that have been taking place in the Middle East since the Arab Spring of 2011, the US invasion of Iraq in 2003, and September 11. Within them, Islamist jihadist groups are powerful vectors of influence that are often poorly understood and poorly studied in the West.

Taken as a whole, these transformations raise fundamental questions about the nature of democracy in a world that is changing politically, technologically, and informationally, but also religiously. The challenges posed by this new era of conflict require in-depth reflection, and an adaptation of the frameworks in which we have traditionally thought about national and international affairs. Transforming politics with the help of new tools is the great challenge facing Europe, and it is one that we must now address.

Conclusion

Since the end of the last century, the ambition of jihadist groups has grown. With each new cycle, the leading organizations, despite repeated failures, have tried to cloak their project in an ever more excessive religious envelope: Islamic *Emirate in* Afghanistan in the 1990s, Islamic *State in* Iraq in the 2000s, and a global *Caliphate* ten years later.

In the same period, the waves have grown in amplitude. A hundred times more Europeans have gone to Syria (6,000 total) than their counterparts in Bosnia twenty years earlier (a few dozen). In the meantime, the movement has both grown younger and older, and above all, it has become more feminized. The phenomenon has taken shape in three types of spaces: for the veterans, in the neighborhoods where they settled; for the pioneers, in prisons, Salafist institutes, and the foreign fronts of their jihad. Whereas the original ideals referred to distant conflicts, sometimes unknown outside militant circles, the jihadist experience today refers to issues internal to European societies or superimposable on them. It now speaks to natives and is spread through social networks. Sympathizers have become aware of themselves and their numbers, and in this sense they present a new challenge.

In the period covered by this book, these militants have benefited from a great deal of misunderstanding about the way they operate and a delay in the production of knowledge about them. Instead of accumulating knowledge as the phenomenon grew in scale, the same diagnostic error was repeated, *mutatis mutandis*, every decade. Thus, on the eve of September 11, 2001, many academics popularized the thesis of "the end of Islamism."[1] Ten years later, the elimination of Osama bin

Laden, combined with the hope raised by the Arab Spring, led others to speculate on "the end of global jihad" and the imminent disappearance of al-Qaeda, just as the phenomenon was about to reach a new level in Syria.[2] Recently, the military defeat of IS in the Levant has led to similar reactions. For example, the star American columnist Fareed Zakaria summarized the prevailing perception in the United States by referring to the "collapse of jihadist militancy" in the spring of 2021, a few months before the return of the Taliban to Kabul.[3]

Western societies have tended to rely on the tactical errors of jihadist organizations rather than creating meaningful legal responses and intellectual, political, and religious antibodies. Europe cannot rely forever on the failures of its declared enemies if it hopes to resolve an issue that is this complex. Such an approach would at best continue to feed identity-based dynamics and political fragmentation; at worst, it would expose the continent to a renewed surge of terrorism.

The destruction of ISIS's territorial entity does not resolve the issue of European jihadism. It marks the start of a new period of low tide that places the question of its future back at the heart of political and social debates, and the decline in the number of attacks should not be allowed to obscure this. Since 2019, we have mainly seen *inspired* attacks, carried out by individuals who are not very organized or very connected to major terrorist organizations, and who are often psychologically unstable. These attacks do not so much herald a new period as end the previous one.

While it is difficult to anticipate future configurations, it is always possible to discuss current ones. Hardcore jihadists, whether in prison or online, are trying to react to the failure of IS by fighting against European democratic values and *salafizing* Islam. They aim to reduce hostility toward them by presenting their actions as a response to the rise of the far right, which they in fact encourage and advocate. The war in Gaza, following the attack and massacres of October 7 in southern Israel, is now being used as a pretext to justify a wide range of terrorist and anti-Semitic projects in Islamist and jihadist circles. Their goal is to turn their positions into a new norm, so that honest believers will break with all but the most rigid form of Islam (per the logic of allegiance and disavowal), and honest citizens will view terrorist violence as justified, or at the very least excusable. This is why two trends must be reckoned with: on the political level, that of people withdrawing into their own communities, and on the religious level, increased connections with larger Islamist groups (the Tabligh, the Muslim Brotherhood, the Hizb ut-Tahrir, the Salafists, etc.) for which these communities have historically provided militants.

Wherever they have asserted themselves, even in the extremely constrained environments of prisons or women's camps in Syria and Iraq, Salafi-jihadists have sought to reorganize social space according to the categories of pure and impure. Halting the preaching machines that have taken shape in certain localities since the 1990s should be a priority. This will require civil societies to be willing to address these issues. Today there is a tendency to place too much responsibility on government services, even though militancy is primarily built on political terrain. Governments in each of the countries we have looked at, whether left wing or right wing, have implemented various measures that take into account the local dimension of Islamist activism: the development of the *Prevent* program over the past fifteen years in Great Britain, the "Separatism" plan launched in France in the fall of 2021, the mobilization of certain German *Länder*, and ongoing discussions in the Netherlands, Denmark, and Sweden. But no lasting solution can emerge without political or civic mobilization within the societies concerned. There is no shortage of will: thirteen million people in France alone are involved in associations and voluntary activities. Jihadists, meanwhile, are not particularly numerous on a European scale – a few thousand in a population of nearly 450 million. They have little capacity for action and are subject to active supervision. Given their small number, they need to attract new recruits if they are not to disappear. In the 2020s, the future of millions of European Muslims is emerging as an issue for European democracies, and is perceived as such by the multiple currents of Islamism.

The phenomenon is therefore at the heart of the major social, economic, political, religious, and digital transformations taking place around the Mediterranean. It is a societal issue that is linked with all the others. As such, responses aimed at strengthening security without considering the other elements of jihadist radicalization are short-sighted and are likely to have only a very limited effect on the causes. Departing from the rule of law will not solve anything and will weaken the entire democratic edifice, which on the contrary should be protected. Similarly, suggesting that the jihadist dynamic in the West is a temporary problem that will disappear once we stop talking about it is irresponsible.

We must improve the quality of the public debate on this issue. It forms a key concern for the coming decade, along with the related issue of education. For too long, we have been caught between denial and hysteria, and these positions are linked to the general polarization of opinion. On the far right, those seeking firmness tend to make no distinction between a Muslim and a jihadist – thus falling into the trap of acknowledging the claims of jihadists to be the sole embodiment of Islam. This gives them considerable leverage and feeds a logic of confrontation that they in turn use to gain ground. Those on the far left, meanwhile, tend, for the laudable reasons of openness and the fight against discrimination, to fail to see Islamist militancy for what it is, thus also failing to distinguish radicals from the ordinary Muslims, who are the first to suffer from their ideas and misdeeds. In this view, everyone is reduced to the role of oppressed, and their potential radicalism stems logically from the injustices they suffer. While the extreme left claims to base its arguments on struggle against oppression, it ignores the anti-progressive, anti-feminist, and supremacist nature of the Salafist project, to give just one example. We must not bury reality under the partisan assumptions of either extreme. Thankfully, there are many other options.

Jihadism appeared in Europe after the fall of the USSR, in an intellectual climate dominated by the misconception that democracy now formed a new "unsurpassable horizon," a political norm that would spread throughout the world. Thirty years later, ideologies based on ideas of decline and even apocalypse are rife on both the left and the right, and are no more correct than democratic triumphalism.

The rapid development of new technologies and, more specifically, the way social networking platforms both shape and fragment public opinion debates, are central issues. It seems unrealistic to expect the jihadism issue to be resolved without answering the question of how to govern in the digital age in a democracy, and by what means.[4]

The European Union will have to find its unity on this subject; ironically, it will also have to come to terms with the unresolved legacy of American wars, some of which, such as the Iraq war, were opposed by France and Germany. Twenty years after September 11, American decision-makers display a lack of interest in, and increasingly a misunderstanding of, issues concerning jihadism, at a time when the latter has become endemic in Europe and the Taliban have regained power in Kabul.

The democratic model is not as fragile as it seems, contrary to what many of the preachers mentioned in this book would have us believe. The cohesion of European societies has been tested, but they have shown impressive resilience and political maturity during the ISIS attacks between 2014 and 2018. But however strong our democracies are, they are also vulnerable, and it would be dangerous to wait for a new wave of terrorism before acting. The current challenge is to prevent the emergence of a new active phase of activism. Periods of low tide, such as the one we are living in now, are by far the most important periods for the future development of jihadism. Over the past thirty years, these periods have been the most poorly understood, even though they determine the next rise of the movement in the West.

The rise of international jihadism occurred in tandem with important technological innovations. It took off during the Soviet withdrawal from Afghanistan in 1989, the year the Web was created. It reached a new level in Europe in the mid-2000s during the jihad in Iraq, at a time when broadband internet access was being rolled out. Ten years later, ISIS emerged as social networks were coming of age. Over this period, jihadism went from being non-existent in Europe to being a major security threat – from a camp in Afghanistan to a millenarian "Caliphate" engaged in a civilizational war against the forces of "disbelief."

Since 1989, a pivotal date if ever there was one, we have seen a succession of breakthrough innovations in the digital domain, leading to an ultra-rapid global dissemination of technical progress, the exponential acceleration of which is impacting institutional and security frameworks long thought to be immutable. These frameworks are proving to be poorly adapted to absorbing the shocks produced by these innovations.

The rise of digital platforms is causing major anthropological upheavals, the first of which concerns the shaping of public opinion. To give just one example, Europe is the world's leading digital space (1.5 times that of the United States), but it has no social network of its own. Yet social networks are the sites where 15–25-year olds gain their political awareness. And TikTok is the network on which young people in Western Europe prefer to socialize.

This situation places the EU in a position of strategic vulnerability that is unique in the world. The lack of algorithmic sovereignty contrasts with the situation of geopolitical and economic rivals (Russia, China, the United States, etc.), which have digital platforms (the tech giants in the United States, Telegram and Vkontakte in Russia, not to mention China's sealed internet) and the technical means to exert influence and defend their worldview and interests. Europe is thus ill-prepared and ill-equipped for struggles for influence, information warfare, cybercrises, the manipulation of mass opinion, and the radicalization of digital power relations, at a time when the costs of all this are falling considerably with the advent of generative artificial intelligence. In the spring of 2024, for example, the first jihadist video entirely generated by AI was posted online.

Since the arrival of ChatGPT 3.5 in the fall of 2022, technological breakthroughs have come one after another, to the point that an autonomous or generalist AI no longer seems fanciful. Humanity thus seems to be approaching a "Cambrian" moment of artificial intelligence. The expression refers to the era that began 540 million years ago, when the increase in the planet's oxygen level led to a rapid diversification of life forms, the emergence of multicellular systems, and the branching of the tree of life towards the living species known today. Sam Altman, founder of OpenAI, and as such the "father" of ChatGPT, shared his vision of what is coming:

> On a short timescale, technological progress follows an exponential curve. [. . .] The coming change will center on our most impressive ability: the phenomenal ability to think, create, understand, and reason. The three great technological revolutions – agricultural, industrial, and computer – will be joined by a fourth: the AI revolution. [. . .] The technological progress we will make over the next 100 years will be far greater than anything we have achieved since we mastered fire and invented the wheel.[5]

Given everything I have said in this book, it is not difficult to understand that the acceleration of the current cycle would bring about an intensification of political and religious unrest, reinforcing apocalyptic sentiments of all kinds. As such, extreme forms of violence, such as those seen under ISIS or on October 7, 2023, could not only be repeated, but find more people to justify them. History teaches us that millenarian projects like those carried out by ISIS almost always fail, but can cause considerable damage along the way, especially in the societies against which they are organized.

These very millenarian movements can also decline, or be channeled. To achieve this, we must put an end to the desynchronization of politics and technology, whereby the latter develops faster than the former's ability to regulate it. This would be possible if politicians were able to understand, act, and intervene in the technological realm – if they could invent a form of democratic control of technological progress and disruptive innovations, and forestall excessive enthusiasm. At the same time, we need to improve our understanding of millenarian ideologies, of which jihadism is a clear example, in order to understand their under-pinnings, for it is these underpinnings that explain their viral nature in the digital age.[6]

Those who have the intellectual tools to think about these changes and the technological tools to control them or influence their course will have a considerable advantage.[7] In a world in which the attributes of power are being partially redefined by the new technological order, Europe must be able to contest the many engineers of chaos with its own engineers of democracy.

To do this, European citizens must reach a new level of political maturity, so that they can evaluate the scale of the global transformations that have occurred since the illusion of the "end of history"[8] dissipated. They will undoubtedly succeed in this, without having to wait for the next crisis, if they come to understand the depth of the ideological threat to European models. Which means that they must get beyond anger and forgetting . . .

I would like to suggest a dozen actions that could be implemented to work towards this goal. I do so with the humility of a researcher who, despite having worked on this subject for more than a decade, is not a public policy specialist.

Protect the rule of law. Faced with a multitude of purveyors of false solutions who claim that a phenomenon that has taken over thirty years to develop can be dealt with in a few weeks with the help of radical solutions, we must stand firm and respect the rule of law. Within the framework of the latter, all necessary measures must be considered in order to confront a phenomenon that has long benefited from a lack of understanding and action.

Bring about a European political union that has its own defense capabilities, so as to safeguard the fundamental democratic principles of EU countries, which are particularly targeted by authoritarian states and totalitarian ideologies. As such, we should make the EU a fully-fledged geopolitical actor, capable of assuming, promoting, and protecting its direct and indirect interests internationally.

Devote more financial and human resources to the study of Islamism in Europe. It is especially important to guarantee complete academic freedom to research teams working on this sensitive subject; such teams should not be confined to studying security. They must also be protected from the excessive politicization of academia around these issues.

Engage in public diplomacy to emphasize that the fight against jihadism and, more broadly, against religious extremism is part of the need to protect European citizens. This includes, *de facto*, all European Muslims, who are the targets of Salafi-jihadist activism and racist or xenophobic acts (which, in turn, are fueled by the growth of this ideology).

Establish a precise map of the geography of Salafi-jihadist activism to understand how its preaching machine is established. Similarly, we must undertake detailed study of the areas where the activists have not managed to establish their preaching machine (for example, in countries such as Italy or numerous cities throughout Europe) and try to understand the objective reasons for this.

Reclaim the disadvantaged areas targeted by these groups. Reclaim the terrain by increasing the range of sporting, social, and cultural activities on offer in these areas, and paying attention to the infiltration of religious ideologies. Similarly, the prison environment must be rethought in the light of the enormous challenges raised in this book.

Develop practices that will allow us to obstruct preaching machines, in particular by filling gaps in our legislative arsenals. We must pay specific attention to non-profit associations, whether in prison or beyond its walls, which conceal activities that aim at ideological radicalization.

Develop legal and digital tools to curb the "virtual preaching machines" that have now taken shape online and on certain social networks. In this respect, TikTok must be given top priority. In European and national parliaments and in public debate, we should openly consider definitively banning it, or temporarily suspending its activity, within the EU. This platform, whose Chinese-developed algorithm is inaccessible to anyone in Europe, is the preferred platform of 15–25-year olds, who spend several hours a day, on average, viewing content of all sorts. For this reason, it is flooded by religious networks, particularly Salafists, who transform it into a "virtual" preaching machine. It is pointless to add an hour of weekly teaching at school to promote "coexistence" or civic education if pupils are overexposed to radical content on this type of platform. Overhauling school curricula is useless without anyone considering the online spaces on which a great deal of radical propaganda is now disseminated.

More effectively control direct or indirect foreign funding of religious associations, regardless of the religion.

Similarly, more closely monitor political funding from outside the EU for European universities and strategic companies. The Russian funding of political and economic networks in Europe since the mid-2000s, the "Qatargate" corruption scandal in the European Parliament (uncovered in 2022), and the Saudi funding of Salafism in the 1990s must all be studied in detail to serve as a basis for an effective policy.

Promote the emergence of healthy online spaces in Europe, by gradually regulating the jungle that has taken shape on social networks. In this regard, the creation of a European agency based on the model of the French ARCOM (the Regulatory Authority for Audiovisual and Digital Communication), which could exploit European regulations such as the *Digital Service Act* to their full potential, would be an interesting avenue to explore.

Similarly, we should promote the creation of a European monitoring center responsible for documenting and reporting campaigns of disinformation and manipulation of public opinion, particularly from foreign actors. The model of *Viginum* (France's service for vigilance and protection against foreign digital interference) can serve as a basis for such an initiative.

More broadly, encouraging and providing financial incentives for the development of a globally competitive European private AI sector would appear to be an essential step towards achieving the technological and algorithmic sovereignty necessary for the creation of a healthy digital democratic space. Europe's infrastructure can allow it to lead the global competition in this regard. It also possesses excellent engineering schools – it must simply be capable of retaining the talented people whom these schools train.

Turn Europe into a champion of AI that focuses on political risk. This field is of interest because it has been somewhat ignored by the United States, which tends to overemphasize the military field. But few issues are more important for the future of the EU than political risk. Europe must encourage the emergence of research centers or companies developing specific AI applications for the protection of democratic values, and the detection of propaganda from violent extremist groups.

Notes

Preface

1 Micheron, 2020, Foreword.

Introduction

1 Reynié, 2021, p. 9.
2 Garapon and Rosenfeld, 2016.
3 Cook and Vale, 2018, p. 17.
4 *Lemonde.fr*, August 29, 2021.
5 Saal, 2021, p. 132.
6 Ranstorp and Gustafsson, 2017; Nilsson and Esholdt, 2022.
7 Leiken, 2015; Varvelli, 2016.
8 Saal, 2021, pp. 132–134.
9 Sageman, 2004; Wiktorowicz, 2004.
10 Shtuni, 2019; Rosenblatt, 2021; Hasbullah and Korf, 2013.
11 Kepel and Jardin, 2015; Roy, 2019.
12 McCants and Meserole, 2016; Fernando, 2014; Baubérot, 2016; Khosrokhavar, 2018.
13 Leiken, 2015.
14 Fukuyama, 2006.
15 *L'Obs*, January 15–21, 1998.
16 *Dabiq*, July 2016.
17 Qutb, 2012; Kepel, 1993.
18 So as not to overburden the text, I have employed a simplified transcription of the Arabic language.
19 Lacroix, 2010.
20 See Louis Wirth's preface to Mannheim.
21 See Nesser, 2015.

Part I The Veterans – The 1990s

1. Afghanistan: Return to the Source

1 These two lines are the Islamic profession of faith.

2 This is the translation of a passage from the Koran, which is present in verse 156 of the cow surah, *al-baqara (inna lillah wa inna ilayhi raajiun)*, used in particular for expressing condolences. It emphasizes that the end of life is merely a return to God.

3 Interview with Usama Hasan, by the author and Magali Serre, London, February 15, 2022. As an accompaniment to this book, a documentary film, produced by Artline and directed by Magali Serre, was broadcast on the television network Arte.

4 Interview with Bruce Riedel by the author and Magali Serre, Washington, DC, June 24, 2022.

5 Curtis, 2012.

6 Continuation of previous testimony.

7 Hoodbhoy, 2005.

8 The investment amounted to between 2.5 and 2.7 billion dollars, according to Bruce Riedel, interview conducted on June 24, 2022. Compare this with the standards of traditional wars: Vietnam cost almost 300 billion dollars, the Iraq War about 1,000 billion, and Afghanistan (2001–2022) 3,000 billion dollars. In addition, where human beings are concerned, the United States registered very few losses during the conflicts of this decade.

9 Cook, 2005; Wright, 2006; Tawil, 2007; Haykel, 2014; Robinson, 2020.

10 Anas, 2019.

11 Rougier, 2008.

12 Interview with Abdullah Anas by the author and Magali Serre, London, February 14, 2022.

13 Religious scholars considered as authorities in matters of dogma.

14 Hegghammer, 2020.

15 Interview with Abdullah Anas by the author and Magali Serre, London, February 14, 2022.

16 Hegghammer, 2020, in the "Icon" chapter.

17 Kepel, 2000.

18 Mouline, 2011.

19 The term "avant garde," frequently employed by Abdullah Azzam and the first jihadists in Afghanistan, was also the name of one of Al Qaeda's well-known propaganda magazines. See Brown and Rassler, 2013.

20 Azzam, 1990.

21 Interview with the author and Magali Serre, Brussels, November 18, 2021.

22 Continuation of previous statement by Bruce Riedel.

23 Rougier, 2008, p. 78.

24 From the interview with Bruce Riedel.

25 Several figures, including Azzam's son-in-law, Abdullah Anas, lean toward the idea of a settling of scores in the midst of jihadist circles, indirectly accusing the Egyptians of the Al-Jama'a al-Islamiyya.

26 Hoodbhoy, 2005.

27 Hafez, 2009.

28 From the interview with Abdullah Anas.

29 Ibid.

30 Rougier, 2008, p. 66.

31 Dorronsoro, 2005.

2. *The Preaching Machines, from Peshawar to London*

1 *Investigative Project on Terrorism*, 2009.

2 London is home to important Middle Eastern newspapers (*Al-Hayat, El-Watan, Al-Qods* . . .), and cable channels that have opened bureaus there (Al Jazeera, Al-Arabiya).

3 From the interview with Usama Hasan.

4 Thomas, 2003; Leiken, 2015; Nesser, 2015; Bowen, 2014; Vidino, 2015.

5 His birth name is Mustafa Kemal.

6 Testimony of Abu Hamza's ex-wife at his trial in New York in May 2014.

7 O'Neill and McGrory, 2010, p. 15.

8 Thomas, 2003, p. 80.

9 Interview with Peter Clarke by the author and Magali Serre, London, May 24, 2022.

10 Continuation of Usama Hasan's previous comments.

11 Leiken, 2015, p. 178.

12 Ibid., p. 45.

13 Interview with Rashad Ali by the author and Magali Serre, London, February 16, 2022.

14 Al-Qahtani, 2012.

15 Continuation of Usama Hasan's previous comments.

16 Stéphane Lacroix, 2010.

17 Leiken, 2015, p. 166.

18 Continuation of the author's interview with Ismaël.

3. Bosnia and Scandinavia: The Periphery of European Jihadism?

1 Continuation of Usama Hasan's previous testimony.
2 Nawaz, 2012.
3 See the book written by his ex-wife, Glück, 2011.
4 Otasevic, 2013.
5 Kosonen, 1993.
6 Interview with Jakob Scharf by the author and Magali Serre, Copenhagen, May 3, 2022.
7 His full name is Fouad Talal Qassim.
8 Kepel, 1993.
9 Jensen, 2006, p. 16.
10 Interview with Ahmed Akkari by the author and Magali Serre, Aarhus, May 4, 2022, translated from the Danish by Martine Selvadjian.
11 The Al-Nour bookshop officially closed its doors in Copenhagen in 1992, but the former postal address of the bookshop, attached to the religious establishment where Saïd Mansour presides, continued to be used for mail-order sales (Jensen, 2006, p. 20).
12 People linked to this mosque would figure in investigations into the preparation of the 2001 World Trade Center attacks in New York and the March 2004 attacks in Madrid.
13 Jensen, 2006, p. 9.
14 *Houston Chronicle*, September 24, 1995.

4. Algeria and Belgium at a Crossroads

1 Vandermotten, 2014, p. 135.
2 Francis, 1975.
3 Interview with Alain Grignard by the author and Magali Serre, Brussels, November 19, 2021.
4 Specifically, the International Union of Muslim Students of the Free University of Brussels, which would later join forces with the Association of Islamic Students in France (Maréchal, 2009, p. 54). Information furnished by Alain Grignard (see previous note).
5 Maréchal and El-Asri, 2012, p. 19.
6 Ibid., p. 30.
7 Torrekens, 2012, p. 260.
8 Interview, by the author, with Mohamed Laroussi, director of the Al-Khalil Mosque, Molenbeek, June 24, 2016.
9 *Au nom du Père, du Fils et du Djihad*, Arte, 2016, https://www.film-documentaire.fr/ 4DACTION/w_fiche_film/48775.

10 RTBF, 7:30pm news program, April 4, 2018.

11 Micheron, 2020.

12 Nesser, 2015, p. 72.

13 Lia and Kjøk, 2001.

14 These demands are reminiscent of those of ISIS, which prioritized imposing so-called Islamic purity on the territory it controlled in Syria above fighting Bashar al-Assad's regime.

15 Nesser, 2015, p. 83.

16 *Guardian*, May 20, 2014.

17 Nesser, 2015, p. 83.

18 Interview with Jean-François Clair by the author and Magali Serre, Paris, November 12, 2021.

19 Ibid.

20 Continuation of interview with Alain Gringnard.

21 *Le Monde*, October 7, 1995.

22 The Clain brothers would later serve as mentors to Mohamed Merah, whose trajectory is reminiscent, in many ways, of that of . . . Khaled Kelkal.

5. London: "The New Peshawar of the Islamic Revival"

1 Continuation of interview with Alain Grignard.

2 From the interview with Rashad Ali.

3 Ibid.

4 Ibid.

5 From the interview with Usama Hasan.

6 Ibid.

7 Myslobodsky, 2004.

8 Bakri, 1996; Thomas, 2003.

9 Ibid., pp. 5–17.

10 From the interview with Usama Hasan.

11 Leiken, 2015, p. 180.

12 Thomas, 2003, p. 187.

6. The Afghanistan Emirate and September 11

1 This was denounced as a betrayal by the jihadists, for whom any non-Islamic settlement was viewed as illegitimate, and who vowed to take revenge.

2 Felbab-Brown, 2022.

3 Lawrence and Howarth, 2005, chs. 3 and 6.

4 Interview with Rashad Ali.

5   Ibid.

6   Thomas, 2003, p. 204.

7   Interview with Mustafa Kastit by the author, Brussels, September 27, 2016.

8   Interview with Alain Grignard.

9   The 1994 event was organized by Hizb at-Tahrir, who spent nearly 50,000 pounds and expected 12,000 participants. Estimates for the 1996 event were around 18,000 pounds (*Telegraph*, September 7, 1996).

10 Thomas, 2003, pp. 201–203.

11 *Telegraph*, August 31, 1996.

12 Shamzai, 2000; see also Zahab and Roy, 2006.

13 Interview with Rashad Ali.

14 Thomas, 2003, pp. 65–103.

15 Baki, fatwa 221, May 15, 2001.

16 Nesser, 2015, p. 95.

17 Interview with Usama Hasan.

Part II The Pioneers – The 2000s

1   From the interview with Usama Hasan.

1. The War on Terror

1   Interview with Bruce Riedel.

2   Reynié, 2005, p. 113.

3   Weiss and Hassan, 2015.

4   From the interview with Bruce Riedel.

2. Europe, Caught in the Middle

1   Kazerouni, 2017.

2   From the interview with Peter Clarke.

3   Thomas, 2003, p. 210.

4   From the interview with Peter Clarke.

5   BBC, May 20, 2014; *Guardian*, May 20, 2014.

6   Reuters, January 6, 2016.

7   *New York Times*, September 13, 2002.

8   From the interview with Abdullah Anas.

9   Leiken, 2015, p. 178.

10 Meleagrou-Hitchens and Amis, 2010, p. 128.

11 King's College, the London School of Economics, Imperial College, and the School of Oriental and African Studies.

12 From the interview with Rashad Ali.

13 Ibid.

14 Lia, 2008; Kepel and Jardin, 2015.

3. From Ulm to Toulouse: Passing the Baton to the Pioneers

1 Thielmann, 2019, and Federal Bureau of Immigrants and Refugees, 2021: https://www. bamf.de/DE/Startseite/startseite_node.html.

2 Nordbruch, 2016.

3 Horst and Zielonka, 2011.

4 Interview with Herbert Müller by the author and Magali Serre, Stuttgart, May 10, 2022. Müller's comments translated from German.

5 Ibid.

6 Horst and Zielonka, 2011.

7 Interview with Reiner Nübel by the author and Magali Serre, Heidelberg, May 10, 2022. Comments translated from German.

8 Micheron, 2020.

9 Interview with Laurent Ridel by the author and Magali Serre, Paris, November 10, 2021.

10 Bellanger, 2007.

11 Amer Makhlouf, a.k.a. Abu Doha, Cited in Brandon, 2009, p. 29.

12 Ibid.

13 Interview with François Molins by the author and Magali Serre, Paris, November 10, 2021.

14 Interview with Bo Yde Sørensen by the author and Magali Serre, Copenhagen, May 3, 2022, translated from the Danish by Martine Selvadjian.

15 Nesser, 2015, p. 132.

4. The Fuse of European Terrorism

1 The first Danish jihadist cell in Denmark, Glostrup, tried to make this claim for itself.

2 Reinares, 2005.

3 Nesser, 2015, p. 140.

4 Ten years later, we would witness ISIS endorsing redemption through jihad for criminals.

5 Dunn, 1991, pp. 93–107.

6 *NRC Handelsblad*, 2000.

7 Eyerman, 2008, ch. 1.

8 Hajer and Uitermark, 2008.

9 *New York Times*, November 3, 2004.

10 Ali, 2008.

11 Eyerman, 2008, ch. 1.

12 Ibid.

13 Among them was Maajid Nawaz, who spoke about the experience. See Nawaz, 2012.

14 From the interview with Rashad Ali.

15 Pantucci, 2015, p. 12.

16 See Vidino, 2013, and Hemmingsen, 2016.

17 *New York Times*, January 16, 2010.

18 Conversation published in *Harper's Magazine*, July 2007, p. 30.

19 From the interview with Peter Clarke.

20 Interview with Flemming Rose by the author and Magali Serre, Copenhagen, May 5, 2022.

21 Interview with Lars Refn by the author and Magali Serre, Copenhagen, May 2, 2022.

22 Ibid.

23 Ibid.

24 From the interview with Ahmed Akkari.

25 Ibid.

26 Ibid.

27 From the interview with Flemming Rose.

28 From the interview with Ahmed Akkari.

29 Interview with Ryan (his name has been changed) by the author and Magali Serre, Copenhagen, May 3, 2022, translated from the Danish by Martine Selvadjian.

30 *Guardian*, February 6, 2006.

31 *Telegraph*, February 4, 2006.

32 Ibid.

33 Pantucci, 2015.

34 The episode was recounted during the hearings of the trial for the *Charlie Hebdo* killings, which took place in Paris between September and November 2020. It is also recounted in an article dated April 5, 2006 on the website "actubd": https://www.actuabd. com/L-affaire-des-caricatures-de-Belleville.

35 From the interview with Flemming Rose.

5. The Acceleration of Salafism in Europe

1 From the interview with Jakob Scharf.

2 From the interview with Herbert Müller.

3 Brandon, 2009, p. 42.

4 In these interviews, he discusses the international situation, as well as

Salafi-jihadist thinkers. See *"Hiouar min dakhil al-sojoun al-britania maa al-cheikh al-olamah abi qatada al-falestini "* ("Discussion from inside British prisons with Sheikh Abu Qatada," 2010).

5 The attackers planned to strike an airport parking lot but were spotted by a patrol. The chase ended in an accident. Cornered by the police, one of the accomplices doused himself with gasoline, set himself on fire with a lighter, and threw himself into the load of explosives in a vain attempt to martyr himself.

6 See the "About Us" section of the Cage website: https://www.cage.ngo/jihad -and-terrorism-war-words.

7 Begg, 2008. He neglects to mention that in the same document, Azzam states that Islam must be spread throughout the world, by violent means if necessary.

8 Legitimate defense consists of using force to directly repel an attack, while retaliation aims to force opponents to modify their behavior. See the commentary by the International Committee of the Red Cross on the aforementioned convention, point 3431 (p. 1007): https://ihl-databases.icrc.org/applic/ihl/dih .nsf/COM/470-750110?OpenDocument.

9 See: https://www.youtube.com/watch?v=5wpGn3VgNMA&ab_channel= TheSpittoon.

10 Meleagrou-Hitchens and Amis, 2010, p. 133.

11 *Observer*, August 23, 2009.

12 From the interview with Rashad Ali.

13 From the interview with Laurent Ridel.

6. The End of Jihad in Iraq and the Digital Revolution of Jihadism

1 McCants, 2015, p. 42.

2 A new administration took over in the mid-2000s, but the mosque's doctrinal orientation remained Salafist, and it continued to be a gathering point for a small radical faction, probably aware of its symbolism.

3 Horst and Zielonka, 2014.

4 Gambetta and Herzog, 2016.

5 Simcox, Stuard, Ahmed, and Murray, 2012.

6 Difraoui, 2013.

7 See: https://www.nytimes.com/2016/08/30/us/al-qaeda-islamic-state-jihad-fbi .html.

8 Morton and Silber, 2018.

9 *New York Times*, August 29, 2016.

10 See: https://www.youtube.com/watch?v=3KSuFN8-tWw&ab_channel= tanyavaldez.

11 The magazine was entitled *Ahul Taqwa* or *People of Conscience*.

12 *Wall Street Journal*, June 3, 2019.

13 Ibid.

Part III The Natives – The 2010s

1. Before ISIS: The Sharia Networks in Europe

1 From the interview with Jakob Scharf.

2 From the interview with Ryan (name changed).

3 Ibid.

4 Ibid.

5 Ibid.

6 From the interview with Ismaël.

7 Around the north–south axis running through Idlib, Aleppo, Hama, Homs, and Damascus.

8 See Kelley, Mohtadi, Cane, Seager, and Kushnir, 2015.

9 In addition to the work of another blogger, Wael Ghonim. See Ghonim, 2012.

10 Interview of Soulé by the author, Fresnes jail, March 2, 2016.

11 Vidino, 2013, p. 13.

12 From the interview with Ryan.

13 Ibid.

14 Ibid.

15 Ibid.

16 In Tingbjerg, for example, bicycles remain unlocked, municipal workers tend to high-quality urban installations, and local residents go about their business in peace.

17 See : http://www.kaldettilislam.com/Izharudeen/shariah-zone-i-danmark.html.

18 From the interview with Ismaël.

19 *Jabhat al-Nusra li-Ahl al-Sham*: Victory Front for the People of the Levant. The group became *Jabhat Fatah al-Sham* ("The Levant Conquest Front") in 2016, then *Hayat Tahrir al-Sham* ("Levant Liberation Movement") in January 2017. For the sake of clarity, and because these different names reflect changes in internal strategy that are not important for our purposes, we will stick to "Al-Nusra."

20 From the interview with Ryan.

21 From the interview with Jakob Scharf.

22 From the interview with Ismaël.

23 Hearings in the trial of group members, which was held at the Paris district court from June 8 to July 10, 2015, and which we attended.

24 Author's interview with a judge from the anti-terrorist sub-directorate of the Paris public prosecutor's office, May 24, 2017.

25 From the interview with Ismaël.

26 *Deutsche Welle*, May 23, 2012.

27 Ibid.

28 *Le Monde*, July 4, 2018.

29 Coolsaet, 2017, p. 59.

30 BBC, December 4, 2013.

31 *L'Obs*, December 8, 2015.

2. ISIS, an Attempt at Jihadist Submersion

1 Bozarslan, 2018.

2 Mouline, 2011.

3 Touzari, 2017.

4 Interview by the author with Amine (not his real name) at the Fleury-Mérogis Prison, June 17, 2016.

5 See: https://nos.nl/video/668781-ik-feliciteer-isis-met-het-kalifaat.html.

6 *Al-Jazeera English*, September 5, 2014.

7 *The Standard*, August 13, 2014.

8 This comparison was made in all the European public debates at the time. See Jung, 2015.

9 Massey and Espinosa, 1997.

10 Weiner, 1995, p. 28.

11 Leiken, 2015, p. 93. More recently, see Regnard-Drouot, 2022.

12 Lahoud, 2014.

13 De Leede, 2018.

14 Cook and Vale, 2018, pp. 4, 14, and 22.

15 We refer the reader to the testimony of one of these women, Nadia Murad, 2018, and the impressive fieldwork Patrick Desbois undertook with Yazidi children who fled the IS (Costel and Desbois, 2016).

16 *Vice News*, November 3, 2014.

17 According to Imam En-Nawawi, regularly cited by Salafists, the opinion of the majority of scholars (ulamas) would make this event one of the signs heralding the end of time. See En-Nawawi, 2017, p. 158. This formula is found in several hadiths considered to be authentic (*sahih*).

18 Saal, 2021, pp. 185–194.

19 Author interview with Aïssam, Fresnes jail, March 1, 2016.

20 Cook and Vale, 2018, p. 3.

21 From the "ask.fm" page of one French jihadist: https//ask.fm/Musulmanooi.

22 Author interview with Yasmina, Fleury-Mérogis Women's Prison, December 5, 2016.

23 Al-Awlaki, 2005, p. 8.

24 Al-Awlaki, 2010, p. 1.

25 Al-Awlaki, 2008, pp. 17–18.

26 From the interview with Ismaël.

27 Due to the very large number of attacks against European democracies during the peak of ISIS, it would be tedious to enumerate them all to the reader. See Reynié (ed.), 2021.

28 Dallemagne and Lamfalussy, 2021, pp. 52 and 65.

29 Such as Amnesty International. See the dossier published in *Le JDD*, June 9, 2018, pp. 2–4.

30 Dallemagne and Lamfalussy, 2021, p. 81.

31 Indictment order for the trial of the November 13 attacks, which we were able to consult.

32 Author interview with Brahim, Lille-Annoeullin prison, October 21, 2016.

33 *Le Monde*, November 13, 2021.

34 See *Le Monde*, June 7, 2017.

35 From the interview with Flemming Rose.

36 Reuters, April 22, 2015.

37 From the interview with Bo Yde Sørensen.

38 Ibid.

39 The slogan "Je suis Charlie," which began with the publication of a cartoon by Joachim Roncin, quickly became a "meme" on social networks and, more broadly, the symbol of the refusal to give up freedom of expression in the face of terrorist violence. To this day, #jesuischarlie is the most shared hashtag in the history of Twitter. However, a debate soon emerged around the possible limits of its use when the far-right leader Jean-Marie Le Pen began using a modified version, "I am Charlie Martel," in reference to the historical figure who stopped the progression of the Saracens in France in 732 at the Battle of Poitiers. Dieudonné, the controversial comedian and close associate of the anti-Semitic far right, came up with "Je suis Charlie Coulibaly," which found favor well beyond his circle of followers, and which led to his conviction by the Paris Court of Appeal in 2016 for advocating terrorism. Finally, some representatives of Islam in France denounced the slogan "Je suis Charlie" as an attack on the honor of Muslims, viewing its success as a symbol of the "Islamophobic" nature of French society. The consequence of the massacres was to make the satirical newspaper, which claims to be radical and marginal, a central symbol of the struggle for freedom of expression in France and throughout the world.

40 *New York Times*, February 16, 2015.

41 Hugo, 1842 (2022), p. 100.

42 Interview with Alain Grignard by the author and Magali Serre, Brussels, November 18, 2021.

43 From the indictment order for the trial of the November 13 attacks.

44 From the indictment order for the trial of the November 13 attacks.

45 RTBF, September 6, 2021, available online at the following address: https://www.radiofrance.fr/franceinter/ce-qu-a-dit-salah-abdeslam-a-la-rtbf-lors-d-un-micro-trottoir-quelques-heures-apres-les-attentats-6154091.

46 From the indictment order for the trial of the November 13 attacks.

47 *Deutsche Welle*, October 18, 2017.

48 BBC, August 19, 2017.

3. After ISIS: The Jihadist Decline and Islamist Reconfigurations in Europe

1 Lister, 2016.

2 These figures are from the European Union: https://civil-protection-humanitarian-aid.ec.europa.eu.

3 Frantzman, 2019.

4 In 2018 alone, 1,800 individuals returned to Europe. The number has increased in the time since. See Cook and Vale, 2018, p. 16.

5 Author interview with a representative of the State Department, Washington, D.C., September 26, 2022.

6 Soz, 2022.

7 Ibid.

8 Ayad, Khan and Al-Tamimi, 2022.

9 *Le Figaro*, February 28, 2019.

10 From the interview with Laurent Ridel.

11 Interview with Olaf (we have changed his name) by the author and Magali Serre, Copenhagen, May 5, 2022, translated from the Danish by Martine Selvadjian.

12 Micheron, 2020.

13 From the interview with Ismaël.

14 From the interview with Brahim.

15 From the interview with Ismaël.

16 Author interview with Amine, Fleury-Mérogis Prison, June 17, 2016.

17 From the interview with Olaf (not his real name).

18 Micheron, 2020, especially the chapter entitled "La katiba de Fleury-Mérogis."

19 Hanane A. and Michaël C. killed a supervisor and injured three others on March 5, 2019, in the Condé-sur-Sarthe Prison.

20 From the interview with Laurent Ridel.

21 *The Local*, May 19, 2017.

22 From the interview with Peter Clarke.

23 From the interview with Bo Yde Sørensen.

24 Ibid.

25 Ibid.

26 *Independent Review of Terrorism Legislation*, April 2022: https://terrorismlegislationreviewer.independent.gov.uk/.

27 From the interview with Peter Clarke.

28 Saal, 2021, p. 109.

29 *Le Point*, June 15, 2018.

30 Nilsson and Esholdt, 2022, p. 1.

31 This research was carried out over a nine-month period in 2016 and is based on semi-structured interviews conducted with a sample of 406 Molenbeek residents (149 women and 257 men), supplemented by non-structured interviews with 100 others (64 women and 36 men). The only existing survey of this type, it had the advantage of providing elements that allowed for an objective view of the ideas that the inhabitants of Molenbeek held on a number of themes related to "living together," to social, political, religious, security, and terrorism issues in this municipality following the 2015 and 2016 attacks and at a time when ISIS was beginning to decline. Published in June 2017 by the European Institute of Peace, it was conducted by a team of researchers under the direction of Professor Rik Coolsaet.

32 Between January 2016 and September 2017, we regularly visited Molenbeek to conduct an in-depth political sociology field survey. More than 50 individuals were interviewed and around 20 semi-structured interviews were conducted.

33 Coolsaet, 2017, p. 10.

34 Ibid., p. 38.

35 Ibid., p. 41.

36 Author interview with the Molenbeek-Saint-Jean police chief, March 26, 2016.

37 *DH Les Sports+*, November 13, 2015.

38 Coolsaet, 2017, pp. 36 and 39.

39 Ibid., pp. 50, 52, and 27. Only fourteen percent consider its imprint as "strong" or "very strong," compared to 34 percent of inhabitants of European origin.

40 Ibid., pp. 7, 29, and 55.

41 Ibid., p. 34.

42 Author interview with the police chief of Molenbeek-Saint-Jean, March 26, 2016.

43 *L'Obs*, December 8, 2015.

44 GNET (The Global Network on Extremism and Technology), 2020. The article can

be found online: https://gnet-research.org/2020/12/09/praising-jihadist-attacks-on-tiktok-and-the-challenge- of-protecting-youths-from-online-extremism.

45 Interview with Laurent Nuñez by the author and Magali Serre, Paris, March 31, 2022.

46 *France Bleu*, November 27, 2020.

47 *New York Times*, October 17, 2020. See the opinion article I published with Bernard Haykel in *Le Monde*, October 21, 2020.

48 Associated Press, October 17, 2020.

49 On this, see the *Washington Post*, October 23, 2020, and the *New York Times*, October 31, 2020.

50 See *Breitbart News*, October 29, 2020, and *Fox News*, October 16, 2020.

51 *Guardian*, November 14, 2022.

52 *Guardian*, June 3, 2022.

4. The Return of Hot Wars and the World after October 7

1 Da Empoli, 2022; and Guriev and Treisman, 2023.

2 For our part, we prefer the term "raid." See "Israël-Hamas: l'Europe dans les failles de la guerre du Soukkot," *Le Grand Continent*, October 27, 2023."

3 DiResta, 2024.

4 On this subject, see Rémy, 2024.

5 Smolar, 2024.

6 Hivert, 2024.

7 Pham-Lê, 2024.

8 Ayad and Seckel, 2024.

9 "TikTok Jihad: Terrorists Leverage Modern Tools to Recruit and Radicalize," August 9, 2024, https://thesoufancenter.org/intelbrief-2024-august-9/. This also explains their fixation on certain Gen Z icons, such as Taylor Swift.

10 It should be noted that the Kurds, who oversee ninety percent of European jihadist prisoners, depend on American support to carry this out.

Conclusion

1 Following Bayat, 1996.

2 Lahoud, 2010; Zelin, 2012; Filiu, 2009; *L'Express*, March 22, 2010.

3 *Washington Post*, April 29, 2001.

4 Da Empoli, 2019.

5 Storchan, 2023.

6 Regarding this theme, see Micheron, 2024.

7 Suleyman and Bhaskar, 2023.

8 Salamé, 2024.

Bibliography

Al-Awlaki, Anwar (2005), *Constants on the Path of Jihad by Shaykh Yusuf al 'Uyayree: Lecture Series by Imam Anwar al Awlaki.*

Al-Awlaki, Anwar (2008), *The Battle of the Hearts and Minds.*

Al-Awlaki, Anwar (2010). *Anwar al-Awlaki: Western Jihad Is Here to Stay.*

Al-Qahtani, Muhammad Saeed (2012), *Al-Wala Wal-Bara. According to the Aqeedah of the Salaf,* Parts 1-2-3.

Ali, Ayaan Hirsi (2008), *Infidel,* New York, Atria.

Anas, Abdullah (2019), *To the Mountains: My Life in Jihad, from Algeria to Afghanistan,* London, Hurst.

Ayad, Christophe and Seckel, Henri (2024), "L'attaque de la synagogue de La Grande-Motte marque un tournant dans la violence antisémite," *Le Monde,* August 27.

Ayad, Moustafa, Khan and Nadeem, Al-Tamimi, Aymenn (2022), "The Terror Times. The Depth and Breadth of The Islamic State Alternative News Outlet Ecosystem Online," *Institute for Strategic Dialogue.*

Azzam, Abdullah (1990), *Al-difa' 'an aradhi al-moslimin, aham foroudh al-a'yan* ["La défense des terres musulmanes, la première des obligations"].

Baki, fatwa 221, May 15, 2001.

Bakri, Omar Muhammad (1996), *The Role of The Mosque,* Khilafah Publishing House.

Baubérot, Jean (2016), Le Cercle des enseignant.e.s laïques, *Petit manuel pour une laïcité apaisée. À l'usage des profs, des élèves et de leurs parents,* Paris, La Découverte.

Bayat, Asef (dir. ; 2013), *Post-Islamism. The Changing Faces of Political Islam,* Oxford, New York, Oxford University Press.

Begg, Moazzam (2008), "Jihad and Terrorism. A War of Words," *Arches Quarterly*, 2 (1), Cordoba Foundation.

Bellanger, Hélène (2007), *Vivre en prison. Histoires de 1945 à nos jours*, Paris, Hachette littératures.

Bowen, Innes (2014), *Medina in Birmingham, Najaf in Brent. Inside British Islam*, London, Hurst & Company.

Bozarslan, Hamit (2018), *Marges et pouvoir dans l'espace (post-)ottoman, xixe–xxe siècle*, Paris, Éditions Karthala.

Brandon, James (2009), *Unlocking Al-Qaeda. Islamist Extremism in British Prisons*, London, Quilliam Foundation.

Brown, Vahid and Rassler, Don (2013), *Fountainhead of Jihad. The Haqqani Nexus, 1973–2012*, New York, Columbia University Press.

Cage website.

Cook, David (2005), *Understanding Jihad*, Berkeley, Los Angeles, University of California Press.

Cook, Joana and Vale, Gina (2018), *From Daesh to "Diaspora". Tracing the Women and Minors of Islamic State*, Londres, ICSR, King's College.

Coolsaet, Rik (2017), "Molenbeek and Violent Radicalisation. A Social Mapping," *European Institute of Peace*.

Costel, Nastasie and Desbois, Patrick (2016), *La Fabrique des terroristes. Dans les secrets de Daesh*, Paris, Librairie Arthème Fayard.

Curtis, Mark (2012), *Secret Affairs. Britain's Collusion with Radical Islam*, London, Serpent's Tail.

Da Empoli, Giuliano (2019), *Les Ingénieurs du chaos*, Paris, JC Lattès.

Da Empoli, Giuliano (2022), *Le mage du Kremlin*, Paris, Gallimard.

Dallemagne, Georges and Lamfalussy, Christophe (2021), *Le Clandestin de Daech*, Loverval, Kennes Éditions.

De Leede, Seran (2018), "Women in Jihad. A Historical Perspective," *Terrorism and Counter-Terrorism Studies*.

Difraoui, Abdelasiem El (2013), *Al-Qaida par l'image. La Prophétie du martyre*, Paris, PUF.

DiResta, Renée (2024), *Invisible Rulers: The People Who Turn Lies into Reality*, Public Affairs.

Dorronsoro, Gilles (2005), *Revolution Unending. Afghanistan, 1979 to the Present*, New York, Columbia University Press.

Dunn, Kevin (1991), "A Great City is A Great Solitude". Descartes's Urban Pastoral," *Yale French Studies*, 80: 93–107.

En-Nawawi (2017), *Résumé de Sahih Mouslim, avec le commentaire de l'imam En-Nawawi,* édition bilingue française-arabe, tome 1, Paris, Librairie Sana.

Eyerman, Ron (2008), *The Assassination of Theo van Gogh. From Social Drama to Cultural Trauma (Politics, History, and Culture)*, Durham, London, Duke University Press.

Federal Bureau of Immigrants and Refugees, 2021: https://www. bamf.de /DE/Startseite/startseite_node.html.

Felbab-Brown, Vanda (2022), "Pipe Dreams. The Taliban and Drugs from The 1990s into its New Regime," *Small Wars Journal.*

Fernando, Mayanthi L. (2014), *The Republic Unsettled. Muslim French and the Contradictions of Secularism*, Durham, London, Duke University Press.

Filiu, Jean-Pierre (2009), *Les Neuf Vies d'Al-Qaïda*, Paris, Librairie Arthème Fayard.

Francis, J. (1975), *La Chanson des rues de Molenbeek Saint Jean*, Bruxelles, Louis Musin.

Frantzman, Seth J. (2019), *After Isis. America, Iran and the Struggle for the Middle East*, Jérusalem, Gefen Publishing House Ltd.

Fukuyama, Francis (2006), *The End of History and The Last Man*, New York, Free Press.

Gambetta, Diego and Hertog, Steffen (2016), *Engineers of Jihad. The Curious Connection between Violent Extremism and Education*, Princeton, Oxford, Princeton University Press.

Garapon, Antoine and Rosenfeld, Michel (2016), *Démocraties sous stress. Les défis du terrorisme global*, Paris, PUF.

Ghassan Salamé (2024), *La Tentation de Mars. Guerre et paix au XXIe siècle*, Paris, Fayard, 2024.

Ghonim, Wael (2012), *Revolution 2.0. The Power of The People is Greater than The People in Power. A Memoir*, Boston, Houghton Mifflin Harcourt.

Glück, Doris (2011), *Niqab. J'étais la femme d'un guerrier d'Allah (récits, témoignages)*, Paris, L'Archipel.

Guriev, Sergei and Treisman, Daniel (2023), *Spin Dictators. Le nouveau visage de la tyrannie au xxie siècle*, Paris, Payot.

Hafez, Mohammed (2009), "Jihad After Iraq. Lessons from the Arab Afghans Phenomenon," *Studies in Conflict & Terrorism*, 32: 73–94.

Hajer, Maarten and Uitermark, Justus (2008), "Performing Authority. Discursive Politics after the Assassination of Theo Van Gogh," *Public Administration*, 86: 5–19.

Hasbullah, Shahul and Korf, Benedikt (2013), "Muslim Geographies, Violence and the Antinomies of Community in Eastern Sri Lanka", *The Geographical Journal*, 179: 32–43.

Haykel, Bernard (2014), "On the Nature of Salafi Thought and Action," in Roel Meijer (ed.) (2009), *Global Salafism. Islam's New Religious Movement*, Oxford, Oxford University Press.

Hegghammer, Thomas (2020), *The Caravan. Abdullah Azzam and the Rise of Global Jihad*, Cambridge, Cambridge University Press.

Hemmingsen, Ann-Sophie (2016), "Plebeian Jihadism in Denmark. An Individualisation and Popularization Predating The Growth of The Islamic State," *Perspectives on Terrorism*, 10 (6).

Hivert, Anne-Françoise (2024), "À Malmö, un concours Eurovision sous haute tension," *Le Monde*, April 17.

Hoodbhoy, Pervez (2005), "Afghanistan and The Genesis of Global Jihad," *Peace Research*, vol. 37, no. 1, pp. 15–30, published by The Canadian Mennonite University.

Horst, Frank W. and Zielonka, Ralf R. (2014), *Salafist Jihadism in Germany. An OSINT Analysis of a Growing Threat*, Kindle.

Hugo, Victor (2022), *OEuvres. Le Rhin. Lettres à un ami*, tome 1, Paris, Hachette.

Jensen, Michael Taarnby (2006), *Jihad in Denmark. An Overview and Analysis of Jihadi Activity in Denmark, 1990-2006*, DIIS Working Paper no. 2006 / 35.

Jung, Dietrich (2015), "Foreign Fighters. Comparative Reflections on Syria and Spain," Middle East Institute / National University of Singapore.

Kazerouni, Alexandre (2017), *Le Miroir des cheikhs. Musée et politique dans les principautés du Golfe persique*, Paris, PUF.

Kelley, Colin, Mohtadi, Shahrzad, Cane, Mark A., Seager, Richard, and Kushnir, Yochanan (2015), "Climate Change in The Fertile Crescent and Implications of the Recent Syrian Drought," *Proceedings of the National Academy of Sciences*, 112: 3241–3246.

Kepel, Gilles (1993), *Le Prophète et Pharaon. Aux sources des mouvements islamistes*, Paris, Le Seuil.

Kepel, Gilles (2000), *Jihad. Expansion et déclin de l'islamisme*, Paris, Gallimard.

Kepel, Gilles and Jardin, Antoine (2015), *Terreur dans l'Hexagone. Genèse du jihad français*, Paris, Gallimard.

Khosrokhavar, Farhad (2018), *Le Nouveau Jihad en Occident*, Paris, Robert Laffont.

Kosonen, Pekka (1993), *The Nordic Welfare State as an Idea and as Reality*, Helsinki, Renvall Institute, University of Helsinki.

Lacroix, Stéphane (2010), *Les Islamistes saoudiens. Une insurrection manquée*, Paris, PUF.

Lahoud, Nelly (2010), *The Jihadis' Path to Self-Destruction*, London, C. Hurst.

Lahoud, Nelly (2014), "The Neglected Sex. The Jihadis' Exclusion of Women from Jihad," *Terrorism and Political Violence*, 26: 780–802.

Lawrence, Bruce and Howarth, James (2005), *Messages to the World. The Statements of Osama Bin Laden*, London, New York, Verso.

Leiken, Robert S. (2015), *Europe's Angry Muslims. The Revolt of The Second Generation*, Oxford, New York, Oxford University Press.

Lia, Brynjar (2008), *Architect of Global Jihad. The Life of Al Qaeda Strategist Abu Mus'ab al-Suri*, New York, Columbia University Press.

Lia, Brynjar and Kjøk, Åshild (2001), "Islamist Insurgencies, Diasporic Support Networks, and Their Host States – The Case of the Algerian GIA in Europe, 1993–2000," *FFI Rapport 2001 / 03789*.

Lister, Charles R. (2016), *The Syrian Jihad. Al-Qaeda, The Islamic State and the Evolution of an Insurgency*, Oxford, Oxford University Press.

Mannheim, Karl (1929; 1956), *Idéologie et Utopie. Une introduction à la sociologie de la connaissance*, traduit de l'édition anglaise par Pauline Rollet, préface de Louis Wirth (1936), Paris, Librairie Marcel Rivière et Cie.

Maréchal, Brigitte and El-Asri, Farid (2012), *Islam belge au pluriel*, Louvain-la-Neuve, Presses universitaires de Louvain.

Massey, Douglas S. and Espinosa, Kristin. E. (1997), "What's Driving Mexico–U.S. Migration? A Theoretical, Empirical, and Policy Analysis," *American Journal of Sociology*, 102.

McCants, William F. (2015), *The ISIS Apocalypse. The History, Strategy, and Doomsday Vision of The Islamic State*, New York, St. Martin's Press.

McCants, William and Meserole, Christopher (2016), "The French Connection. Explaining Sunni Militancy Around The World," Foreign Affairs, March 24.

Meleagrou-Hitchens Alexander and Amis, Jacob (2010), "The Making of the Christmas Day Bomber," *Current Trends in Islamist Ideology*, 10.

Micheron, Hugo (2020), *Le Jihadisme français. Quartiers, Syrie, prisons*, Paris, Gallimard.

Micheron, Hugo (2024), "La Terreur et l'IA : la violence millénariste à l'ère de ChatGPT," in *Le Grand Continent, Portrait d'un monde cassé*, Paris, Gallimard.

Morton, Jesse and Silber, Mitchell (2018), "NYPD vs. Revolution Muslim: The Inside Story of the Defeat of a Local Radicalization Hub," *CTC Sentinel at West Point*, 11 (4).

Mouline, Nabil (2011), *Les Clercs de l'islam. Autorité religieuse et pouvoir politique en Arabie saoudite, xviiie-xxie siècle*, Paris, PUF.

Murad, Nadia (2018), *Pour que je sois la dernière*, Paris, Librairie Arthème Fayard.

Myslobodsky, Michael S. (2004), *The Fallacy of Mother's Wisdom. A Critical Perspective on Health Psychology*, Singapore, World Scientific Publishing Company.

Nawaz, Maajid Usman (2012), *Radical. My Journey from Islamist Extremism to a Democratic Awakening*, with Tom Bromley, London, Allen.

Nesser, Petter (2015), *Islamist Terrorism in Europe. A History*, Oxford, New York, Oxford University Press.

Nilsson, Marco and Frees Esholdt, Henriette (2022), "After The Caliphate. Changing Mobilization in the Swedish Salafi-Jihadist Environment Following the Fall of ISIS," *Studies in Conflict & Terrorism*.

Nordbruch, Götz (2016), "Les jeunes musulmans en Allemagne. Entre normalité, racisme et discours salafistes," *Migrations Société*, 166: 95–110.

O'Neill, Sean and McGrory, Daniel (2010), The Suicide Factory. Abu Hamza and The Finsbury Park Mosque, London, Harper Perennial.

Otasevic, Ana (2013), "Les organisations combattantes irrégulières en Bosnie-Herzégovine," *Stratégique*, 103: 219–231.

Pantucci, Raffaello (2015), *We Love Death as You Love Life. Britain's Suburban Terrorists*, London, Hurst.

Pham-Lê, Jérémie (2024), "Dominique Bernard était la cible finale": le terroriste d'Arras raconte son crime et sa radicalisation," *Le Parisien*, February 5.

Qutb, Sayyid (2012), *Milestones. Maalim fil-tariq*, Dar Al-Wahi Publication.

Ranstorp, Magnus and Gustafsson, Linus (2017), *Swedish Foreign Fighters in Syria and Iraq. An Analysis of Open-Source Intelligence and Statistical Data*, Centre for Asymmetric Threats Studies, Swedish Defence University.

Regnard-Drouot, Céline (2022), *En transit. Les Syriens à Beyrouth, Marseille, Le Havre, New York (1880–1914)*, Paris, Anamosa.

Reinares, Fernando (2005), "Spain, 11th March and International Terrorism," site de l'Institut européen de la Méditerranée.

Rémy, Jean-Philippe (2024), "À Gaza, une frappe israélienne tue près de cent personnes, rendant encore plus improbable un cessez-le-feu," *Le Monde*, August 10.

Reynié, Dominique (2005), "L'idée d'une 'opinion européenne,'" *Raisons politiques*, 19: 99–117.

Reynié, Dominique (dir. ; 2021), *Les Attentats islamistes dans le monde, 1979-2021*, Fondation pour l'innovation politique; https://www.fondapol.org/etude/les-attentats-islamistes-dans-lemonde-1979–2021/.

Robinson, Glenn E. (2020), *Global Jihad. A Brief History*, Stanford, Stanford University Press.

Rosenblatt, Nathaniel (2021), *All Jihad is local*, PhD. Thesis, Oxford, University of Oxford.

Rougier, Bernard (2008), *Qu'est-ce que le salafisme ?*, Paris, PUF.

Saal, Johannes (2021), *The Dark Social Capital of Religious Radicals. Jihadi Networks and Mobilization in Germany, Austria and Switzerland, 1998–2018*, Wiesbaden, Springer.

Sageman, Marc (2004), *Understanding Terror Networks*, Philadelphia, University of Pennsylvania Press.

Salamé, Ghassan (2024), *La Tentation de Mars. Guerre et paix au XXIe siècle*, Paris, Fayard, 2024.

Shamzai, N. (2000), *An Exemplary Rule of an Exemplary State*, Maktaba al-Ansar, Birmingham.

Shtuni, Adrian (2019), "Western Balkans Foreign Fighters and Homegrown Jihadis. Trends and Implications," CTC *Sentinel at West Point*, 12 (7).

Simcox, Robin, Stuart, Hannah, Ahmed, Houriya, Murray, Douglas (2012), "Islamist Terrorism. The British Connections," *The Henry Jackson Society*.

Smolar, Piotr, "Entre Israël et l'Iran, après la guerre de l'ombre, le péril de la confrontation directe," *Le Monde*, April 14, 2024.

Soz, Jiwan (2022), "The Crisis of Female Jihadists in Al-Hawl Displacement Camp," *Carnegie Endowment for International Peace*.

Storchan, Victor (2023), "Sam Altman: la loi fondamentale de l'IA," *Le Grand Continent*, April 14.

Suleyman, Mustafa and Bhaskar, Michael (2023), *The Coming Wave: Technology, Power, and the Twenty-First Century's Greatest Dilemma*, London, Crown.

Tawil, Kamil (2007), Al-Qaidah Wa-Akhawatuha. Qissat Al-Jihadiyin Al-Arab, Beyrouth, Dar Al-Saqi.

Thielmann, Jörn (2019), "Histoire de la présence musulmane en Allemagne," in Élise Voguet and Anne Troadec (eds), *Islams de France, Islams d'Europe*, Paris, Institut d'études de l'Islam et des sociétés du monde musulman, pp. 37–45.

Thomas, Dominique (2003), *Le Londonistan. La voix du djihad*, Paris, Michalon.

Torrekens, Corinne (2012), "La gestion publique du culte musulman en Belgique : le cas de trois communes bruxelloises", in Brigitte Maréchal, Farid El Asri (éd.), Islam belge au pluriel, Louvain, Presses universitaires de Louvain, pp. 259–271.

Touzari Greenwood, Maja (2017), "Islamic State and al-Qaeda's Foreign Fighters," *Connections. Quarterly Journal*, 16 (1): 87–97.

Vandermotten, Christian (2014), *Bruxelles, une lecture de la ville. De l'Europe des marchands à la capitale de l'Europe*, Bruxelles, Éditions de l'université de Bruxelles.

Varvelli, Arturo (ed.) (2016), *Jihadist Hotbeds. Understanding Local. Radicalization Processes*, Milan, Edizioni Epoké.

Vidino, Lorenzo (2013), "Hisba in Europe? Assessing a Murky Phenomenon," *European Foundation for Democracy.*

Vidino, Lorenzo (2015), "Sharia4. From Confrontational Activism to Militancy," *Perspectives on Terrorism*, 9 (2).

Weiner, Myron (1995), *The Global Migration Crisis. Challenge to States and to Human Rights*, New York, HarperCollins College Publishers.

Weiss, Michael Douglas and Hassan, Hassan (2015), *ISIS. Inside The Army of Terror*, New York, Regan Arts.

Wiktorowicz, Quintan (2004), *Islamic Activism. A Social Movement Theory Approach,* Bloomington, Indiana University Press.

Wright, Lawrence (2006), *The Looming Tower. Al-Qaeda and The Road to 9/11*, New York, Knopf.

Zahab, Mariam Abou and Roy, Olivier (2006), *Islamist Networks. The Afghan-Pakistan Connection*, New York, Columbia University Press.

Zelin, Aaron Y. (2012), "Know Your Ansar al-Sharia," *Foreign Policy.*

Articles

Ahul Taqwa or *People of Conscience.*
Al-Jazeera English, September 5, 2014.
Associated Press, October 17, 2020.

Au nom du Père, du Fils et du Djihad, Arte, 2016, https://www.film-documentaire.fr/ 4DACTION/w_fiche_film/48775.

BBC, December 4, 2013.

BBC, May 20, 2014.

BBC, August 19, 2017.

Breitbart News, October 29, 2020.

Dabiq, magazine de propagande de l'EI, numéro de juillet 2016.

Jihad and Terrorism. A War of the Words (2013, 28 décembre), Cage: https:// www.cage.ngo/jihad-and-terrorism-war-words

Deutsche Welle, May 23, 2012.

Deutsche Welle, October 18, 2017.

DH Les Sports+, November 13, 2015.

L'Express, March 22, 2010.

Le Figaro, February 28, 2019.

Fox News, October 16, 2020.

France Bleu, November 27, 2020.

GNET (The Global Network on Extremism and Technology), 2020.

Guardian, May 20, 2014.

Guardian, June 3, 2022.

Guardian, November 14, 2022.

Harper's Magazine, July 2007, p. 30.

Houston Chronicle, September 24, 1995.

International Committee of the Red Cross on "Israël-Hamas: l'Europe dans les failles de la guerre du Soukkot," *Le Grand Continent*, October 27, 2023.

Le JDD, June 9, 2018.

Le Monde, October 7, 1995.

Le Monde, June 7, 2017.

Le Monde, July 4, 2018.

Le Monde, October 21, 2020.

Lemonde.fr, August 29, 2021.

Le Monde, November 13, 2021.

Le Monde, 17 April, 2024.

The Local, May 19, 2017.

New York Times, September 13, 2002.

New York Times, November 3, 2004.

New York Times, January 16, 2010.

New York Times, February 16, 2015.

New York Times, August 29, 2016.

New York Times, October 17, 2020.

New York Times, October 31, 2020.

NRC Handelsblad (2000), Paul Scheffer: "Het Multiculturele Drama."

L'Obs, January 15–21, 1998.

L'Obs, December 8, 2015.

Observer, August 23, 2009.

Le Point, June 15, 2018.

Reuters, April 22, 2015.

Reuters, January 6, 2016.

RTBF, 7:30pm news program, April 4, 2018.

RTBF, September 6, 2021, available online at the following address: https:// www.radiofrance.fr/franceinter/ce-qu-a-dit-salah-abdeslam-a-la-rtbf-lors -d-un-micro-trottoir-quelques-heures-apres-les-attentats-6154091.

Standard, August 13, 2014.

Telegraph, August 31, 1996.

Telegraph, September 7, 1996.

"TikTok Jihad : Terrorists Leverage Modern Tools to Recruit and Radicalize," August 9, 2024, https://thesoufancenter.org/intelbrief-2024-august-9/.

Vice News, November 3, 2014.

Wall Street Journal, June 3, 2019.

Washington Post, April 29, 2001.

Washington Post, October 23, 2020.